Policing Matters

Policing and Criminal Justice

Christopher Blake

Barrie Sheldon

Peter Williams

Series editors

P A J Waddington

Martin Wright

LearningMatters

First published in 2010 by Learning Matters Ltd

British Library Cataloguing in Publication Data
A CIP record for this book is available from the British Library.

ISBN: 978 1 84445 345 0

Cover and text design by Toucan Graphic Design Ltd.
Project Management by Diana Chambers
Typeset by Kelly Winter
Printed and bound in Great Britain by TJ International, Padstow, Cornwall

Learning Matters Ltd
33 Southernhay East
Exeter EX1 1NX
Tel: 01392 215560
info@learningmatters.co.uk
www.learningmatters.co.uk

All weblinks and web addresses in the book have been carefully checked prior to publication, but for up-to-date information please visit the Learning Matters website, www.learningmatters.co.uk.

FSC
Mixed Sources
Product group from well-managed
forests and other controlled sources

Cert no. SGS-COC-2482
www.fsc.org
© 1996 Forest Stewardship Council

Policing Matters

Policing and Criminal Justice

-001

Contents

1   Criminal justice   1

2   Courts of Justice   22

3   Arrest and detention   43

4   The prosecution process   59

5   Crime and punishment   75

6   Victims and the Criminal Justice System   96

7   Youth justice   111

8   Multi-agency approach   127

9   Criminological perspectives   147

10   Future directions   166

Index   184

1 Criminal justice

Introduction

Criminal Justice is a particularly complex process through which the state decides what particular forms of behaviour are to be considered unacceptable and then proceeds through a series of stages – arrest, charge, prosecution, trial sentence, appeal, punishment – in order to 'bring the guilty to justice'.

(Muncie and Wilson, 2006, p ix)

Criminal justice is an issue for us all and, with the growth of crime during the latter stages of the twentieth century, it became a key issue for all political parties, who were faced with the challenge of effectively tackling the problems of crime and disorder responsible for public disquiet. Crime figures have risen dramatically since the end of the Second World War and a peak of nearly 20 million crimes per year within England and Wales was reported by the British Crime Survey in 1995.

Let us consider the concept of 'criminal justice' in simple terms. When a person commits a crime society will expect the state to do something about it and bring the offender to account so that justice can be seen to be done. Those convicted of crime should be suitably punished and steps taken to prevent further offending. The state also has a duty to protect innocent and vulnerable persons and to help victims of crime.

As you proceed through the book we will explore some of these issues in greater detail.

Overview

Chapter 2 outlines the structure and role of the courts and the part they play within the CJS. The courts are responsible for sentencing decisions and society has an expectation that justice is seen to be done within the courtroom.

Chapter 3 examines issues surrounding the arrest and detention of an individual and the safeguards that are currently in place to ensure that individual human rights are protected and that the processes used by agencies of the state are ethical and transparent.

Chapter 4 explores the prosecution process and the role of the Crown Prosecution Service (CPS), including the controversy of recent criminal justice innovations, such as Simple, Speedy, Summary Justice (SSSJ).

Chapter 5 explores the wide range of sentencing options that are now available to the courts and considers some of the challenges currently facing the CJS, such as overcrowded prisons and implementing effective community sentences.

Chapter 6 deals with the plight of victims within the CJS and more particularly the impact of legislation since 1997, which was intended to place victims at the heart of the CJS. We will briefly discuss the emergence of 'victimology' as a science that examines the harm that victims suffer through illegal activities. We will also consider some models within victimology and criminal justice theory, and conclude by asking whether the notion of restorative justice and reparation have a place in the CJS.

Chapter 7 provides a historical perspective of the development of youth justice services, and explores contemporaneous approaches to youth justice. Young people feature heavily within the CJS as both victims and offenders and will form an integral part of any criminal justice strategy.

Chapter 8 outlines the implications of the Crime and Disorder Act 1998, which provided a statutory requirement for local councils and the police to jointly carry out crime audits and prepare community safety strategies in conjunction with the Probation Service and Health Authorities. This has had a profound effect on the CJS and has moved the focus away from perceptions that the police alone are responsible for crime and disorder problems.

Chapter 9 explains some criminological theories with explanations that have shaped both local and international contemporary criminal justice policies.

Chapter 10 provides a summary of the book content and also considers some future directions within the CJS. The growth of terrorism, the worldwide recession, miscarriages of justice and changes of government are just some examples of events that could have an impact on criminal justice and those agencies, such as the police, who have a key role to play within the CJS.

Within this chapter we shall provide a brief historical perspective of criminal justice and consider a number of paradigms (models) together with associated theories. Further, we shall explore recent government criminal justice interventions and discover how the Labour Party has transformed the CJS following their election in 1997.

REFLECTIVE TASK

What would you consider to be the objectives of a Criminal Justice System? Write down your thoughts, outlining how an offender, victim or member of the public might expect criminal justice to be approached.

In any society there will be a diversity of views, ranging from a harsh punitive regime to a more liberal rehabilitative approach. The government is challenged to reflect the views of the general populace with expectations to reduce crime and disorder, deliver safer communities and provide security. Those persons who are brought into the realms of the CJS expect to be treated fairly.

When an individual is charged by the state, what approach should be adopted when dealing with the crime committed? Table 1.1 provides examples of some of the approaches that can be adopted.

Table 1.1 Various approaches to dealing with crime

Retribution	Punishment that is seen as vengeance or just deserts.
Incapacitation	Sending offenders to jail or detention centre.
Deterrence	Punishment that deters others from committing crime.
Rehabilitation	Preventing reoffending, providing treatment and reintegrating offenders into public life.
Reparation	Making good the harm done, e.g. compensation, repair, restorative justice.

Within the UK and other Western societies it is rare to find a purely retributivist or rehabilitative approach by government. The UK government has tended to adopt a blend of approaches to criminal justice rather than developing a pure doctrine (Cavadino et al., 1999, p11).

REFLECTIVE TASK

Consider the responsibility of government today and the problems it is facing regarding crime and disorder.

- *What would you consider to be an effective criminal justice policy?*

- *Put yourself in the shoes of an offender, victim and member of the public – what would be your expectations of the CJS and could government meet your expectations?*

- *Where are the problems and how does the government meet the needs and expectations of the majority?*

- *If you were to develop a strategy (plan) to shape and reform the CJS, what would you need to know? Write down a list of some of your early thoughts and expand/develop these thoughts as you progress through the chapters.*

Historical perspectives

Since time immemorial communities have faced problems of crime and deviancy. To maintain social control community leaders or those persons who have been given certain powers by the state have been required to deal with those deemed to have committed crime.

Having conquered Britain, the Romans imposed their own harsh laws and cruel punishments, such as crucifixion and torture. By 603 the Romans had been replaced by the invading Jutes, Saxons and Angles, who knew nothing of Roman law and introduced their own laws and customs. As the invaders prospered and gained in wealth, the great landowners started to take a lead in village communities and developed their own peace and customs. Justice was very much a system of self-protection with vengeance of kin and neighbours against wrongdoers. The law was primitive and harsh with constant blood feuds and self-help was the primary means of law (Hostettler, 2009).

The land was developed into 'shires' and 'hundreds', where separate assemblies formed with judicial and administrative powers. Existing customs became laws (known as dooms) and the concept of breaching the King's Peace was introduced and enforced by landowners, with fines being directed to the king. Early Anglo-Saxon law was concerned with compensating victims rather than punishment; however, savage punishments were evident, including hanging, beheading, branding, removal of hands, feet and tongues, and castration (Hostettler, 2009).

As the centuries passed law became more sophisticated, with criminal justice evolving in line with social, economic and political events, which saw the development of policing, the courts, the trial process and penal approaches. As democracy emerged and the voice of civil liberty groups became heard, the modern era has seen significant attention given to issues such as youth justice, human rights and the victims of crime. Some of these historical developments will be explored further in subsequent chapters.

The modern era

Following the Second World War, while recovering from the aftermath and rebuilding the country's infrastructure, crime was not a priority for government; however, as the century progressed, crime levels dramatically increased and confidence in the CJS diminished owing to alleged police corruption and abuse of powers, riots and miscarriages of justice, resulting in criminal justice becoming a key issue for the political parties.

From the middle of the century to the 1970s, the treatment and rehabilitation of offenders was the main focus of the CJS but, in the 1990s, a more punitive stance was adopted by the Conservative government together with some treatment programmes, and attempts were being made to find out 'what works' within the CJS (Cavadino et al., 1999).

Between 1979 and 1997, Parliament debated at least one major piece of legislation originating from the Home Office every session, compared with just five pieces of legislation of equivalent significance in the previous 50 years (James and Raine, 1998, p3).

During the past decade, the Labour Party, which was elected to government in 1997, has carried out a major upheaval of the current CJS, with a series of reviews and major changes, many of which will be highlighted in subsequent chapters. Legislation continues to be produced at an alarming rate. Between 1997 and 2004 it was estimated that nearly 50 Acts of Parliament were produced relating to crime, disorder, policing, criminal justice and punishment (Solomon et al., 2007, p16). This trend continues unabated at present, with the government continuing to legislate, thus adding new challenges and burdens to those working within the CJS.

Government criminal justice strategy

Working Together to Cut Crime and Deliver Justice is the current government's strategic plan for criminal justice published in November 2007. Its purpose is to 'Deliver a fair and effective criminal justice service that puts victims of crime and law abiding citizens first' (Home Office 2007a:3). Criminal justice agencies are identified as the police, prosecution, courts, probation, prison and youth offending services, and a stated aim of the strategy is for the services to work together to respond more effectively to crime, to bring more offences to justice and help tackle crime, and to reduce reoffending.

The plan also sets out the government's vision for criminal justice by 2011:

- a CJS that is more effective in bringing offences, especially serious offences, to justice and assisting with reducing crime and reoffending;

- a public that has been properly consulted and are confident that the CJS is fair, effective and meets local needs;

- people of all races being treated fairly;

- victims placed at the heart of the CJS and both victims and witnesses receiving a high level of service;

- speedy and simple processes, supported by modern technology with improved efficiency, enabling the police to focus on tackling crime.

(Home Office, 2007a, p4)

REFLECTIVE TASK

Go online and download the following three documents.

- *Labour Party's* Criminal Justice Strategic Plan 2008–2011*: www.cjsonline.gov.uk/ downloads/application/pdf/1_CJS_Public_ALL.pdf;*

- *Labour Party's* Criminal Justice Strategy 2001: The Way Ahead*: www.archive.official-documents.co.uk/document/cm50/5074/5074.htm;*

- *Ten Years of Criminal Justice under Labour: An Independent Audit: www.crimeand justice.org.uk/opus55/ten-years-of-labour-2007.pdf.*

Read through the 2008–11 strategy and establish how the government intends to achieve its vision, and compare this with the previous 2001 criminal justice strategy (tip: reading through the introduction and executive summary will provide the information required; detail can be found within the main bodies of the documents).

Consider whether the government has made significant improvements since 2001 or is the current strategy saying very much the same thing? Further, compare your findings with the last study, where an alternative view is provided. How effective do you consider the strategy to be?

The government is clearly attempting to deliver change and suggests that considerable improvements are being made, providing certain statistics to evidence the progress; however, the Centre for Crime and Justice Studies provides a significant challenge:

> *Overall the results of this audit are mixed. The ambition to overhaul the criminal justice system has certainly been very high. There has been substantial extra investment and major changes are evident. But there has not been a significant step change in outcomes. Claims of success have been overstated and at times have been misleading. Despite a decade of reform, crime and victimisation levels remain high and the proportion of crimes dealt with is extremely low.*

(Solomon et al., 2007, p13)

The effectiveness of the government approach to criminal justice provides an excellent topic for further research and discussion, and the basis for an assignment topic.

Models of criminal justice

Models can assist us in our understanding of the CJS, which today is very complex. Modern government is very reactive and tends to respond quickly to significant events and public reaction with an array of new legislation, policy and guidance. As Muncie and Wilson point out, '"Paradigms" or, more broadly, models . . . help us to think more critically about the general characteristics, themes, and principles that make up the criminal justice system' (2006, p27).

Within this section we shall briefly look at a number of models of criminal justice and consider how they relate to practice.

Welfare versus justice

The *welfare model* of criminal justice is focused on the offender and sets out to discover why the offender committed the crime. When a reason has been established, attempts are made to find solutions to prevent further offending. The result is a series of perspectives that focus on three aspects:

- determining and resolving the causes of the crime;
- reforming the behaviour of those who offend;
- reintegrating offenders within the community.

In contrast, the *justice model* of criminal justice is concerned with examining the crime committed and sometimes the person or group offended against. It considers what the appropriate penalty is for the offence and takes into account what is just and fair and what might deter reoffending. The approach is retributive and may or may not include restorative considerations (James and Raine, 1998, p11).

Crime control versus due process

These two models were introduced by Herbert Packer in 1968 in his book, *The Limits of Criminal Sanction*, and relate to the criminal process. The *crime control model* is about the repression of criminal behaviour, considered as the main aim of the criminal process, whereas the *due process model* is aligned to the formal structure of the law and is concerned with the protection of the innocent. The models provide two extremes but appear to have the same objectives of punishing criminals and protecting the innocent.

The crime control model is focused on reducing crime and to achieve its goal may be detrimental to the human rights of an individual. The criminal process should be quick and efficient, and can often overlook quality within the process to achieve quantity, for example the priority of detecting crime and convicting offenders at any cost.

In contrast, the due process model attempts to ensure adherence to rights and liberties that are likely to impact on the reduction of crime and prosecution of offenders. A premise of English law is that a person is innocent until proved guilty. Agencies of the state are required to work within the rule of law, which provides certain safeguards for the accused from the initial investigation of a crime, to arrest, charge and through to trial. It may be fairly clear that a person is guilty of a crime but, if the evidence against them has been improperly obtained, under this model the evidence would not be allowed. Here the process is concerned with quality rather than quantity to ensure fairness, integrity of evidence and protection of individuals, and to engender public confidence (Packer, 1968).

PRACTICAL TASK

Governments continue to innovate and adopt various strategies in their search for solutions to tackle crime and disorder. Consider the following innovations and apply the above models, defining where each innovation may sit between the extremities of crime control and due process. Make a list of the advantages and disadvantages of the approaches adopted.

- *Diplock Courts, Northern Ireland – introduced in 1973 to hear certain terrorist cases. The use of a jury was removed, and evidential standards relating to confessions, inferences from silence, and statements from police officers were relaxed.*

- *Police and Criminal Evidence Act 1984 – introduced rules, conduct and guidance for the use of powers relating to search, seizure of property, arrest, detention, questioning and identification.*

- *Regulation of Investigatory Powers Act 2000 – introduced a series of safeguards for intrusive and directive surveillance of citizens.*

- *Use and expansion of CCTV (closed-circuit television) as a crime prevention measure heavily funded by government.*

It is interesting to note the comments made by the human rights group *JUSTICE* in their response to Lord Justice Auld's review of the criminal courts in 2001 (JUSTICE, 2002). They see Packer's work as being disproportionately influential and continuing to affect contemporary analysis of criminal justice. They suggested that Lord Justice Auld had adopted a crime control approach with a focus on efficiency (a primary government objective). They did not see the two models as being automatically in opposition, describing crime control as an objective and due process as a method that may or may not be a means of achieving crime control (JUSTICE, 2002, p3). (These models will be explored further in Chapter 6 in the context of their application to the victims of crime.)

Packer's two models have been further extended by Michael King (1981) and Davies et al. (1995), briefly explained below.

- *Medical model* – concerned with rehabilitation, and treating the condition that has caused the crime, e.g. alcohol or drugs dependence.

- *Bureaucratic model* – concerned with the management of crime and criminals. Adheres to rules and procedures and processing offenders with speed and efficiency, e.g. focuses on targets to detect crime, reducing time between arrest and conviction.

- *Status passage model* – concerned with denunciation and degradation. Focuses on public values and attitudes about the immorality of crime and the shaming of offenders, e.g. Community 'Payback' schemes.

- *Power model* – concerned with the maintenance of class domination. Examines the role of law makers and in whose interest laws are implemented, e.g. are the laws designed for the rich, powerful and elite or democratically drafted to serve all?

- *Just deserts model* – concerned with the priority of punishment. Focuses on the offender with the seriousness of the offence and culpability of the offender being considered so that the punishment reflects the crime committed, e.g. minimum sentences for rapists and drug traffickers and sending burglars to jail on a third conviction.

(Muncie and Wilson, 2006, pp27–9)

Inquisitorial versus adversarial

The UK and the USA adopt an *adversarial* approach to criminal justice as opposed to our neighbours in France and other parts of Europe, who adopt an *inquisitorial* approach. The adversarial approach allows both parties within criminal proceedings (prosecution and defence) to investigate, define and argue the facts of a case and it is the Crown prosecutor or the defence lawyer who presents the facts to the court. The facts presented are often conflicting and it is up to the fact finders (jury or lay magistrates) to decide which version of the facts is closest to the truth in order to establish guilt.

With this approach the lawyers representing the parties concerned are not obliged to assist the court in a search for the truth; their role is to represent their respective clients and put forward their version of the facts.

With an inquisitorial approach the judge rather than the parties concerned actively takes on the responsibility of establishing the facts, rather than acting as an impartial referee between the two parties concerned within the criminal process. The judge will supervise the gathering of evidence required to resolve the case, including the search for evidence and the questioning of witnesses and the defendant. The judge will take the lead, with lawyers taking on a more passive role in the process. Table 1.2 provides an example of some of the differences between the two systems.

Table 1.2 Differences between the adversarial and inquisitorial approaches

Adversarial	Inquisitorial
Lawyers investigate and present evidence/facts to the court. Judge's role is to advise and arbitrate.	Judge has primary investigation role.
Parties compete against each other with hope that competition will reveal truth.	Seeks the truth by questioning those most familiar with the events in dispute.
Focus on individual rights of accused.	Rights of accused secondary to search for the truth.

REFLECTIVE TASK

> Judge: 'Am I not to hear the truth?' Barrister: 'No, your honour is to hear the evidence.'
>
> (Hannibal and Mountford, 2002, p5)

This is an apocryphal story used to demonstrate the process of an adversarial criminal trial.

Consider the adversarial approach within our CJS – does it work in the best interests of the public, bringing those guilty of criminal offences to justice and allowing those who are innocent to go free? It is suggested that, in some cases, the rules of evidence prevent the truth from being revealed and that the guilty go free.

Compare the two approaches and produce an argument in favour of either approach.

Structure and management of the CJS

During the last decade considerable changes have been made to both the structure and management of the CJS. Figure 1.1 shows a simple model of the current structure together with heads of department and responsibilities.

The 'Firewall' shown in Figure 1.1 is to signify the independence of the judiciary from the executive (government) and the legislature (Parliament) or, to put it simply, removing politics from the judicial process. The doctrine of the 'separation of powers' between the judiciary and government is important, in order to ensure that the citizen is defended 'From arbitrary actions undertaken by the state' (Joyce, 2006, p294). Surprisingly, it is not until recently that this separation of powers has been fully achieved. The issue came to the fore following the conviction of two boys for the murder in 1993 of Jamie Bulger, resulting in the Home Secretary becoming embroiled in the sentencing decisions made by the judiciary. Following rulings from the House of Lords and the European Commission for Human Rights, and the introduction of the Human Rights Act 1998, politicians' ability to interfere with sentencing decisions has been seriously eroded.

Lord Chancellor

The office of Lord Chancellor is steeped in history and can be traced back to the Middle Ages. The Lord Chancellor was a member of the legislature, member of the executive and the head of the judiciary, which clearly compromised the separation of powers doctrine. On 12 June 2003, the Prime Minister announced the introduction of the Department for Constitutional Affairs (DCA), headed by the Lord Chancellor with an additional title of Secretary of State for Constitutional Affairs. This ended the previous role of the Lord Chancellor as a judge and speaker in the House of Lords:

> Once the reforms are in place, the post of Lord Chancellor will be abolished, putting the relationship between executive, legislature and judiciary on a modern footing.
>
> (Number10.gov.uk, 2003)

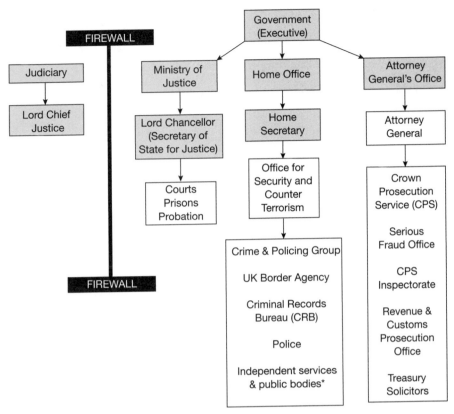

Figure 1.1 The current structure of the Criminal Justice System

* Independent services and public bodies include organisations such as the Independent Police Complaints Authority, National Police Improvement Agency, Serious Organised Crime Agency, Her Majesty's Inspectorate of Constabulary, and Forensic Science Service.

Part 2 of the Constitutional Reform Act 2005 provided statutory authority for redefining the Lord Chancellor's role, but the title has not yet been abolished.

We shall now consider the roles of the three government departments whose responsibility it is to provide the policy, framework, objectives and targets, support and funding for the CJS:

- Home Office;
- Ministry of Justice;
- Attorney General.

Home Office

The Home Office is a government department that is responsible for immigration and passports, drugs policy, policing and counter-terrorism. It is headed by the Home Secretary, who is a cabinet minister supported by a *Permanent Secretary*, who is a senior civil servant responsible for ensuring that departmental objectives are met.

The Home Office *Strategic Plan 2008–2011* sets these objectives:

- to help people feel secure in their homes and local communities;
- to cut crime, especially violent, drug- and alcohol-related crime;
- to lead visible, responsive and accountable policing;
- to support the efficient and effective delivery of justice;
- to protect the public from terrorism;
- to secure our borders and control migration for the benefit of our country;
- to safeguard people's identity and the privileges of citizenship.

(Home Office, 2007a, p2)

PRACTICAL TASK

For any student studying criminal justice, certain websites provide key resources to assist with research and assignment completion. Go online to www.homeoffice.gov.uk and discover what this site can offer you. Search for and explore the following links, which will provide you with information and resources to assist with your studies.

- *Left-hand menu – 'About us' provides links to latest news and publications.*
- *Left-hand menu – also provides links to crime and victims, anti-social behaviour, drugs, police and others.*
- *'Other Home Office Websites' drop-down menu provides links to other key sites, such as 'Police', 'Crime Reduction' and 'Tackling Drugs, Changing Lives'.*

Find the document, Summary of the 2009 Home Office Departmental Report *(access through the following links from the homepage: About us/Publications/Corporate publications and strategy documents), go to page 6 and find out how the Home Office has done in meeting its objective to 'lead visible, responsible and accountable policing'.*

Ministry of Justice

The Ministry of Justice (MoJ) replaced the DCA on 9 May 2007 and became responsible for a number of agencies that had previously been under the remit of the Home Office. There were a number of factors that contributed to this change. The threat of terrorism was increasing and, in 2006, the Home Office had faced considerable criticism following the discovery that, between 1999 and 2003, over 1,000 foreign prisoners had not been considered for deportation and, later, revelations that some of those released had committed further serious offences, including violent crime and, in one case, a rape.

In March 2007, the then Prime Minister, Tony Blair, announced a new office for 'Security and Counter Terrorism' within the Home Office to strengthen the capacity for dealing with the terrorist threat. At the same time, he announced the creation of the MoJ, with the purpose of bringing together the main agencies responsible for dealing with offenders within the CJS, that is, the National Offender Management Service (NOMS), the Prison Service and the Probation Service. These responsibilities, together with those of the DCA, formed the basis of the newly formed MoJ.

> *The Ministry of Justice will take a leading role in delivering a fairer, more effective, speedy and efficient justice system, and also in reducing re-offending. In doing so it will, with the Home Office and the Attorney General's Office, respect the vital roles and independence of the judiciary and the Prosecuting authorities.*
>
> (Number10.gov.uk, 2007)

The MoJ has four strategic objectives:

- to strengthen democracy, rights and responsibilities;

- to deliver fair and simple routes to civil and family justice;

- to protect the public and reduce reoffending;

- to ensure a more effective, transparent and responsive CJS for victims and the public.

(MoJ, 2009)

REFLECTIVE TASK

- *Consider the last objective outlined above. How would you go about putting together a more effective, transparent and responsive CJS for victims and the public?*

- *Write down your answers and then compare with the MoJ Departmental Report 2008–09, pages 44–60 (can be found on the MoJ website under 'Publications': www.justice.gov.uk/publications/docs/justice-annual-report-08-09ii.pdf).*

- *Having made the comparison with your answers, consider how effective the MoJ is, and question whether it is really making a difference in tackling the problems of crime and disorder.*

PRACTICAL TASK

The MoJ website also provides a useful and key resource for students.

- *Go to the MoJ website, www.justice.gov.uk/index.htm, and explore the 'Publications' link on the homepage header.*

- *Make a note of the types of document that may be of use to you and where they can be found.*

Attorney General's Office

The role of Attorney General (AG) originated in 1315 with the responsibility of prosecuting on behalf of the Crown. The AG has a deputy called the Solicitor General (SG), who can be traced back to 1461 and who was earlier known as the king's solicitor. In the seventeenth century the AG became the legal adviser to the Crown, and both the AG and SG are now known as law officers of the Crown (Attorney General's Office, 2009).

The AG and SG, together with the Advocate General for Scotland, have three main functions:

- as guardians of the public interest;
- as chief legal advisers to government;
- as criminal justice ministers.

They are responsible for a number of organisations (see Figure 1.1), including the CPS, which prosecutes offenders on behalf of the Police Service. The offices of AG and SG also provide the holders with additional powers in law, such as referring cases to the Court of Appeal on points of law or taking action for appeals against unduly lenient sentences. They also contribute to making changes within the CJS and currently have a number of responsibilities for CJS reform, such as bringing more offenders to justice.

Criminal justice agencies

The three government departments are responsible for a number of agencies that deliver services within the CJS. Some of the key agencies are:

- Courts Service;
- Police Service;
- Crown Prosecution Service;
- Probation Service;
- Prison Service;
- National Offender Management Service (NOMS);
- Criminal Defence Service;
- Criminal Injuries Compensation Authority;
- other victim and witness care services.

Some of these agencies will be considered in more detail later (see Chapters 2, 4 and 6, which relate to the courts, prosecution process and victims respectively). Brief overviews will be provided of the Police, Probation and Prison Services and NOMS.

The Police Service

The modern Police Service was introduced in 1829 by Sir Robert Peel (Home Secretary). The aims of the service were threefold:

- to prevent crime;

- to protect life;

- to preserve public tranquillity.

REFLECTIVE TASK

Consider the initial aims of the modern Police Service and their application within the twenty-first century.

- *Do these early aims encompass what you consider to be the role of a contemporary police officer or is their scope limited?*

- *What do you think should be the aims of the Police Service? Make a list of what you consider should be the aims of the Police Service within society today.*

This is what the government tells us are the aims of the Police Service today:

- to uphold the law fairly and firmly;

- to prevent crime;

- to pursue and bring to justice those who break the law;

- to keep the Queen's Peace;

- to protect, help and reassure the community;

- to be seen to do all things with integrity, common sense and sound judgement.

(Home Office, 2007b)

The Police Service is governed through a tripartite arrangement set up by the Police Act 1964, which provided clear lines of responsibility for the Home Secretary, the Police Committee (now Police Authority) and the Chief Constable. Table 1.3 briefly outlines the role of each.

The purpose of this relationship is to ensure that there is no direct political interference with the operational aspects of policing, and to ensure accountability and the delivery of an efficient and effective Police Service.

Table 1.3 Police Service roles

Home Secretary	Overall efficiency of Police Service
Police Authority	Maintenance of an adequate and efficient police force
Chief Constable	Direction and control of police force

Since the Police Act 1964, additional legislation has been introduced that has provided the Home Secretary with greater powers over the Police Service. The Police and Magistrates' Courts Act 1994 gave the Home Secretary power to impose key national objectives, together with targets for the Police Service, thus asserting some control over Chief Constables, who are now required to adhere to central government direction. This control and direction was enhanced even further when the Police Reform Act 2002 introduced an annual national policing plan, setting out priorities and further targets for the Police Service. The plan is prepared in consultation with the Association of Chief Police Officers (ACPO) and the Association of Police Authorities (APA) and provides the strategic direction for the Police Service.

The Probation Service

Prior to 1907, charitable organisations such as the Church of England Temperance Society and the Police Court Commission provided volunteers who would offer their services to the court to supervise offenders in the community. This was put on a statutory footing with the introduction of the Probation of Offenders Act 1907, which signalled the birth of what is now known as the Probation Service. The act gave powers to the courts to issue probation orders and appoint probation officers to 'advise, assist and befriend those who had been sentenced' (Joyce, 2009, p53).

The Criminal Justice and Court Services Act 2000 provided for a unified National Probation Service for England and Wales divided into 42 areas, aligned with the 42 areas of both the Police and the CPS (Northern Ireland and Scotland have their own Probation Service).

The aims of the Probation Service are to:

- protect the public;
- reduce reoffending;
- properly punish offenders in the community;
- ensure offenders' awareness of the effects of crime on the victims of crime and the public;
- rehabilitate offenders.

The workload of the Probation Service is extensive and annually they deal with the supervision of 175,000 offenders, supervise 8 million hours of unpaid work, and provide 246,000 pre-sentence reports for the courts and 87,000 reports relating to the early release of prisoners (National Probation Service, 2009).

The work is very demanding and intensive, with probation officers having to assess the risk and dangerousness of offenders so that others can make informed decisions in the interests of community safety.

Consider the case of Dano Sonnex, who was convicted in June 2009 of murdering two French students in London. An internet search will provide details about the crime, which was reported widely by the media, and the MoJ website provides an overview of the case and subsequent investigations: www.justice.gov.uk/news/announcement040609a.htm.

- Carry out some research and identify the criticisms levelled at the Probation Service and others.

- Consider what this case says about our current CJS and its effectiveness, writing down a list of its strengths and weaknesses.

The Prison Service

Prisons are usually a place of last resort for an offender when other remedies to rehabilitate, treat and prevent further offending have failed. Some offences are so serious that, as a matter of public safety, prison is the only option, for example terrorism and murder.

The overarching aim of the Prison Service is to protect the public and its objectives are to hold prisoners securely, to reduce the risks of prisoners reoffending (recidivism) and to provide safe and well-ordered establishments in which prisoners are treated humanely, decently and lawfully (HM Prison Service, 2009).

Historically, prisons were places with a retributivist and punitive regime and it was the Gladstone Report of 1895 that recommended that prisons should be rehabilitative institutions, and the Prison Act 1898 that provided for a rehabilitative approach. During the twentieth century, prisons adopted the rehabilitative approach that gave rise to the *treatment model*, which is very evident today in criminal justice policy. However, between 1979 and 1999 Conservative governments were seen to adopt a more punitive approach and reverted to the 'justice model' (see page 7), in their attempts to appease the public by getting tough with the criminal (Joyce, 2009, p59). The Conservative government firmly believed that prison worked and, as a result, the prison population was seen to increase dramatically. (See Chapter 5, where the premise that 'prison works' is discussed.)

Post-1997, the Labour government has continued to face the problem of rising prison numbers, but has intervened to ensure that prison regimes are constructive by providing purposeful activities. The main focus currently is to reduce offending by those released from prison and this was a key purpose for the creation of NOMS (Joyce, 2009, p61).

National Offender Management Service

Lord Carter of Coles was asked by the government in March 2003 to review correctional services in England and Wales and he produced a report in December of the same year entitled *Managing Offenders, Reducing Crime*. Within his foreword, addressed to the Prime Minister, he made the following observation:

We have found an urgent need for the different parts of the criminal justice system to work closer together. At its simplest, each part of the system has little regard for the consequences of its actions on the other parts. This means that resources are not always used effectively. Further, few of the players are focused on the overall aim of crime reduction.

(Carter, 2003)

A number of recommendations were made that included the setting up of a National Offender Management Service (NOMS) and also the introduction of *National Offender Managers*. Problems had been recognised in the two separate agencies, that is, the Prison and Probation Services, of not being able to effectively manage offenders. NOMS is now able to provide continuity and a service that manages an offender from conviction, through sentence, treatment and beyond, working towards the goals of preventing reoffending and the reduction of crime.

Criminal Justice Boards

Before we conclude this chapter, it will be appropriate to outline the function of Criminal Justice Boards (CJBs) and the important role they now play within the CJS. As part of the Labour government's reform of the CJS, it set out its policy in a white paper, *Justice for All*, presented to Parliament in July 2002, in which it stated that a national CJB would be set up, together with 42 local CJBs within England and Wales.

The CJBs were introduced in April 2003 with the purpose of:

- delivering public service agreement targets;
- improving delays in justice;
- improving service provided to victims and witnesses;
- securing public confidence in the CJS.

(Audit Commission, 2003, p8)

The introduction of the CJBs provides an excellent example of the multi-agency approach adopted by the Labour government to tackle crime and disorder (see Chapter 8, which explores further this multi-agency approach). It brings together locally all of the key agencies responsible for criminal justice and provides them with a focus for common aims and objectives that should result in improved services and efficiency.

PRACTICAL TASK

- *Go online to http://lcjb.cjsonline.gov.uk and select a link to one of the 42 CJBs and find out which agencies are involved.*

- *Scan through and access some of the links on the menu provided and find out about the work and services provided by the CJB.*

- *Consider and make a list of the advantages and disadvantages of this type of approach within the CJS.*

C H A P T E R   S U M M A R Y

Within this chapter we have considered the structure of the modern CJS and explored a number of criminal justice models that will assist you with knowledge and understanding of some of the theoretical concepts relating to criminal justice. We have also provided an insight into how government develops policy to tackle the ever challenging problem of effectively tackling crime and disorder issues and the balances required to meet the needs of the public, victim and offender.

The tasks that you have completed will have introduced further information and resources that will assist with your criminal justice studies and have opened up areas for debate that could provide an assignment theme. The content of this chapter is limited, providing you with an overview of the CJS and some key issues, and it is recommended that further reading and research is completed to develop some of the information and concepts introduced.

REFERENCES

Attorney General's Office (2009) *History*. Available online at www.attorneygeneral.gov.uk/sub_about_us_history.htm (accessed 29 September 2009).

Audit Commission (2003) *Local Criminal Justice Boards: Supporting Change Management*. London: Audit Commission.

Carter, Lord Patrick (2003) *Managing Offenders, Reducing Crime: A New Approach*. Available online at www.cabinetoffice.gov.uk/media/cabinetoffice/strategy/assets/managingoffenders.pdf (accessed 30 September 2009).

Cavadino, M, Crow, I and Dignan, J (1999) *Criminal Justice 2000*. Winchester: Waterside Press.

Hannibal, M and Mountford, L (2002) *The Law of Criminal and Civil Evidence: Principles and Practice*. Harlow: Pearson Education.

HM Prison Service (2009) *About the Service: Statement of Purpose*. Available online at www.hmprisonservice.gov.uk/abouttheservice/statementofpurpose (accessed 30 September 2009).

Home Office (2007a) *Working Together to Cut Crime and Deliver Justice: A Strategic Plan for Criminal Justice 2008–2011 – An Overview*. London: Office for Criminal Justice Reform.

Home Office (2007b) *The Role of the Police Service*. Available online at www.asb.homeoffice.gov.uk/members/article.aspx?id=8214 (accessed 29 September 2009).

Hostettler, J (2009) *A History of Criminal Justice in England and Wales*. Sheffield: Waterside Press.

James, A and Raine, J (1998) *The New Politics of Criminal Justice*. Harlow: Addison Wesley Longman.

Joyce, P (2006) *Criminal Justice: An Introduction to Crime and the Criminal Justice System*. Cullompton: Willan.

Joyce, P (2009) *Criminology and Criminal Justice: A Study Guide*. Cullompton: Willan.

JUSTICE (2002) *JUSTICE's Response to the Auld Review*. London: JUSTICE.

Ministry of Justice (MoJ) (2009) *Our Strategy*. Available online at www.justice.gov.uk/about/our-strategy.htm (accessed 2 October 2009).

Muncie, J and Wilson, D (2006) *Student Handbook of Criminal Justice and Criminology*. Abingdon: Routledge-Cavendish.

National Probation Service (2009) *About Us*. Available online at www.probation.homeoffice.gov.uk/output/page2.asp (accessed 30 September 2009).

Number10.gov.uk (2003) *Lord Falconer Appointed as Secretary of State for Constitutional Affairs*. Available online at: www.number10.gov.uk/Page3892 (accessed 29 September 2009).

Number10.gov.uk (2007) *Home Office Machinery of Government Changes*. Available online at www.number10.gov.uk/Page11377 (accessed 29 September 2009).

Packer, H L (1968) Two models of the criminal process, in Newburn, T (ed., 2009) *Key Readings in Criminology*. Cullompton: Willan.

Solomon, E, Eades, C, Garside, R and Rutherford, M (2007) *Ten Years of Criminal Justice under Labour: An Independent Audit*. London: Centre for Crime and Justice Studies.

USEFUL WEBSITES

All weblinks and web addresses in the book have been carefully checked prior to publication, but for up-to-date information please visit the Learning Matters website, www.learningmatters.co.uk.

www.attorneygeneral.gov.uk (Attorney General's Office)

www.cica.gov.uk (Criminal Injuries Compensation Authority)

www.cjsonline.gov.uk (Criminal Justice System)

www.hmcourts-service.gov.uk (Her Majesty's Courts Service)

www.hmprisonservice.gov.uk (Her Majesty's Prison Service)

www.homeoffice.gov.uk (Home Office)

www.justice.gov.uk (Ministry of Justice)

www.legalservices.gov.uk (Legal Services Commission)

www.noms.homeoffice.gov.uk (National Offender Management Service)

www.number10.gov.uk (official site of the Prime Minister's Office)

www.police.homeoffice.gov.uk (official Police website)

www.probation.homeoffice.gov.uk (National Probation Service)

www.victimsupport.org.uk (Victim Support)

LEGISLATION

Constitutional Reform Act 2005

Crime and Disorder Act 1998

Criminal Justice and Court Services Act 2000

Human Rights Act 1998

Police Act 1964

Police and Criminal Evidence Act 1984

Police and Magistrates' Court Act 1994

Police Reform Act 2002

Prison Act 1898

Probation of Offenders Act 1907

Regulation of Investigatory Powers Act 2000

2   Courts of Justice

Introduction

The courts play a pivotal role within the Criminal Justice System (CJS) and are responsible for making key decisions that impact on all sectors of society. There are the victims who are seeking justice; members of the public who are drawn into the courts system as witnesses; the general public who are seeking reassurance and confidence from the decisions and action taken by the courts; and the accused who have certain human rights that need to be respected.

The public also provide a vital role within the courts, acting as jurors in certain trials and, where suitably qualified, as lay magistrates (justices of the peace).

This chapter will provide you with an overview of the Courts of Justice and provide you with a number of activities to encourage debate, learning and reflection.

Historical perspectives

Courts are not a new phenomenon and have been about in various forms since time immemorial. Courts of Justice are places where people acting on behalf of the sovereign make decisions or judgments against those who have been brought before the courts for both civil and criminal actions.

Early years

During the reign of Edward 1 (1272–1307) the main courts were:

- the ancient courts of the shire and hundred, which dealt locally with both criminal and civil cases;

- the feudal courts, which had their origins in resolving disputes between lord and tenant;

- courts held by the King's itinerant justices (judges), who visited the shires on a regular basis to preside over assize courts on behalf of the King;

- the King's central courts, which had several functions, including hearing cases of special interest to the King, e.g. breach of the King's special peace, protection such as the death of or injury to servants of the King, or treason.

(Maitland, 2008, p106)

A series of Statutes of the Realm between 1327 and 1388 saw the introduction of justices of the peace (JPs), who had local powers to indict (charge) and imprison those brought before them to be tried later by a King's judge when visiting the shire. The powers were later extended, empowering the JPs to hear certain cases. Each shire was required to hold courts four times a year and the courts became known as the 'Quarter Sessions'.

Nineteenth and twentieth centuries

This early structuring of the court system remained intact for many centuries, with criminal cases being heard in three different types of court. First, the most serious cases were heard in the Assize Courts, which met at least twice a year. The Assize Court in London was the Old Bailey, which became known as the Central Criminal Court after 1834. Second, the Quarter Sessions continued to hear a range of criminal cases and, third, JPs heard the less serious offences in what was termed 'Petty Sessions'. As legislation developed from the late eighteenth century, more power was given to JPs to hear a wider range of criminal cases and, by 1900, 80 per cent of the offences coming before the court were being dealt with by JPs (Bentley, 1998, cited in Emsley, 2002).

The Supreme Court of Judicature Act 1873 saw a restructuring of the higher courts. A High Court with three divisions was created, together with a Court of Appeal, which dealt mainly with civil cases. The Criminal Appeal Act 1907 created a separate Court of Criminal Appeal and, in 1966, as a result of a further Criminal Appeal Act, a single Court of Appeal with both a civil and a criminal division was established.

Following a Royal Commission (Beeching, 1969), the Assize Courts and Quarter Sessions were abolished as a result of the Courts Act 1971, when the Crown Court was introduced.

PRACTICAL TASK

- *Visit the website www.oldbaileyonline.org, which contains a digitalised archive of about 197,000 trials heard at the Old Bailey between 1674 and 1913.*

- *Access the link 'Historical Background' and then 'Crime, Justice and Punishment', and explore the historical information provided relating to policing, types of crime, conduct of proceedings, judges and juries, types of verdict and methods of punishment.*

- *Make notes of key information and later, having completed your reading and research, contrast and compare this with how the courts are conducted today.*

Police officers are mainly concerned with the criminal courts; however, there will be occasions when a police officer may be required to present evidence in a civil court. Today both criminal and civil cases within England and Wales are administered through a hierarchy of courts, from the locally based Magistrates' Courts to the European Courts.

Figure 2.1 is an outline of the hierarchy of courts within England and Wales. Northern Ireland and Scotland have similar, but slightly different structures, but do come within the jurisdiction of some of the higher courts.

For the purposes of this chapter we will be concerned with courts responsible for criminal cases (highlighted in grey on Figure 2.1).

Her Majesty's Courts Service

The courts are the responsibility of the Crown, and the Lord Chancellor's Department (LCD) has historically played a key role in the management of the courts. In 1977, the LCD became a major government department and, in 1995, the 'Courts Service' was launched as an executive agency of the LCD to manage the Crown, County and Supreme Courts. At this time the Magistrates' Courts were managed separately.

Lord Justice Auld, in his review of the criminal courts published in 2001, recommended that courts services should be brought together to provide a single administration. In June 2003, the LCD became known as the Department for Constitutional Affairs (DCA), headed by a Secretary of State retaining the office of Lord Chancellor. It was in November of that year that the Courts Act 2003 set out a framework for the introduction of Her Majesty's Courts Service (HMCS).

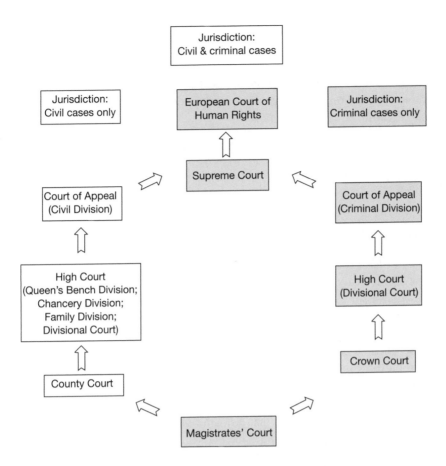

Figure 2.1 The structure of the courts

HMCS was introduced in April 2005 as an executive agency of the DCA (now Ministry of Justice) and its remit is to deliver justice effectively and efficiently to the public. It is responsible for managing the Magistrates' Courts, the Crown Court, the County Court, High Court, and Court of Appeal in England and Wales.

Magistrates' Courts

The Magistrates' Court is the place where justices of the peace (now more commonly known as magistrates) continue to deal with people for breaches of the law, resolving disputes, and maintaining good order within the community. During the year 2008–09 these courts were responsible for hearing two million criminal cases (HMCS, 2009a, p7), which is nearly 95 per cent of all criminal cases heard within England and Wales.

Magistrates' role is to sit in judgment on those people who are brought before them and includes:

- determining guilt and sentencing a person;
- dealing with requests for a remand in custody;

- dealing with applications for bail;

- committing persons to the Crown Court for trial or sentence.

Magistrates also have a civil jurisdiction and deal with a range of cases, for example care proceedings, non-payment of fines, non-payment of council tax, anti-social behaviour, family and domestic issues, and injunctions.

There are limitations as to the type of offence the courts can hear and the sentences that can be awarded. There are three types of offences:

- summary;

- either-way;

- indictable.

A summary offence is one that is dealt with at the Magistrates' Court and is an offence where the accused cannot elect trial by jury at the Crown Court. The offences are usually of a less serious nature, such as minor theft, assault and criminal damage, public disorder and motoring offences. Section 40 of the Criminal Justice Act 1988 allows certain summary offences, such as common assault, taking a vehicle without consent, and driving while disqualified, to be heard by a higher court subject to certain criteria, for example if it is founded on the same facts or evidence supporting an indictable or either-way offence. Sentencing is restricted and magistrates can only award a maximum of six months' imprisonment (or twelve months for consecutive sentences), and a fine not exceeding £5,000. When magistrates consider that a greater sentence is required, the case must be referred to the Crown Court for a sentencing decision.

An either-way offence can be dealt with either at the Magistrates' Court or the Crown Court. Magistrates can only hear the case if the accused consents and waives the right for the case to be heard by a jury at the Crown Court. Theft and handling stolen property are examples of either-way offences.

An indictable offence relates to a more serious crime and includes offences such as murder, rape, blackmail and robbery. These offences can only be heard by a jury at the Crown Court.

Cases in the Magistrates' Court are usually heard by a panel of three magistrates supported by a justice's clerk, who is legally qualified and is required to advise the magistrates on matters of law. Both lay magistrates and district judges can be found presiding in a Magistrates' Court.

Lay magistrates

There are around 30,000 lay magistrates in England and Wales (HMCS, 2009b) who are appointed by the Crown. A lay magistrate can be recruited between the ages of 18 and 65 and must retire by 70. They are volunteers and receive no payment, but may claim expenses. Most magistrates have no legal qualifications, but receive appropriate training to carry out their role. Certain members of the public are disqualified from applying for the role, such as serving or recently retired police officers, undischarged bankrupts, serving members of HM Forces, or persons with convictions for serious offences or a series of minor offences. An applicant will also require certain qualities of:

- good character;
- good understanding and communication;
- good social awareness;
- sound judgement;
- maturity and sound temperament;
- commitment and reliability.

District judges

In addition to lay magistrates, there are also about 130 district judges (prior to August 2000 these were known as stipendiary magistrates). District judges are legally qualified and are required to have at least seven years' experience as a barrister or solicitor and two years' experience as a deputy district judge. They are mainly found sitting in the metropolitan and major urban areas and sit alone, dealing with the longer and more complex cases. Some district judges have the power to hear extradition proceedings and certain terrorist offences.

REFLECTIVE TASK

The use of lay magistrates within the CJS has caused some commentators concern. Some suggest that our magistrates are middle class, middle minded and middle aged.

- *Consider whether our magistrates are currently representative of the communities they serve.*
- *Further consider some of the decisions that a lay magistrate has to make, such as deciding whether an accused is granted bail or remanded in custody.*
- *Are they suitably qualified to make these decisions and do they get them right?*
- *Go to the Prison Reform Trust website at www.prisonreformtrust.org.uk/subsection. asp?id=1497 and discover what they have to say about remanding people to prison.*

Youth Courts

Most 10–17 year olds will have their cases heard in a Youth Court that is not open to the general public, and only those who have direct involvement with the case will normally be present. If a young person is charged with an adult, the hearing can take place in a Magistrates' Court. The Youth Court is usually located in the same building as the Magistrates' Court and the proceedings are less formal than an adult hearing.

Crown Court

The Crown Court is responsible for hearing the more serious criminal cases and, in the year 2008–09 dealt with about 150,000 cases (HMCS, 2009a, p7). A person who commits an indictable offence can only be dealt with at the Crown Court. The court also deals with either-way offences, appeals from the Magistrates' Court, and those offences referred to them by the Magistrates' Court.

The Crown Court is presided over by a single judge who will have had at least ten years' experience as a lawyer. There are three types of judge who can sit in a Crown Court:

- High Court judge, who is a member of the Queen's Bench Division based in London;

- circuit judge;

- recorder, who is a part-time judge.

The High Court judge will hear the most serious criminal cases with the circuit judge and recorder dealing with about 95 per cent of all the cases referred to the Crown Court (Uglow, 2005, p460). A district judge, in certain circumstances, can sit as a recorder within the Crown Court (Courts Act 2003, s65).

Until 1971, the most serious cases were always heard by a travelling High Court judge at the County Assizes, with the lesser cases being dealt with at the Quarter Sessions. A Royal Commission recognised that these courts could not cope with the ever increasing demand and the Crown Court system was introduced, initially setting up 90 (now 77) different Crown Court centres within England and Wales (Beeching, 1969).

The centres provide three different tiers of Crown Court.

- *Tier One.* Based in key areas of business, e.g. Bristol, Birmingham, Leeds and Manchester. They have both a High Court and a Crown Court with separate judges for civil and criminal work. The Crown Court is staffed by all three types of judges and deals with all categories of indictable offences.

- *Tier Two.* Crown Court only, staffed by all three types of judges and dealing with all categories of indictable offences.

- *Tier Three.* Crown Court only, not attended by a High Court judge and not dealing with the more serious offences such as murder, manslaughter and rape.

(Martin, 2005, p166)

PRACTICAL TASK

- *Find out where your nearest Crown Court is and establish which tier it is.*

- *Establish which judges sit at the court and the types of offences they hear.*

- *If possible, pay a visit to the court and sit in on a trial.*

The judge has an important role to play in the Crown Court, being responsible for the proceedings and solely responsible for matters of law. He or she advises the jury on legal issues; provides a summary of the evidence; and explains the burden of proof which, in criminal cases, is beyond all reasonable doubt.

The role of the jury

The traditions of the jury can be traced back to Henry II (1154–89), who formed local juries of 12 knights to settle disputes over ownership of land. The jury's role is to establish matters of fact within a criminal trial and, having heard the evidence, provide a verdict. Any law issues that are raised during the trial will be dealt with by the judge alone.

A juror is selected from the electoral roll and must be aged between 18 and 70 years. He or she must have been resident within the UK, Channel Islands or Isle of Man for the previous five years, must not be mentally disordered, and must not be disqualified. The Courts Act 2003 tightened up the provisions relating to persons who can be excused or disqualified from jury service. People who have received certain sentences for criminal offences can be disqualified for life or 10 years depending on the type of sentence received. Police officers used to be excluded from jury service but are no longer exempt.

Today questions are continually asked about the ability of jurors to make sound decisions. Some trials are lengthy and complex; acquittal rates are very high in the Crown Court; some jurors are exposed to horrific evidence; some are exposed to extortion and threats by certain criminals; and the values and attitudes of some jurors can influence the trial outcome.

PRACTICAL TASK

Make a list of what you consider to be the advantages and disadvantages of the use of a jury in a criminal trial (this may require some further research). When your list is completed, produce an argument either for or against reform of the jury system.

Appeal courts

There is a system in place that provides the opportunity for a person convicted of a criminal offence to appeal against a conviction or the sentence that has been awarded. An appeal can also be made on a point of law by way of case stated. Figure 2.2 provides details of the routes of appeal that are available.

Appeal from a Magistrates' Court

The defence can appeal to the Crown Court against the conviction and/or sentence imposed by a Magistrates' Court. The case will usually be heard by a circuit judge assisted by two magistrates and will be a complete rehearing of the case together with the original

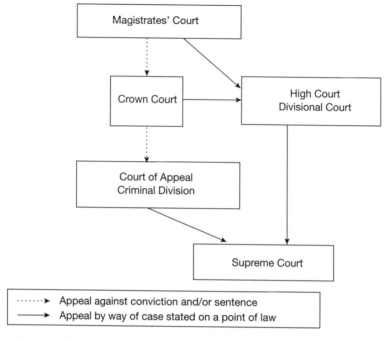

Figure 2.2 Routes of appeal

witnesses and legal arguments. Following the hearing, three decisions can be made: to uphold the conviction; to quash the conviction; or to vary the sentence.

The second route for an appeal is by way of case stated on a point of law direct to the Divisional Court of the High Court. This route can only be used by the defence against a conviction or the prosecution against an acquittal. The facts of the case are outlined, and the legal issues considered, and when forwarded to the higher court it will only be interested in the points of law and will not be concerned with the facts or sentence.

CASE STUDY

In a drink-drive offence, a decision was taken not to call a witness living in Bulgaria who was responsible for analysing the blood sample. The accused was found guilty and the decision not to produce the witness was challenged. The 'point of law' was posed in a question:

> *Was the Court right to admit in evidence a certificate of analysis of a blood specimen served under s.16 of the Road Traffic Offenders Act 1988 when notice had been given pursuant to s.16(4) of the Act, requiring the attendance at the hearing of the analyst.*

> *(Brett v. DPP [2009])*

Appeal from the Crown Court

As with the Magistrates' Court, the defence can appeal to the Court of Appeal (Criminal Division) against the conviction and/or sentence imposed by the Crown Court. Leave (permission) for appeal needs to be granted and the Criminal Appeals Act 1995 requires the trial judge to produce a certificate to be lodged with the Court of Appeal within 28 days, stating that the case is fit for appeal. A single judge will then consider the application for leave to appeal and, if refused, in certain circumstances a further application for leave to appeal can be made to the full Court of Appeal.

The conduct of the appeal is different from that heard in the Crown Court. The Court of Appeal has the discretion to hear evidence, but rarely does so, because their main purpose is to review the initial trial; however, the rules do allow for the introduction of fresh evidence that would require examination and assessment by the Court. The appeal will be allowed only if there is evidence to show that the conviction is 'unsafe'. An unsafe conviction is where a judge has made an error in explaining the law to the jury; if inadmissible evidence has been allowed; or if there has been some other significant procedural error. Upon allowing an appeal, the judges have the power to quash the conviction, vary the sentence or order a retrial.

In 2008, 7,240 applications were received by the Court of Appeal – 5,422 against sentence and 1,588 against conviction, of which 1,204 (33 per cent) and 212 (21 per cent) respectively were granted leave to appeal. Of the appeals actually heard by the Court during the year, 1,567 (75 per cent) against sentence and 188 (43 per cent) against conviction were allowed (Ministry of Justice, 2009, p14).

REFLECTIVE TASK

Access Westlaw or Lexis Library online and find the case of R v. Nazir Ahmed [2009]. Reflect on the issues raised and consider whether you agree with the findings of Lady Justice Hallett. Explain your reasoning.

As with the Magistrates' Court, a second route for an appeal is by way of case stated on a point of law direct to the Divisional Court of the High Court.

Post-appeal mechanisms and the Criminal Cases Review Commission

While considering the criminal appeal courts, it is appropriate to mention the key role the Criminal Cases Review Commission (CCRC) plays in investigating and referring cases to the Court of Appeal. Post-appeal mechanisms come into play once an individual has exhausted all normal appeal rights and has either lost an appeal or has been refused leave to appeal.

During the 1980s and early 1990s, there was a series of high-profile miscarriages of justice that began to seriously undermine the public's confidence in the CJS. Where appeals had failed and miscarriages of justice were suspected, cases could only be referred back to the Court of Appeal by the Home Secretary. This was felt to be an unsatisfactory way of dealing with miscarriages of justice, due to numerous political, procedural and bureaucratic issues. The Home Secretary announced a Royal Commission on Criminal Justice in 1991, chaired by Viscount Runciman of Doxford. On the very same day of the announcement, six men who had been convicted in 1974 of killing 21 people in a series of bombings in Birmingham City Centre were freed by the Court of Appeal.

The Commission reported in 1993 and one of their recommendations was to set up an independent body to review potential miscarriages of justice and refer them to the Court of Appeal where appropriate. Following the Criminal Appeal Act 1995, the CCRC was established in March 1997 and became responsible for referring cases to the Court of Appeal rather than the Home Secretary.

The CCRC jurisdiction extends to England, Wales and Northern Ireland and they deal with all applications relating to alleged miscarriages of justice (Scotland has its own CCRC). It carries out an investigation and considers whether there is any new evidence available to cast doubt on the original conviction (section 23 of the Criminal Appeal Act 1968 provides the courts with the power to receive 'fresh' evidence). It has the power to refer the conviction or sentence back to the Court of Appeal (Criminal Appeal Act 1995, s13). It does not consider issues of innocence or guilt.

By December 2009, the CCRC had received 12,325 applications since 1997. Of these, 11,605 of the applications had been completed but only 444 were referred to the Court of Appeal. Of those referred, 411 have been heard by the Court with 290 cases quashed and 118 upheld (CCRC, 2009).

Appeals to the House of Lords

Prior to 1 October 2009, the House of Lords was the highest court in the land and the supreme court of appeal. It acted as the final court on points of law for the whole of the UK in civil cases, and in England, Wales and Northern Ireland in criminal cases, and its decisions were binding on all courts below. Appeals could be made to the House of Lords from the Court of Appeal (Criminal Division) and the Divisional Court of the High Court.

Appeals to the Supreme Court

The House of Lords has now been replaced by a Supreme Court for the United Kingdom and has moved to new premises at the Middlesex Guildhall, Parliament Square, Westminster. Section 23 of the Constitutional Reform Act 2003 provides the legal authority for the constitution of the Supreme Court, which is presided over by 12 judges known as 'Justices of the Supreme Court'. The purpose of the move is to provide greater clarity in constitutional arrangements and further separate the judiciary from the legislature and the executive.

In criminal cases, leave to appeal is necessary and a certificate from the court dealing with the initial appeal is required. The certificate will state that a point of law of general public importance is involved and outline the details of the point of law. Upon receipt of the petition (application for leave of appeal), an appeal committee of at least three justices will consider it and decide whether to give leave for the appeal to proceed or to reject it. Previously, the law lords (House of Lords) dealt with about 200–250 civil and criminal petitions for leave to appeal each year. In 2008, 28 criminal petitions were considered, of which only 10 were allowed (Ministry of Justice, 2009, p19).

Following consideration of the case, each justice will provide a written opinion that sets out his or her interpretation of the law and judgment in respect of the appeal.

PRACTICAL TASK

Go online to: www.publications.parliament.uk/pa/ld/ldjudgmt.htm, which will give you access to all House of Lords appeal decisions from 1996 to 2009. Find an appeal considered by the Court of Appeal (Criminal Division), explore how it is set out and identify the point of law being considered.

European Court of Human Rights

In 1950, the UK signed the European Convention on Human Rights, which was set up after the Second World War to protect individual rights and freedoms and the development of democratic principles. The agreement included recognition of the binding jurisdiction of the Convention, meaning that its decisions should be reflected within domestic law.

The European Court of Human Rights (ECHR) was first introduced in 1959 and, from 1966, individuals within the UK had the right to petition the court for breaches of the Convention. The ECHR is currently based in Strasbourg, France, and is staffed by member states of the European Council.

Since 1998, the Court has operated on a full-time basis and is made up of 47 judges, one for each state that has signed up to the Convention. The Human Rights Act 1998, introduced in 2000, provided for any breaches of the Convention to be dealt with in the first instance by the courts within the UK. Where a case is not resolved, an application can be made to the ECHR to consider it accordingly.

The work of the Court has grown considerably, from 8,400 applications in 1999 to 49,900 in 2008 with 97,300 applications pending (as at 1 January 2009). During the period 1959 to 2009, 404 judgments were made on applications received from the UK (ECHR, 2009).

CASE STUDY

The three cases highlighted below provide a good contrast of how the government has responded to decisions made by the ECHR.

- *Golder v. UK [1975] relates to the right to privacy (article 8) and concerned a prisoner who was not allowed to send confidential information to his solicitor. The appeal was successful and the UK Prison Rules were changed to allow confidentiality.*

- *Abdulaziz v. UK [1985] relates to prohibition against discrimination (article 14) and concerned immigration law and alleged discrimination against women, who were not allowed to bring their husbands or fiancés to the UK, in contrast to men, who were* allowed to bring wives and fiancées. The appeal was successful and the government changed the law to avoid any further discrimination.

- Brogan v. UK [1988] relates to the right to liberty and security (article 5) and concerned the seven-day detention period for terrorists, preventing a suspect being brought quickly before a judge. In this case, the government refused to change the law in the interest of national security.

(Martin, 2005, p281)

All of the above cases can be accessed via the 'HUDOC database' on the ECHR website.

PRACTICAL TASK

Research the implications of the ECHR decision in Osman v. UK [1998] and its impact on policing. Most forces now have a 'Threat to life' policy, which includes an 'Osman' warning. Using 'Google', find one of these policies on the internet and discover how the Police Service is reacting to the ECHR decision.

Other courts

Community Justice Courts

Community Justice Courts are a new innovation within the CJS and they are part of what are termed 'community justice centres'. The centres are based on a similar scheme in Red Hook, Brooklyn, New York and have been introduced by the Labour government as part of their strategy to tackle crime and disorder. It is a multi-agency approach involving a number of key players, including the Local Criminal Justice Board, the judiciary and magistrates, local councils, Crime and Disorder Reduction Partnerships, Safer Neighbourhood Teams and other volunteer services.

The first centres were introduced in North Liverpool and Salford (Manchester) in the autumn of 2005 and 11 further centres have been established in Bradford, Birmingham, Devon & Cornwall, Leicester, Merthyr Tydfil, Middlesbrough, Nottingham and three in the London area. The aim of each centre is for the agencies concerned to join together with the local community and seek solutions to tackle crime and disorder effectively.

Judges and magistrates will meet on a regular basis with the local community and sentencing decisions are focused on problem solving, addressing underlying causes of offending, punishment and reparation to the community.

The Liverpool Court is presided over by a single Community Justice Judge, which is a new judicial post that was awarded to a district judge who receives the salary of a circuit judge.

In contrast, the Salford Community Justice Court is presided over by an experienced and dedicated bench of magistrates. The first evaluations to explore the effectiveness of the centres were completed in 2007 and below are some examples of the results provided from the evaluation of the Liverpool Court.

- Evidence of a more efficient court that avoids unnecessary delays and bureaucracy.

- Guilty plea rate of 82 per cent compared against national rate of 68 per cent.

- Effective case management and information exchange.

- Average hearings per case 2.2 compared with a regional average of 2.8.

- Reduced times from first hearing to sentence.

- Evidence of the problem-solving approach reducing reoffending.

(McKenna, 2007)

PRACTICAL TASK

Go to the website www.communityjustice.gov.uk, read about Community Justice Courts and make a list of what you consider to be the advantages of this approach. Links are provided to all of the currently established centres and copies of evaluations are available for further study. Some excellent resources and links are available for those of you considering writing assignments about the effectiveness of the multi-agency approach to tackling crime and disorder or exploring the concepts of restorative justice.

Dedicated domestic violence courts

These are specialised courts that were introduced in 2006 to provide a part solution to effectively tackling the well-documented problems of domestic abuse. This is another partnership approach involving agencies such as the Police, Crown Prosecution Service, court staff, the Probation Service and other specialist support services.

The courts are presided over by magistrates who have received additional training for dealing with domestic abuse and, by April 2008, 98 courts had been established in England and Wales.

Dedicated drug courts

The use of dedicated drug courts provides a further example of a multi-agency approach in tackling the problems of drugs abuse and its link to acquisitive crime. The court will manage the case from conviction and throughout the sentence to completion or breach of a community order with a drug rehabilitation requirement (DRR). The DRR was introduced by the Drugs Act 2005 with an aim to increase the effectiveness of the Drug Interventions Programme by getting more offenders into treatment.

Coroner's Courts

The office of Coroner was first established in 1194, primarily to gather tax, but the Coroner is now an independent judicial officer who investigates sudden, violent or unnatural death. In some cases, the Coroner will be required to hold an inquest, which is a legal enquiry that takes the form of a public hearing in a court building or other place designated as a Coroner's Court.

In certain circumstances the Coroner will be required to summon a jury of between seven and eleven people to sit at an inquest. The jury will be selected from the electoral roll and must be aged between 18 and 70 years. It is the role of the jury to establish certain facts, such as the identity of the deceased and when, where and how the deceased died, and to obtain information required to register the death. The inquest is not a trial where there is a finding of guilt but a legal enquiry into the causes and circumstances of the death. Relatives are able to ask questions of witnesses and can be represented by a lawyer, but there is no legal aid provision.

A jury will be required to sit at an inquest where the death:

- has occurred in prison;

- has occurred in police custody, or resulted from an injury caused by a police officer;

- was caused by an accident, poisoning or disease, where legislation requires reporting to a government department or other officer, or to the Health and Safety Executive;

- has occurred in circumstances prejudicial to the health or safety of the public.

(Coroners Act 1988, s8(3))

Following an inquest, the Coroner can deliver a number of different verdicts, including natural causes, accident, suicide, unlawful or lawful killing, industrial disease or open verdict.

Tribunals

The use of tribunals has grown considerably during the latter part of the twentieth century and they work alongside the civil and criminal court systems. Many have been created by legislation and deal with issues such as social security, rent, immigration, mental health and employment. Not all tribunals will operate in the same way, but usually consist of a panel of three with a legally qualified chair and two lay members who have expertise in the field of the tribunal.

A Tribunals Service was created in 2006 and is an executive arm of the Ministry of Justice with the aim of producing a unified administration for the tribunals system. The Tribunals, Courts and Enforcement Act 2007 has established a judicial and legal framework that has created a new unified structure for tribunals. There are two tiers of a first and upper tribunal that are split into a number of chambers. The chambers have specific jurisdictions with appropriate experts and, during the first phase of the implementation of restructuring, the following chambers have been introduced:

- social entitlement;

- health, education and social care;

- war pensions and armed forces.

The social entitlement chamber includes criminal injuries compensation and this is one tribunal where a police officer may have to attend and provide evidence.

Criminal Injuries Compensation Authority

The Criminal Injuries Compensation Authority (CICA) is a government body that is responsible for administering the criminal injuries compensation scheme within England, Scotland and Wales. The scheme was first introduced in 1964 and later revised in 2001, providing compensation for victims of violent crime of from £1,000 to £500,000. Where a person is not satisfied by the compensation awarded, they can appeal to a first-tier tribunal. The tribunal is not a court of law and will be presided over by at least two judges/members who have expertise in the field of criminal compensation. The hearing is informal and claimants have the right to question witnesses.

A police officer is very likely to have been involved in receiving the initial complaint of the crime that resulted in the injury to the victim and will have completed an investigation. The Police Service has processes in place to ensure that each victim of violent crime is informed of the scheme and how to access it. It is important that proper records have been maintained and are readily available for the tribunal.

Preparing for court and giving evidence

Any policing practitioner will be required at some time to provide evidence in a court or tribunal and will need to be fully prepared to present evidence effectively. All exhibits, notes and relevant materials should be identified and made readily available. There may also be a responsibility to liaise with relevant parties and to take any action necessary to resolve problems or difficulties that may arise. Examples of relevant parties include victims, witnesses, defence and prosecution personnel, court ushers and supporting agencies.

You must be able to present evidence in an effective manner, complying with rules of evidence, court procedures and acceptable professional standards. It will also be necessary to ensure that all relevant aspects of community and race relations, diversity and human rights are adhered to.

Preparing for the court

Once a time and date have been received to attend court, arrangements should be made to obtain any statements, notes or exhibits that will be required by the court. When you take responsibility for any exhibit there is a need to ensure that it is readily available, and that continuity and integrity of the exhibit are maintained.

It will be good practice to consider your evidence prior to a case and ensure that you are in possession of any notes and materials that may be required at court, for example witness statements, pocket notebooks and original notes.

If you have not been to the court before, find out where it is and make plans to arrive in plenty of time. Some court buildings contain many courts and upon arrival you may have to establish which court is hearing your particular case. Once the court is found, inform the court usher that you have arrived. You will be required to wait in the vicinity until called to give evidence and it is advised that the case or evidence that you are to present is not discussed with anyone else as this may compromise the trial.

Presenting evidence in court

When called, you will be required to walk to the witness box in the courtroom and take the oath or affirmation. Each witness is required to hold a New Testament Bible (Old Testament in the case of a Jewish person) in their right hand and repeat the oath:

> *I swear by Almighty God that the evidence I give shall be the truth, the whole truth and nothing but the truth.*

(Oaths Act 1978, s1)

Where the witness is not Christian or Jewish, they can affirm or take an oath upon a holy book aligned to their religious belief, for example Vadas (Hindu) or Koran (Muslim). The affirmation will commence:

> *I (name) do solemnly, sincerely and truly declare and affirm . . .*

Personnel within the courts should be addressed in certain ways as shown in Table 2.1.

Once you have taken the oath/affirmation and have been introduced to the court, the prosecution will start the process of examining (questioning) you – referred to as 'examination in chief'. The prosecution will lead you through the evidence and ask questions where appropriate. Section 139 of the Criminal Justice Act 2003 allows a witness with the permission of the court to refresh their memory by referring to notes made at an earlier date. For example, a police officer may make some notes of a conversation with the accused at the time of arrest, and many months later is called to court to give evidence. Details of the initial conversation may be difficult to recall; however, notes made at the time would provide an accurate account of the actual conversation.

The next phase of the process allows the defence team to cross-examine you and test the evidence provided. Defence questioning can be challenging and it is important to

Table 2.1 Forms of address in the courts

High Court judge	My Lord or My Lady
Circuit judge	Your Honour
Recorder or district judge	Sir or Madam
Magistrate	Your Worship
Tribunal chair	Sir or Madam

concentrate, stay calm and take time in answering questions posed. Answers provided should remain concise and accurate without embellishment, as any additional information provided may give the defence team a further avenue to explore and an opportunity to discredit you.

Following the cross-examination, the prosecution will sometimes want to re-examine a witness on issues raised during the cross-examination. This is permitted in certain circumstances, with the proviso that the prosecution does not ask any leading questions.

After giving evidence you should remain nearby until formally released by the court.

PRACTICAL TASK

It is likely that, at some time in the future, you will be required to give evidence. Consider how you will prepare to give evidence in a court and write out a checklist of what will be required.

If you have already had the experience of giving evidence in court, assess the effectiveness of your preparation and how the evidence was delivered, and write out an action plan for any areas of development identified.

CHAPTER SUMMARY

Within this chapter you have been provided with a brief historical background of the development of the courts within England and Wales, together with details of the current structures and purpose of the courts with a focus on criminal cases. Opportunities have been provided for further research, and there has been analysis of certain issues relating to the courts that will provide stimuli, sources and evidence for completion of NOS and assignments. Further reading around this topic area will provide a clearer and more detailed understanding of the key role that courts play within the CJS.

REFERENCES

Beeching, Lord Richard (1969) *Report of the Royal Commission on Assizes and Quarter Sessions 1966–69* (Cmnd 4153). London: HMSO.

Criminal Cases Review Commission (CCRC) (2009) *Case Library: Case Statistics.* Available online at www.ccrc.gov.uk/cases/case_44.htm (accessed 18 January 2010).

Emsley, C (2002) The history of crime and control institutions, in Maguire M, Morgan, R and Reiner, R (eds) *The Oxford Handbook of Criminology.* Oxford: Oxford University Press.

European Court of Human Rights (ECHR) (2009) *Some Facts and Figures 1959–2009.* Strasbourg: European Court of Human Rights. Available online at www.echr.coe.int (accessed 19 January 2010).

Her Majesty's Courts Service (HMCS) (2009a) *Annual Report and Accounts 2008/09.* Available online at www.hmcourts-service.gov.uk/cms/files/HMCS-AnnualReportAndAccounts-2008-09.pdf (accessed 26 November 2009).

Her Majesty's Courts Service (HMCS) (2009b) *Magistrates and Magistrates' Courts.* Available online at http://212.137.36.113/infoabout/magistrates/index.htm (accessed 19 January 2010).

Maitland, F W (2008) *The Constitutional History of England: A Course of Lectures Delivered.* London: Maitland Press.

Martin, J (2005) *The English Legal System*, 4th edition. London: Hodder Arnold.

McKenna, K (2007) *Evaluation of North Liverpool Community Justice Centre* (Ministry of Justice Research Series 12/07). London: Ministry of Justice Research Unit.

Ministry of Justice (MoJ) (2009) *Judicial and Court Statistics 2008.* Norwich: The Stationery Office.

Uglow Steve (2005) The Criminal Justice System, in Hale, C, Hayward, K, Wahidin, A and Wincup, Emma (eds) *Criminology.* Oxford: Oxford University Press.

USEFUL WEBSITES

www.ccrc.gov.uk (Criminal Case Review Commission)

www.cica.gov.uk (Criminal Injuries Compensation Authority)

www.communityjustice.gov.uk (Community Justice)

www.crimereduction.homeoffice.gov.uk (Crime Reduction)

www.echr.coe.int (European Court of Human Rights)

www.hmcourts-service.gov.uk (Her Majesty's Courts Service)

www.judiciary.gov.uk (Judiciary of England and Wales)

www.justice.gov.uk (Ministry of Justice)

www.magistrates-association.org.uk (Magistrates Association)

www.parliament.uk (Houses of Commons and Lords)

www.supremecourt.gov.uk (UK Supreme Court)

CASES

Brett v *DPP* [2009] EWHC 440 (Admin)

R v. *Nazir Ahmed* [2009] EWCA Crim. 669

Coroners Act 1988

Courts Act 1971

Courts Act 2003

Courts and Legal Services Act 1990

Criminal Appeal Act 1907

Criminal Appeal Act 1966

Criminal Appeal Act 1968

Criminal Appeal Act 1995

Criminal Justice Act 1988

Criminal Justice Act 2003

Constitutional Reform Act 2003

Drugs Act 2005

Human Rights Act 1998

Oaths Act 1978

The Supreme Court of Judicature Act 1873

Tribunals, Courts and Enforcement Act 2007

3 Arrest and detention

CHAPTER OBJECTIVES

By the end of this chapter you should be able to:

- give a brief overview of the history of arrest and detention;
- understand police discretion and the implications for arrest and detention;
- identify some of the differences between key pieces of legislation;
- understand some of the legal requirements for arrest and detention;
- appreciate how the Police and Criminal Evidence Act (PACE) 1984 affects the detention and questioning of suspects;
- analyse a number of key issues regarding the right to silence and its impact within the Criminal Justice System (CJS).

LINKS TO STANDARDS

This chapter provides opportunities for links with the following Skills for Justice, National Occupational Standards (NOS) for Policing and Law Enforcement 2008.

Unit CD1
1:1 Identify the legislation, policies, procedures, codes of practice and/or guidelines that relate to human rights.

Unit CD5
1:1 Identify the legislation, policies, procedures, codes of practice and/or guidelines that relate to arrest and detention.

Unit CJ201
1:1 Identify the legislation, policies, procedures, codes of practice, professional practice and organisational requirements and guidelines in relation to conducting interviews with suspects.

Introduction

Have you ever considered why the police arrest in some circumstances but not in others?

Police officers must and should be able to exercise discretion in deciding whether to detain and arrest; however, allowing the police to use their professional judgement should not be seen as an endorsement of random or arbitrary policing. Contemporary policing should operate on the basis of public consent without which the police would be ineffective. But knowing whether and when to arrest and to do so in a way that protects the public can be problematic, as history has demonstrated!

This chapter will provide you with an overview of arrest and detention, and the various activities will allow for further independent study, group discussion and critical reflection.

Arrest: a brief history

As London expanded during the eighteenth and nineteenth centuries, the issues of law and order became a matter of public concern, resulting in the setting up of parliamentary committees in 1812, 1818 and 1822. The Vagrancy Act 1824 was introduced as a method of dealing with the large numbers of soldiers who found themselves on the streets after the Napoleonic Wars, as well as an influx of economic migrants travelling in search of work. Sections 4 and 6 of the Act made it illegal for a suspected person or reputed thief to frequent or loiter in a public place with intent to commit an arrestable offence. The Metropolitan Police Act 1839 also allowed a constable within the Metropolitan Police area to stop, search and detain any person who was reasonably suspected of having, or conveying, anything stolen or unlawfully obtained. These powers allowed the police to stop, search and arrest anyone based on 'suspicion' alone, which led to assertions among black and ethnic minority groups that they were being deliberately and indiscriminately targeted. The laws were abolished after assertions that they had contributed to race riots, which first erupted in the St Paul's district of Bristol and later spread during 1981 to Brixton and Southall, Toxteth in Liverpool, Moss Side in Manchester, Handsworth in Birmingham, Sheffield, Nottingham and other major cities. I shall return to the problem of urban unrest later in the chapter.

You may be familiar with the euphemism 'helping police with their enquiries'. Historically, arrest was used as a means of securing the attendance of a suspect at court, where they were first interviewed and afterwards arrested on warrant for a suspected offence, provided that there was sufficient evidence on which to base a prosecution. Arrest and detention is now a more formal process, generally occurring at the start of any investigation. This has largely come about by the introduction of some key pieces of legislation, namely:

- Criminal Law Act 1967;

- Police and Criminal Evidence Act (PACE) 1984;

- Serious Organised Crime and Police Act (SOCAP) 2005.

Originally, all crimes in English law were categorised in a hierarchy of *treason*, *felony* and *misdemeanour*, each with its own rules of procedure and evidence. The Criminal Law Act

1967 abolished these distinctions and created a new category of 'arrestable offences', which were crimes attracting a maximum prison sentence for an adult on conviction of five or more years. The Act also defined the circumstances in which a citizen or a constable could arrest somebody without a warrant.

At common law a constable can still arrest a person where it's genuinely suspected that conduct is likely to result in a breach of the peace, whether in public or in private. While shouting and swearing alone does not constitute a breach of the peace, it is an offence under the Town Police Clauses Act 1847, which is arrestable under the 'general arrest' conditions of section 25 of PACE. Where a course of conduct results in harassment, alarm or distress, it may constitute an offence under section 5 of the Public Order Act 1986.

Arrestable offences were later repealed and replaced by PACE, which also created new powers (for constables only) to arrest without a warrant, in certain circumstances, those suspected of committing 'non-arrestable offences'. PACE was then modified by SOCAP which came into force in January 2006. SOCAP abolished the differences between arrestable and non-arrestable offences and replaced them with a new general power of arrest for all offences irrespective of the maximum sentence. Under the new SOCAP provisions a police officer can arrest for any offence provided that certain conditions exist. SOCAP also extends the powers of Police Community Support Officers (PCSOs) and other persons designated or accredited under provisions of the Police Reform Act 2002. We will return to some of the reasons for the introduction of PACE and SOCAP later in this chapter.

REFLECTIVE TASK

In England and Wales policing is undertaken with the public's support and cooperation.

Debate whether the principle of 'policing by consent' has been affected by the key legislative changes referred to.

Arrest procedures and what the law demands

Before the introduction of PACE, compulsion had been a necessary element of arrest, for example by some 'physical' restraint such as taking someone by the arm and then clearly explaining that they were under arrest. Where words alone were used, it was necessary for the detainee to consent to the arrest. There was a danger, however, that where only words were used, they might not be clear enough. In *Sandon* v. *Jervis* [1859] it was held that there was no arrest where the detainer said 'I arrest you' and the detainee ran off before they could be touched.

These principles remain good law today and, according to PACE, no arrest is lawful unless the detainee is informed of the ground(s) for arrest at the time of, or as soon as is reasonably practicable after, the arrest (s28(3)). This applies regardless of whether the ground is obvious and, once it is given, the arrest becomes lawful (s28(4)). In the case of *Lewis* v. *Chief Constable of South Wales Constabulary* [1991], officers informed the two plaintiffs that they were under arrest but delayed explaining the grounds to them for 10 minutes and 23 minutes respectively. It was held that arrest arose factually from the deprivation of a person's liberty and it was a continuing act. In this case, what had begun as an unlawful act became lawful as soon as the grounds had been explained.

A person arrested by a constable, or handed over to one, must be taken to a police station as soon as is practicable, unless his or her presence elsewhere is 'necessary in order to carry out such investigations as it is reasonable to carry out immediately' (s30(1)(10)). Where a citizen makes an arrest they 'must, as soon as they reasonably can, hand the man over to a constable or take him to a police station or before a magistrate'.

Let's now consider what constitutes an arrest. In *Spicer v. Holt* [1977], Lord Dilhorne stated:

> *Whether or not a person has been arrested depends not upon the legality of the arrest but on whether he has been deprived of his liberty to go where he pleases.*

Where the liberty of an individual is at stake, the arrest must be justified and there is certainly no legal police power to detain someone against their will in order to make enquiries about the person. This is confirmed in the case of *R v. Lemsatef* [1977] and by section 29 of PACE, which clearly states that someone who attends a police station for the purpose of 'assisting with an investigation' is entitled to leave at any time unless placed under arrest. If a decision is taken to 'prevent him from leaving at will', he must be arrested and informed of the grounds.

Unlawful arrest

Where the arrest of someone is deemed to be unlawful, there are a number of remedies open to the person wrongly arrested.

First, the detainee can invoke the ancient prerogative of *habeas corpus*. Defined as 'you must have the body', habeas corpus is intended to protect those who have been unlawfully detained in prison, hospital, in a police station or in private custody. A writ can be issued by a judge in chambers where there is prima facie evidence (accepted as so until proved otherwise) that the detention is unlawful and, because every detention is primarily unlawful, the burden of proof is on the detainer to justify their actions. Similar to habeas corpus and an equally important safeguard, articles 5(4) and 5(5) of the Human Rights Act (HRA) 1998 provide that everyone shall have the right to petition a court to question the appropriateness of any detention and that, where it is found to be unlawful, there should be an automatic right to compensation.

Second, the detainee can use unlawful detention to argue that any subsequent prosecution should fail. However, it's rare to succeed with this type of argument as the court has no discretion to exclude evidence simply because it has been obtained improperly (*R v. Sang* [1979]). This has prompted some to argue that the moral underpinnings of the CJS should demand that, if evidence has been obtained by 'foul means', defendants should be acquitted even if they appear to be guilty. An extreme example might involve the admissibility of confession evidence obtained by torture in another country.

The current position is that relevant evidence can only be excluded where its effect would be 'unduly prejudicial' to an accused, and this tends to be more an issue for the Crown Court where the admissibility of evidence seems to be challenged more often; section 78(1) of PACE allows the exclusion of any prosecution evidence if the prejudicial effects outweigh its *probative value*. The court has to consider what negative inferences could be unfairly drawn against a defendant compared to the evidence it 'proves', or its probative value. But just because evidence might be adverse doesn't automatically exclude it. It should be that it doesn't assist the jury in determining something factual, while at the same time leading them to wrongly infer guilt from it. Where it does assist the jury, but is only slightly prejudicial, it is likely that it would be admitted.

PRACTICAL TASK

Refer to a copy of the Spring 2009 newsletter of Liberty, which can be found under the 'Publications/newsletter' links at www.liberty-human-rights.org.uk.

Read the football article on page 3 and then visit the website www.opsi.gov.uk. Search for the article 5 of the Human Rights Act (HRA) 1998 and section 27 of the Violent Crime Reduction Act 2006. Consider the major themes and debate with a friend, a family member or fellow student officer whether:

- *the HRA is a 'rogue's charter' that unacceptably hinders the effective investigation of offences;*

- *despite the HRA, police powers are still open to abuse, which includes the arbitrary use of arrest and detention.*

Street detention

In determining whether an arrest is legal, the detainer's conduct needs to be considered. In the case of *Kenlin v. Gardiner* [1967] a police officer, while wearing plain clothes, took hold of the arm of a boy he wished to question. Not believing the man to be a police officer, despite being shown a warrant card, the boy punched the officer in order to escape. The court held that the officer's conduct in trying to physically apprehend the boy was unlawful and that the boy had acted in self-defence.

In the case of *Donnelly v. Jackman* [1970] an officer approached the suspect to ask some questions. The officer followed the suspect after he was first ignored and then tapped him on the shoulder. The suspect tapped the officer back, saying 'now we are even, copper'. The suspect forcibly punched the officer after he had been tapped on the shoulder a second time. This case was distinguished from *Kenlin v. Gardiner* and it was held that not every trivial interference with a citizen's liberty amounted to a course of conduct sufficient to take the officer beyond the course of his duties.

In *Bentley v. Brudzinksy* [1982] two boys were stopped by a constable while running barefoot down the street in the early hours. They were questioned about a stolen vehicle as they fitted the description of the suspects. After waiting for ten minutes while their details were confirmed they started to walk away. Another constable arrived and placed his hand on the defendant's shoulder, who then punched the officer in the face. Unlike the *Donnelly* v. *Jackman* case, it was held that the officer's conduct was more than trivial interference and had amounted to an unlawful attempt to detain the boy.

Reasonable grounds for suspecting an offence

A considerable number of police arrest powers require reasonable 'suspicion', 'cause' or a 'belief' that a suspect is involved, actually or potentially, in a crime. The precedent for determining what is 'reasonable' was established in the 1948 case of *Associated Provincial Picture Houses Ltd* v. *Wednesbury Corporation* and the resulting 'Wednesbury Principles'. The case considered whether the conditions imposed by a local authority on Sunday cinema opening were reasonable. In determining whether the Corporation had acted reasonably, Lord Green MR said:

> *A person entrusted with a discretion must . . . call his own attention to matters which he is bound to consider. He must exclude . . . matters which are irrelevant . . . If he does not obey those rules, he may be truly said, and often is said, to be acting 'unreasonably'.*

PRACTICAL TASK

Access Westlaw or Lexis Library online and find the case of Armstrong v. Chief Constable of West Yorkshire Police [2008] All ER (D) 69 (Dec). This Court of Appeal case considers a case of rape and the arrest grounds.

Reflect on the issues highlighted and decide whether you agree with the court's judgments.

Discretion in the exercise of police powers

In the Wednesbury case, Lord Green refers to the notion of discretion, which is defined by Gelsthorpe and Padfield as:

> *The freedom, power, authority, decision or leeway of an official, organisation or individual to decide, discern or determine to make a judgment, choice or decision about alternative courses of action or inaction.*

(2003, p1)

The recognition that police officers are required to interpret and selectively apply the law has been a recurring theme of much police research since the early 1960s. Studies by Herman Goldstein (1964) and Joseph Goldstein (1960) suggest that full law enforcement doesn't actually exist. This is particularly the case for 'low-visibility' police work carried out beyond the scope of line managers. Here, police officers have been allowed considerable autonomy, especially in deciding whether and how to apply the law. Recent studies also suggest that officers tend to evade policy that doesn't correspond with their perception of the police role. They also suggest that a police subculture contributes to the abuse of police discretion and bias against disorganised and economically deprived sections of the working class and minority ethnic groups. For example, someone from the lower working classes is more likely to be scrutinised and, therefore, to be observed and arrested when in violation of the law (Rowe, 2004; Box, 2009). This particular theme is also addressed by Chambliss (1969), who provides one of the most instructive assessments of the organising principles in the administration of justice.

> *Those persons arrested, tried and sentenced . . . can offer the fewest rewards for non-enforcement of the laws and . . . can be processed without creating any undue strain for the organisations which complete the legal system.*
>
> (Chambliss, 1969, pp84–5)

Paradoxically, some commentators have argued that police discretion is necessary, particularly where limited resources mean that not every law can be enforced and because even the most precise laws require some interpretation, even in the most concrete situations (Waddington, 1999; Reiner, 2000). While the police have considerable discretion in deciding whether to enforce the law, the final decision is usually determined by a range of factors both intrinsic and extrinsic to policing. The police can be constrained from enforcing the law because of discontinuity with ever changing moral standards. You might recall some of the debates on the harmful effects of cannabis and issues around the classification of drugs. There is a continuing strand of thought which suggests that legalisation should be preferred to policing and enforcement.

PRACTICAL TASK

Use the internet to research UK law on the possession of Class A, B and C drugs. Then research the equivalent law(s) in the Netherlands and decide:

- *if the police should have complete discretion in whether or not to enforce the law for the possession of cannabis – what are the implications for your decision?*

- *if there should be a stricter or more lenient approach to arrest and detention for the possession of controlled drugs.*

Whatever your views on the legalisation of cannabis, the public needs to be confident that crime is being managed effectively and this can only be achieved by striking a healthy balance between enforcement and non-enforcement of law, policy and practice.

There are, of course, certain ideological approaches that tend to be underpinned by respect and 'protocol'. In schools, for example, the police might strictly enforce the law in accordance with agreed protocols. Then there is a more sociological debate, which focuses on the role of the police in society and its recognition of criminal types. It has been argued that the typical officer is conservative and purist, and believes that crime and criminality are associated with the least well off in society, against whom police enforcement is biased, so the decision to arrest is frequently coloured by moral standards and beliefs about the stereotypical conceptions of criminals. Finally, there is the issue of class. Box (2009) describes the symbolic or 'implied' threat by someone of privilege, influence or power who is more likely to complain or appeal against an arrest decision.

REFLECTIVE TASK

Access Westlaw or Lexis Library online and find the case of Mohammed Holgate v. Duke [1984] QB 209, [1983] 3 All ER 526.

The case involves an action for wrongful arrest in which the plaintiff argued that she was detained in police custody solely for the purpose of inducing a confession.

Identify and reflect on the issues in this case and decide with fellow student officers whether you agree with the findings of Sir John Arnold and Justice Latey.

Discretion – justifiable control or unnecessary restraint?

New public management is intended as a rigorous, objective measure of whether individual police services are operating effectively and efficiently. It requires officers to account for, and measure, certain of their activities, which some argue curtails, but doesn't eliminate, personal discretion. So why is the monitoring of police activity so important? Part of the answer can be found in the interim report on *Reducing Bureaucracy* (Berry, 2008), which suggests the inability of many officers to exercise professional judgement. The Reducing Bureaucracy Practitioners Group was set up in October 2008 following the Flanagan (2008) *Review of Policing*, which challenges government and the Police Service to remove and/or reduce overly bureaucratic systems or processes and to tackle risk aversion.

The Home Office has since changed the way that it measures the effectiveness of the Police Service by scrapping most top-down police targets. There is now a single target that focuses on public confidence, a core theme of the Policing Pledge, which sets out minimum standards of delivery. In order to achieve value for money savings and to increase public satisfaction the Home Office has also introduced a QUEST initiative, which focuses on streamlining processes to help police effectiveness. The *Reducing Bureaucracy* report (Berry, 2008, para. 1:12) highlights some of the benefits of a 'lean principle' approach, which seeks to eliminate anything without value and to empower front-line workers. It also suggests that QUEST is restoring the use of discretion and common sense and is improving public confidence.

Although detecting crime and arresting offenders continues to be a policing priority, QUEST suggests that the focus is gradually shifting towards resolving problems and building public confidence. This is particularly important where values need to be balanced against providing sufficient scope to prevent and detect offending. An infringement against privacy laws can lead to public disapproval, especially by the lower classes where, for example, the use of 'sus laws' and contingent events led to urban unrest in 1981 (Box, 2009).

The Brixton riots

Because of an increase in street robberies in Brixton, Lambeth, in early 1981, the police adopted a week-long police initiative entitled Operation Swamp. The use of sus laws during this operation saw unprecedented levels of racial violence, rioting and public disorder, culminating in further rioting some three months later when police targeted houses in the Railton Road area of Brixton. A report into the disorder found that poor social and economic conditions, fears about rising crime and drug use, growing black youth unemployment, the lack of consultation with community representatives prior to the operation and the use of heavy-handed police tactics had contributed to the riot (Scarman, 1981). In January of the same year, the Royal Commission on Criminal Procedure (RCCP) (1981) reported the need for additional safeguards and standardised procedures, particularly in relation to police stop and search.

REFLECTIVE TASK

The paragraph below is taken from the RCCP report (also known as the Philips Report). In a group debate its currency and admissibility.

> *Because arrest deprives the citizen of his liberty its use is to be restricted generally to offences that carry the penalty of imprisonment . . . and to persons against whom the summons procedure will not be effective.*
>
> *(RCCP, 1981, para. 3.65)*

Miscarriages of justice and criminal justice reform

In recent decades we have witnessed a significant number of high-profile miscarriages of justice. These include the 'Guildford Four' who were jailed for life in 1975, the 'Birmingham Six' who were also convicted in 1975, and more recently the 'Cardiff Three' who were wrongly convicted for the murder of Lynette White in 1988. The exposure of wrongful convictions severely undermines the fair and effective delivery of criminal justice. It could be suggested, too, that these miscarriages occurred because of the absence of clear rules about how police powers should be exercised. But these failings have also strengthened citizens' rights by now making those responsible for the administration of justice more accountable. This is illustrated in the case of Maxwell Confait, which led to some key legislative changes and ultimately to the implementation of PACE.

In 1972, Ronald Leighton and Colin Lattimore were convicted of the murder of Maxwell Confait. Leighton, who was 16 years old, had the reading age of a ten year old. Lattimore, who was 19 years old, had the mental age of a 14 year old. They claimed that their confessions had been obtained under duress. Despite pleading not guilty, they were both convicted. Their convictions were overturned by the Court of Appeal in 1975. An official inquiry by Sir Henry Fisher was critical both of the treatment of the suspects and of system failures throughout the criminal justice process. It also found flaws in the prosecution decision-making and evidential processes, which paved the way for the Prosecution of

Offences Act 1985 and the creation of the Crown Prosecution Service (CPS) (Fisher, 1977, pp19–22). The report also set the agenda for the RCCP.

The Police and Criminal Evidence Act 1984

PACE was implemented in 1986, based on the recommendation of the RCCP, and its provisions cover:

* stop and search in the street;

* entry, search and seizure;

* arrest;

* detention;

* questioning and treatment of persons;

* evidence at trial;

* complaints against the police and disciplinary proceedings.

PACE also includes codes of practice drawn up by the Home Secretary that offer guidance on the interpretation and application of its main provisions. While breaches of PACE might constitute a civil wrong or a criminal offence, the codes aren't law, so that breaches cannot result in criminal or civil proceedings.

Police detention

Because arrest confers significant powers of investigation, it's important that we consider and understand suspects' rights in custody. The RCCP acknowledged that the time a suspect spends in custody is determined both by the nature of the alleged offence and by the demands placed on the police at the time. Of central concern to the Commission was the actual treatment of detainees while in custody together with the amount of time spent in custody before charge, as well as suspects' overall rights:

> There are two complementary elements to developing safeguards. The first is to provide for overall limits upon the length of the detention . . . and the protection of his rights so long as he is detained.

> (RCCP, 1981, para. 3.94)

Arrest and detention should also be considered against article 5 of the Human Rights Act (HRA) 1998, which guarantees a right to liberty. The article also requires that, for the purpose of bringing the detainee before an authority, the arrest must have been lawful or that detention is necessary to prevent the commission of an offence.

These issues reflect what was arguably the most significant change to custody procedures in the last 170 years: the introduction by PACE of the 'custody officer', a police officer of sergeant rank who is independent from any arrest and subsequent investigation. The custody officer is responsible for supervising the detention process and for maintaining an audit of the detainee's custody (PACE 1984, s54 and Code C, para. 4.1).

The custody record contains information such as the time(s) of arrest and authorised detention, the time, place and duration of suspect interviews and any request for legal representation. But first the custody officer needs to determine whether there is sufficient evidence to charge the suspect. If so, they must be charged and released unconditionally, bailed to return to the police station or to appear before a Magistrates' Court, or detained in custody to be brought before the next Magistrates' Court. If there is insufficient evidence to charge, the suspect must be released unless the custody officer considers that further detention is necessary to preserve evidence, or to secure evidence by questioning. There is also a duty to order the immediate release of suspects if the grounds to detain cease.

After six hours' detention there must be a review of the investigation by someone independent of the custody officer. If further detention is authorised there must be further reviews every nine hours. The normal maximum period of detention without charge is 24 hours, but in the case of arrestable offences a senior officer can authorise a further 12 hours' detention if he or she believes that it is necessary and that the investigation is being carried out expeditiously. If detention is necessary beyond 36 hours the police may apply to the Magistrates' Court for a warrant of further detention for further periods up to a total of 96 hours. As soon as the suspect is charged, he or she must be released, unless:

- the person has refused to give his or her name and address;

- there are reasonable grounds for believing that detention is necessary to protect the suspect, or to protect others, or to prevent damage to property;

- there are reasonable grounds for believing that the suspect will fail to attend court, or will interfere with the administration of justice.

REFLECTIVE TASK

Visit the website http://police.homeoffice.gov.uk/operational-policing/powers-pace-codes/pace-code-intro/, which relates to PACE and accompanying Codes of Practice. Access the link to Code C, which sets out the requirements for the detention, treatment and questioning of suspects not related to terrorism in police custody by police officers.

Consider Jo, who is 15 years old but has a mental age of ten. Jo, who resides at a special needs care home, is in custody for assaulting another resident at the home. S/he was accompanied to the police station by a residential care worker to whom s/he admitted the offence prior to arrest. The police now wish to interview Jo.

- *How does the Code relate to appropriate adults and legal representatives when dealing with vulnerable young persons?*

- *How effective is Code C in affording rights for persons like Jo?*

- *Do you believe that the procedural requirements for dealing with vulnerable suspects constrain the police?*

Right to legal advice

PACE has now replaced the Judges' Rules, which previously regulated access to legal advice. Since the implementation of PACE anyone in custody is entitled to free and independent legal advice and has a right to see a solicitor 'as soon as is practicable', which can give scope for delay. The Youth Justice and Criminal Evidence Act 1999 has also amended section 34 of PACE by excluding adverse inferences when the suspect has not been allowed to consult a solicitor prior to being questioned or charged. This meets the ruling in *Murray v. UK* [1996] that delay in access to a solicitor, even if lawful, could amount to a breach of article 6 of the HRA 1998, given the risk of adverse inferences being drawn.

As a result of the above provisions, requests and consultation rates for custodial legal advice increased from around 7 and 6 per cent, respectively, in the 1970s to 38 and 33 per cent, respectively, in 1998 (Phillips and Brown, 1998; Sanders and Young, 1994). But increased attendance hasn't always resulted in providing competent, legal advice and, until quite recently, it was practice that trainees or ex-police officers employed by solicitors' firms would attend at police stations. But poor standards of advice have led to the compulsory training of advisers, which is particularly important in relation to changes to the right of silence.

Duty to answer police questions and the right to silence

The police have a right to ask questions of anyone and, while there is no general requirement to provide an answer, there are circumstances where a member of the public is under a duty to respond. Where, for example, a vehicle has been involved in an accident the person keeping the vehicle is required to name the driver. Section 25(3) of PACE also provides a power of arrest for a non-arrestable offence in cases where the suspect's details can't be established for the purpose of serving a summons. The only restriction is that questioning should cease once a suspect is charged. But until 1994, there was no legal requirement for an *arrested* person to answer police questions.

Since the abolition of the Star Chamber in 1641, no English court has been able to 'extract' confessions from a suspect and the 'right to silence' meant that a court could not make adverse comments to the jury about such a silence. You might consider that this actually encouraged the 'abuse' of criminal justice by allowing professional and hardened criminals the opportunity to 'ambush' the prosecution with late defences that were virtually impossible to confirm or rebut, certainly within the constraints of the trial process. And, of course, it can be argued that the right to silence has contributed to allegations of police malpractice. High-profile cases such as those of the Guildford Four, the Birmingham Six and the Maguire Seven saw convictions overturned after long campaigns that challenged the legitimacy of the police, and that highlighted the fabrication of confession evidence.

One of the most notorious miscarriages of justice is the case of the Bridgwater Four, who were convicted of the murder of 13-year-old Carl Bridgwater in 1979. The suspects were cleared some 18 years later after it was discovered that police had falsified and fabricated the evidence. The case had been investigated in 1978 before the implementation of PACE and it might now be argued that the right to legal advice and the need for interviews to be recorded have reduced the opportunity for police malpractice. Indeed, there are provisions in PACE designed specifically to address such concerns, particularly coercive detention and the unethical questioning of suspects. Section 78 of PACE states that 'no interviewer may try to obtain answers or elicit a statement from a suspect by the use of oppression'. But despite the implementation of PACE, the use of 'oppressive and persuasive tactics' continued.

In 1993, George Heron was acquitted of murdering Nikki Allan after the trial judge ruled that seven of the twelve interview tapes were inadmissible because of oppressive conduct in the interviews. Heron repeatedly denied the allegations and although he was represented in interview, his adviser failed to object as interviewing officers repeatedly asserted his guilt, misrepresented the strength of evidence against him and pointed out that it was in his interest to confess. In a later examination of the case it was stated that the interviewing techniques used by officers had been 'common police practice at the time' (Sanders and Young, 1994, p1).

There has been intense debate on the right to silence and its role in the real workings of the CJS, with suggestions that it is not as significant as is often argued. Most defendants tend to plead guilty, so the right to silence isn't important in such a context. Similarly, common law rules permit the judge to mention the defendant's silence and, in some limited circumstances, not to mention it. Studies also found that silence at the police station hasn't necessarily resulted in any advantage at court (Motson et al., 1992). But supporters of the right to silence have argued that suspects should not be forced to answer questions that could prejudice their safety or privacy. After intense debate the 1993 Royal Commission on Criminal Justice eventually decided that the right to silence should be retained. Its report states:

> The majority of us feel that adverse inferences should not be drawn from silence at the police station and recommend retaining the present caution and trial direction.
>
> (RCCJ, 1993, para. 82)

Despite the Commission's recommendations the government felt that there was sufficient legal provision in PACE, including the right to free legal advice, and that this was enough to protect suspects' rights. The Criminal Justice and Public Order Act 1994 was subsequently introduced and this effectively ended the right to silence. Now, if a suspect refuses to answer questions during interview the court may draw an 'adverse inference' as to their guilt if their defence relies on facts that could reasonably have been disclosed during interview (ss34–7). The abolition of the right to silence can be seen as a clear move towards a more inquisitorial, crime-control model of justice, such as those used in France or Germany, where the suspect is seen as the focus of the investigation process. Instead of a right to silence, they are regarded as having a 'right to speak' in order to assist in the discovery of the truth.

C   H   A   P   T   E   R   S   U   M   M   A   R   Y

When reviewing arrest and police detention, we need to be aware of a range of issues, particularly legislation, policy and those practices that govern the use of police powers. There had been a range of statutory and common law sources before PACE and, some would argue, insufficient guidance on how the police should exercise their powers. This allowed for a wide measure of discretion in the exercise of powers, and the absence of any concise rules contributed to malpractice and miscarriages of justice. But if you accept that it is neither desirable nor possible to enforce the law in every circumstance, striking a healthy balance between enforcement and non-enforcement can be problematic.

The growing problems of crime and the fear of crime continue to be important concerns of the government, as well as balancing the notion of justice with efficiency and funding. Enforcement that interferes with the rights of private individuals can lead to disapproval, but not enforcing the law attracts similar criticism and the assertion that the police are failing to protect society. Consequently, we see a tension between the need for wider police powers and the tightening of rules of evidence and procedure that govern the investigation and prosecution of crime, although there would seem to be a trend towards the strengthening of police powers. The Criminal Justice Act 1967, PACE 1984 and SOCAP 2005 provide the legal framework for policing and, while it appears that there is a willingness to allow the police greater discretion in the exercise of their powers, policy and practice clearly depends on the prevailing culture of the police and of society as a whole.

REFERENCES

Berry, J (2008) *Reducing Bureaucracy in Policing: An Interim Report*. London: Home Office.

Box, S (2009) The social construction of official statistics on criminal deviance, in Newburn, T (ed.) *Key Readings in Criminology*.Cullompton: Willan.

Chambliss, W J (1969) *Crime and the Legal Process*. New York: McGraw-Hill.

Fisher, H (1977) *The Confait Case: Report*. London: HMSO.

Flanagan, Sir Ronnie (2008) *The Review of Policing: Final Report*. London: Home Office.

Gelsthorpe, L and Padfield, N (2003) *Exercising Discretion: Decision Making in the Official Criminal Justice System and Beyond*. Cullompton: Willan.

Goldstein, H (1964) Police discretion: the ideal versus the real. *Public Administration Review*, 23(3): 140–8.

Goldstein, J (1960) Police discretion not to invoke the criminal process: low-visibility decisions in the administration of justice. *Yale Law Journal*, 69(4): 543–94.

Motson, S, Stephenson, G and Williamson, T (1992) The effects of case characteristics on suspect behaviour during police questioning. *British Journal of Criminology*, 32(1): 23–40.

Phillips, C and Brown, D (1998) *Entry into the Criminal Justice System: A Survey of Police Arrests and their Outcomes*, London: HMSO.

Reiner, R (2000) *The Politics of the Police*, 3rd edition. Oxford: Oxford University Press.

Rowe, M (2004) *Policing, Race and Racism*, Cullompton: Willan.

Royal Commission on Criminal Justice (RCCJ) (1993) *Runciman Report* (Cmnd 2263). London: HMSO.

Royal Commission on Criminal Procedure (RCCP) (1981) *Philips Report* (Cmnd 8092). London: HMSO.

Sanders, A and Young, R (1994) *Criminal Justice*. London: Butterworths.

Scarman, Lord Leslie (1981) *The Brixton Disorders 10–12 April 1981: Report of an Enquiry by the Rt Hon. the Lord Scarman, OBE* (Cmnd 8247). London: HMSO.

Waddington, P A J (1999) *Policing Citizens*. London: UCL Press.

USEFUL WEBSITES

www.cjsonline.gov.uk (Criminal Justice System)

www.homeoffice.gov.uk (Home Office)

CASES

Armstrong v. Chief Constable of West Yorkshire Police [2008] All ER (D) 69 (Dec)

Associated Provincial Picture Houses v. Wednesbury Corporation [1948] 1 KB 223; [1947] 2 All ER 137

Bentley v. Brudzinksy [1982] Crim LR 825

Donnelly v. Jackman [1970] 1 WLR 562, CA

Holgate-Mohammed v. Duke [1984] 2 WLR 660, CA

Kenlin v. Gardiner [1967] 2 QB 510; [1967] 2 WLR 129

Lewis v. Chief Constable South Wales Constabulary [1991] 1 All ER 206, CA

Mohammed Holgate v. Duke [1984] QB 209, [1983] 3 All ER 526

Murray v. UK (1996) 22 EHRR 29

R v. Lemsatef [1977] 1 WLR 812, CA

R v. Sang [1979] 3 WLR 263, CA

Sandon v. Jervis [1859] EB & E 942

Spicer v. Holt [1977] Crim LR 364

LEGISLATION

Criminal Justice Act 1967

Criminal Justice and Public Order Act 1994

Criminal Law Act 1967

Human Rights Act 1998

Metropolitan Police Act 1839

Police and Criminal Evidence Act 1984

Police Reform Act 2002

Prosecution of Offences Act 1985

Public Order Act 1986

Serious Organised Crime and Police Act 2005

Town Police Clauses Act 1847

Vagrancy Act 1824

Violent Crime Reduction Act 2006

Youth Justice and Criminal Evidence Act 1999

4 The prosecution process

Introduction

This chapter will provide you with an overview of the prosecution process and the various activities will allow for further independent study, group discussion and critical reflection.

It has been argued that the prosecution process, which is based on adversarial principles, only reflects the 'legal truth' and that, when investigating offences, the police are preoccupied only in selecting, interpreting and sometimes 'creating facts' that sometimes bear little resemblance to what the suspect can actually recall. McBarnett (1981) makes

59

the point that adversaries don't need to establish what 'actually happened', but simply argue their case. It's also argued that establishing the 'truth' isn't a primary issue for the court; it's more about deciding on the veracity of competing stories. It follows, therefore, that conviction doesn't mean that the prosecution case is any more truthful or accurate than the defence case; it is more a by-product of the pre-trial criminal procedure(s) (McBarnett, 1981).

So why do we have an adversarial prosecution system, which some argue does little to deter future offending, allows plea bargaining and discontinuance, and undermines the notion of victimhood through discontinuations and acquittals? You might wish to consider whether the existing structural relationship between the Crown Prosecution Service (CPS) and the Police Service is an effective one, particularly where it concerns the reviewing of cases and when deciding the real meaning of 'public interest'!

A brief history of the prosecution process

If we look back some 300 years the state would generally prosecute the more serious offences, such as treason. Then, minor criminality was accepted as part of everyday life and cases would be dealt with mainly through private prosecutions, and sometimes through community associations on payment of a fee. While this enabled people to have their cases heard, it was usually the wealthy who benefited.

Before 1879, there was no single supervision of criminal prosecutions. The Attorney General had the right to institute and conduct criminal proceedings, and to take over a private prosecution and either continue or end it. The Home Office advised police forces and magistrates' clerks in the more important cases and sometimes instructed the Treasury Solicitor to commence proceedings in matters affecting Crown revenue.

In the eighteenth century, 'thief taking' became an accepted method of addressing the general rise in crime. Private individuals were hired by crime victims to apprehend offenders and bring them to justice. Sometimes they would act as go-betweens, negotiating the return of stolen property in return for a fee. However, corruption was prevalent and it was common for thief takers to blackmail more felony suspects than they actually brought to trial. This was largely because of the cost of bringing a prosecution and the risk of acquittal or conviction on a lesser charge for which no reward was offered. Jonathan Wild was a notorious thief taker and, by his testimony, over 60 thieves were sent to the gallows. Wild was executed in 1725 after devising a scheme that saw him run one of the most successful gangs of thieves at that time.

It was during the early part of the nineteenth century that the balance in bringing prosecutions shifted markedly towards the state, particularly after the emergence of the New Police in 1829. But Godfrey and Lawrence (2005, p45) make the point that this wasn't a watershed event, but part of a more gradual shift in the balance of criminal justice: 'We can't say that because a formal policing and prosecuting structure had arrived, so the prosecution associations, the need and/or right of citizens to defend themselves, or extra-judicial initiatives disappeared.'

The police gradually assumed responsibility for prosecution, but it wasn't until the enactment of the County and Borough Police Act 1856 that they were permitted to act formally as a prosecuting authority. Before this most criminal cases were private prosecutions that didn't involve professional lawyers. The office of public prosecutor, more commonly referred to as the Director of Public Prosecutions (DPP), was eventually created by the Prosecution of Offences Act 1879 and, by the latter part of the nineteenth century, most cases were being prosecuted by a police prosecutor.

After 1908, although the most serious cases in England and Wales were being referred to the DPP for prosecution, most charges continued to be investigated and prosecuted by police officers. By 1981 a number of different provisions had developed for the conduct of criminal prosecutions. For all non-serious cases, one of three broad approaches was used. In some areas a local authority prosecuting solicitor's department would prosecute all cases, while others retained one or more firms of private solicitors. The Metropolitan Police Service had its own solicitor's branch. However, the decision to prosecute, or to continue with a prosecution, ultimately remained with the Chief Constable.

Until 1986 England was one of only a few countries that allowed the police to prosecute rather than a state agency, such as the US District Attorney or the Scottish Procurator Fiscal. Each of the 43 police services in England and Wales was allowed to implement its own prosecutions, but inconsistencies in charging standards caused some disquiet over the independence of the police. Ashworth and Redmayne (2005, p175) argue that the police prosecuted 'too many weak cases', causing undue stress to both victims and suspects, wasted time and avoidable costs. They attribute this to the adversarial nature of the prosecution process where, after gathering evidence *against* the accused, and having established a prima facie case, the police were allowed to charge or summons.

As Lord Devlin states:

> Once he finds a reasonable quantity of pros, he will act decisively without too much anxiety about the cons. When a police officer charges a man it is because he believes him to be guilty, not just because he thinks there is a case for a trial.
>
> (1979, p72)

The prosecution process after 1986

The fact that legal aid is provided in most cases seems to reflect the interest that the police have in securing successful prosecutions. By using testimony from lay witnesses, victims, expert witnesses and the police themselves, cases are constructed to prove the charge. But each of these parties is prone to perceive events in line with their own types of experiences and, according to Sanders (1985), the prosecution case is sometimes nothing more than an approximation of the truth. And while it should never be that suspected criminal offences are automatically the subject of prosecution, there is evidence that the police have tended to focus their attention on particular types of conduct. For example, research indicated a bias in favour of prosecuting working-class offenders, as well as in prosecutions that reflect the principle of 'let the court' decide (Sanders, 1985).

It has also been argued that the police construct their case to prove the charge and it follows that any defence is usually reactive in nature. That is, the grounds for an argument can't be chosen, for it's about the charge which is, of course, selected by the police. But the police also have a responsibility to assist the defence, for example by disclosing information in their possession that might undermine the prosecution case – see the Criminal Proceedings and Investigations Act (CPIA) 1996. And of course, the Simple, Speedy, Summary Justice (SSSJ) initiative requires the prosecution and defence to identify trial issues at the first court hearing, with a trial date usually set within six weeks of that hearing. This is discussed later in the chapter. But the police still have a responsibility to prepare the case for the prosecution. Devlin points to the consequence of this: 'The tendency of the police, once their mind is made up . . . [is] . . . to treat as mistakes any evidence that contradicts the proof of guilt' (1979, p73).

PRACTICAL TASK

Refer to the CPIA 1996 Code of Practice, which can be found at the website http://www. opsi.gov.uk.

In a group or with a colleague, decide whether the linking of prosecution and defence disclosure represents another example of the tendency towards an inquisitorial approach to the Criminal Justice System (CJS).

Devlin's point is also argued by McConville and Baldwin (1981, p190), who suggest that once the guilt of a suspect is established, the police are only concerned with constructing a case that is able to withstand the scrutiny of the court. Moody and Tombs (1981, p45) also remind us that the police need to build a clear and unambiguous case that reduces any uncertainty and maximises the strength of the prosecution case. But officers don't just find strong cases; they make them by removing those features that undermine the case. But this doesn't mean that they try to make strong cases out of every case. The police also construct cases in ways that justify non-prosecution, for example with reprimands and warnings. The point here is that Crown prosecutors are usually presented only with cases that the police *want* them to prosecute.

It's been argued that, as soon as a certain threshold of evidence is reached, the police rarely look further into the matter and, indeed, the potential for actually discounting evidence is particularly high, especially when that evidence relies on lay assessment; and neither do the police actively seek information that could establish innocence (Zander, 1979, p203). Paradoxically, it could be argued that the police are entitled to build any case with a legally valid basis and, since most facts tend to be vague and malleable, that there is no distinction between building and then aligning the investigation with a decision to prosecute! Indeed, the police have argued that, in most cases of acquittal, especially those involving miscarriages of justice, the decision to prosecute is usually taken by a lawyer.

Because of the issues around police accountability and independence, the Philips Royal Commission (RCCP, 1981) was set up to review police powers and to examine the prosecution process. It concluded that a new system was needed based on several distinct features, including:

- that the initial decision to charge a suspect should rest with the police;

- that thereafter all decisions on whether to proceed with, alter or drop the charges should rest with another state prosecuting authority;

- that this agency should provide advocates for all cases in the Magistrates' Courts, apart from guilty pleas by post;

- that it should also provide legal advice to the police and instruct counsel in all cases tried on indictment.

The CPS was established by the Prosecution of Offences Act 1985 under the general direction of the DPP, which is responsible to the Attorney General. The Attorney General, like the Lord Chancellor, is a political appointee whose role is to act as legal adviser to the government. As well as deciding whether or not to prosecute in sensitive and serious cases, the Attorney General alone has the authority to advise on matters of national importance. For example, in 2003 the former Attorney General, Lord Goldsmith, controversially advised the government that there was a legal basis for its use of military force against Iraq. As head of the CPS, the DPP oversees the prosecution of criminal offences and the decision to prosecute, or not, is always subject to judicial review in the courts. In *R v. DPP ex p C* [1994], it was stated that such powers should be used sparingly and only on grounds of unlawful policy and perversity.

PRACTICAL TASK

Carry out some internet research and establish the role of the CPS, for example by visiting the CPS website or by accessing the following link to the Justice Committee – Ninth Report: www.parliament.the-stationery-office.co.uk/pa/cm200809/cmselect/cmjust/186/ 18602.htm. This considers the CPS as the gatekeeper to the CJS.

The CPS as gatekeeper to the prosecution process

The CPS has been repeatedly accused of discontinuing or downgrading in a large number of inappropriate cases. This is particularly the case with serious assaults, which are downgraded to the summary offence of 'common assault' and subsequently dealt with in the Magistrates' Court at a lesser cost. In the light of this and other more general criticisms, Sir Iain Glidewell (1999) was appointed to conduct a review of the CPS. His report describes the CPS as bureaucratic, ineffective and inefficient. A further report from the independent CPS Inspectorate identified serious weaknesses in the prosecution system (HMCPSI, 2002). The then DPP, Dame Barbara Mills, resigned shortly after the release of the Glidewell Report, which then saw the CPS established in 43 areas, each corresponding to a Police Service area. The exception is in London, where the CPS operates in a single area that includes the City of London and Metropolitan Police services. Each CPS area is headed by a Chief Crown Prosecutor, who has authority delegated from the DPP for decision making in their particular area.

The Statutory Charging Scheme

The role of the CPS, when first created, was to take over responsibility for cases where a person had been charged and to decide whether or not to withdraw or proceed with the case. Increasingly, however, the service has become more involved with the charging process itself. This was partly in response to the Glidewell Report, which recommended that the CPS should take full responsibility for the prosecution process, after charge. Further impetus for change arose from a review of the practices and procedures of the criminal courts by Lord Justice Auld (1999), published in 2001. Recommendation 154 states that:

> The Crown Prosecution Service should determine the charge in all but minor, routine offences or where, because of the circumstances, there is a need for a holding charge before seeking the advice of the Service.

PRACTICAL TASK

> The practice of prosecutors and police holding face-to-face meetings to advise on charging leads to delay, the quality of police files is often wanting and there are wide variations in practice.
>
> *(Gibb, 2008)*

Visit the CPS Inspectorate website and research the November 2008 joint thematic review of the 'new charging arrangements' and decide whether the above headline is a true reflection of the way that statutory charging is currently working.

In March 2002, the CPS commenced a six-month pilot of the Statutory Charging Scheme, the essence of which is that the CPS and not the police has responsibility in deciding whether an offender should be charged in the more serious or contested cases. This was to minimise the number of inappropriate charges and discontinuations. Table 4.1 shows dismissals in the Magistrates' Court on a 'no case to answer' basis, which is attributable to failings in the review process. This amounted to 0.011 per cent or 11 per 100,000 in 2001–02, compared with 0.0085 per cent or 8.5 per 100,000 in 2000–01 (CPS, 2002).

The table shows figures for:

- *hearings*: cases which proceeded either to a guilty plea or to a not guilty plea and full trial;

- *discontinuances*: when proceedings had to be discontinued in accordance with the code for Crown prosecutors;

- *committals*: when the defendant in a more serious case was committed or sent for trial in the Crown Court;

- *other disposals*: cases in which the defendant was bound over to keep the peace, and committal proceedings in which the defendant was discharged after the court considered evidence.

Table 4.1 Breakdown of cases heard at Magistrates' Courts

	1990–2000	%	2000–01	%	2001–02	%
Hearings	998,717	73	942,528	72	944,929	72.5
Discontinuances	166,861	12.2	167,988	13.0	171,381	13.1
Committals	87,885	6.4	83,400	6.4	86,794	6.7
Other disposals	114,017	8.3	100,131	7.7	100,260	7.7
Totals	1,367,480		1,294,047		1,303,364	

Source: Figures taken from CPS (2002).

The pilot Charging Scheme was followed by publication of the white paper, *Justice for All* (Home Office, 2002) and the subsequent enactment of the Criminal Justice Act (CJA) 2003, which placed it on a statutory footing. The main migration to statutory charging took place in 2005, with the last CPS area moving to a statutory status in 2006.

Section 37 of the Police and Criminal Evidence Act (PACE) 1984 now permits that, where a person is being investigated by the police, the custody officer may take one of four actions.

1. Release the suspect on bail, without charge to enable the CPS to decide whether to prosecute.

2. Release the suspect on bail to permit further investigations to be made.

3. Release the suspect without charge and without bail.

4. Charge the suspect.

These changes prompted a 'twin track' response by the CPS, the first being the availability of a duty prosecutor at designated police stations during normal working hours. This permits discussion with the prosecutor so that an appropriate charge decision(s) can be made. The second is the creation of CPS Direct, a system of 'on-call' prosecutors, which allows the police access to 'around the clock' decisions. Since 2006, the scheme has been responsible for providing out-of-hours charging advice to every police force in England and Wales. In January 2010, the CPS Direct service was expanded across England and Wales to operate 24 hours a day. This should provide police officers with immediate access to CPS prosecutors when seeking advice and authorisation on the less serious charging decisions. Consultation in serious or complex cases will continue to operate on a face-to-face basis, with charging decisions ultimately remaining with the CPS. At the same time, some charging decisions will return to the police in a pilot scheme aimed at streamlining the current charging boundary. A test period of six months will consider if a roll-out of these provisions is appropriate.

REFLECTIVE TASK

(This task links to the task on page 62.)

The Statutory Charging Scheme saw the police hand over the job of charging serious offences to Crown prosecutors.

Do you consider that prosecutors who are familiar with the rules of evidence and the intricacies of law can always be objective in what is still a fundamentally inquisitorial role? Please provide reasons for your answer.

The *Code for Crown Prosecutors*

The *Code for Crown Prosecutors* (DPP, 1986) is issued by the DPP under the authority of the Prosecution of Offences Act 1985. It provides guidelines on the delivery of justice to victims and witnesses and, like the PACE codes of practice, is periodically revised to reflect changing attitudes and circumstances. For example, in 2001 emphasis was placed on the victim, especially for offences motivated by discrimination. This reflects the drive to tackle racist crimes in the light of the Macpherson Report into the death of Stephen Lawrence. The *Code* states that prosecutors should select charges that reflect both the gravity and depth of the offence, as well as giving the court sufficient powers to sentence and impose appropriate post-conviction orders. The *Code* was last revised in 2004 to take account of the Statutory Charging Scheme and, while fundamental evidential considerations were unaffected, key developments included new public interest factors, alternatives to prosecution such as conditional cautioning, and restarting a prosecution.

Conditional cautions

Conditional cautions were created by the CJA 2003 (s22) as a means of diverting from court those who admit an offence in circumstances where the suspect, victim and community may be better served by the suspect agreeing to undertake rehabilitative or reparative activities. But before a caution can be offered the prosecutor must be satisfied that the prospect of a conviction is real and that a prosecution would otherwise be in the public interest. This is in case the conditional caution offer is refused or the offender fails to comply with the conditions of the caution (see the *Code for Crown Prosecutors* (DPP, 1986, para. 8.5).

Restarting a prosecution

While it's not normal to commence a prosecution once a suspect is informed that he or she will not be prosecuted, there *are* occasions when the CPS will start or restart a prosecution, particularly if the case is serious. This includes cases where:

- the original decision was clearly wrong;
- more evidence can be collected reasonably quickly, in which case the suspect will be informed that the prosecution may well start again;

- there is an initial lack of evidence but more significant evidence is later discovered;

- after acquittal for a serious offence, the defendant is retried in accordance with part 10 of the CJA 2003 – an order of the court that quashes the acquittal.

PRACTICAL TASK

Access Westlaw or Lexis Library online and find the case of Guest v. DPP [2009] EWHC 594. This High Court case concerns a CPS decision to authorise the conditional caution of a suspect for an offence of assault occasioning actual bodily harm. The court subsequently ruled that the decision not to prosecute was unlawful and that the conditional caution was accordingly inappropriate, although not unlawful.

- *Which of the Full Test criteria do you think outweigh those given as CPS reasons for administering the caution?*

In response to a pre-action letter from the complainant's solicitor, the Chief Crown Prosecutor wrote:

> *I have concluded that it would not be appropriate for the CPS to institute proceedings in these circumstances. My reasons are that it would be an abuse of the process of the court.*

- *Had you been able to respond to the letter, what would you have said and why?*

- *Do you agree with the Prosecutor that an offender should be confident that any formal procedure to which they first agree should represent a final disposal of the matter? Give reasons for your answer.*

The need for case review

The *Code* provides detailed guidance to Crown prosecutors on the general principles that have to be applied when making prosecution decisions and, indeed, the same guidance is followed in cases where the police determine the charge. The origins of the *Code* can be linked to Lord Shawcross, the then Attorney General, who said:

> *It has never been the rule of this country . . . I hope it never will be . . . that suspected criminal offences must automatically be the subject of prosecution.*
>
> (Hansard, 1951)

This has led to the current position, where the CPS should not ordinarily allow a prosecution to start or continue if this might be seen as an abuse of the prosecution process. This requires an ongoing review of every case and, in circumstances where it's considered necessary to amend the charge(s) or to discontinue the case, the police will normally be consulted beforehand.

The *Code* provides detailed guidance to prosecutors on the general principles that should be applied when making prosecution decisions. Unless the Threshold Test applies, the CPS will only start or continue with a prosecution when the case has passed the evidential and public interest tests, otherwise called the Full Code Test.

The Threshold Test

There is a significant body of cases in which the suspect is arrested but the evidential test can't be applied because of the need to obtain outstanding evidence. The police, nevertheless, prefer a holding charge on the 'common sense' basis that further evidence will be secured in the course of the investigation. The Threshold Test now applies in cases where the release of the suspect on bail would be inappropriate, for example by presenting a substantial risk on bail or perhaps because medical evidence is still required. In applying the Threshold Test the CPS must determine, first, whether there is some reasonable suspicion that the suspect has committed an offence and, second, whether it is in the public interest to prosecute. Here, the meaning of 'public interest' is the same as in the Full Code Test. But because time spent in custody without charge is based on statutory limits, the Threshold Test can only apply for a limited period and requires consideration of:

- the nature of the available evidence;

- the likelihood of further evidence being obtained and its likely impact on the case;

- the time needed to obtain further evidence;

- the steps being taken to obtain further evidence.

The evidential test

The evidential test requires the CPS to be satisfied that any evidence provided is admissible, reliable and sufficient to provide a 'realistic prospect of a conviction' against *each* defendant on *each* charge. 'Realistic prospect' is an objective test, which means that a jury or a bench of magistrates, properly directed within the law, will be more likely than not to convict the defendant of the alleged charge. The *Code* points out that this test is separate from the one applied by the court itself. That is, it should only convict if satisfied that it is sure of the defendant's guilt. In terms of the admissibility of evidence, the CPS needs to consider whether it is likely to be excluded by the court because legal rules mean that it cannot be presented at a trial. For example, has it been obtained unfairly and, if the answer is yes, does the remaining evidence meet the realistic prospect rule? In determining the reliability of evidence, the CPS must consider the following.

- Is the evidence likely to support or undermine the reliability of a confession?

- What explanation has the defendant provided and does it support an innocent explanation?

- Is the identity of the defendant in question?

- Is the background of a witness likely to undermine the prosecution case, for example through their previous conviction(s)?

- Is further evidence required to confirm the accuracy or credibility of any witness?

If the case does not pass the evidential test, it must not proceed, irrespective of how important or serious it may be.

The public interest test

Once the evidential test has been passed, the CPS must then decide whether it is in the public interest to prosecute. A charge is usually preferred where the CPS decides that the interest factors for a prosecution outweigh those against and where it's not appropriate, in all the circumstances, to divert the person away from prosecution. Although there may be public interest factors against prosecution in a particular case, the CPS might take the decision to charge to allow those factors to be put to the court for consideration when sentence is being passed.

The *Code for Crown Prosecutors* lists the factors that are considered to favour a prosecution. These include the following.

- A conviction is likely to result in a significant sentence or in a confiscation or any other order.

- A weapon was used or violence was threatened during the commission of the offence.

- The offence was committed against a person serving the public, for example a police or prison officer, or a nurse.

- The defendant was in a position of authority or trust.

- The evidence shows that the defendant was a ring leader or an organiser of the offence.

- There is evidence that the offence was premeditated.

- There is evidence that the offence was carried out by a group.

- The victim of the offence was vulnerable, has been put in considerable fear or has suffered personal attack, damage or disturbance.

- The offence was committed in the presence of, or in close proximity to, a child.

- The offence was motivated by any form of discrimination against the victim's ethnic or national origin, disability, sex, religious beliefs, political views or sexual orientation, or the suspect demonstrated hostility towards the victim based on any of those characteristics.

- There is a marked difference between the actual or mental ages of the defendant and the victim, or if there is any element of corruption.

- The defendant's previous convictions or cautions are relevant to the present offence.

- The defendant is alleged to have committed the offence while under an order of the court.

- There are grounds for believing that the offence is likely to be continued or repeated, for example by a history of recurring conduct.

- The offence, although not serious in itself, is widespread in the area where it was committed.

- A prosecution would have a significant positive impact on maintaining community confidence.

The *Code for Crown Prosecutors* lists main public interest factors that are likely to prevent a prosecution. These include the following.

- The court is likely to impose a nominal penalty.

- The defendant has already been made the subject of a sentence and a further conviction is unlikely to result in the imposition of an additional sentence or order, unless the nature of the particular offence requires a prosecution or the defendant withdraws consent to have an offence taken into consideration during sentencing.

- The offence was committed as a result of a genuine mistake or misunderstanding – these factors must be balanced against the seriousness of the offence.

- The loss or harm can be described as minor and was the result of a single incident, particularly if it was caused by a misjudgement.

- There has been a long delay between the offence taking place and the date of the trial, unless:

  - the offence is serious;

  - the delay has been caused in part by the defendant;

  - the offence has only recently come to light; or

  - the complexity of the offence has meant that there has been a long investigation.

REFLECTIVE TASK

Access Westlaw or Lexis Library online and find the case of Alford v. Chief Constable of Cambridgeshire Police [2009] All ER (D) 232. This Court of Appeal case concerns a police officer's appeal against the dismissal of his claim for false imprisonment following his arrest for causing death by dangerous driving during a vehicle pursuit.

Identify and reflect on the public interest issues in this case and decide whether you agree with the following statement of Lord Justice Richards.

> *If those concerned in . . . the decision to prosecute had had full cognisance of the Parker report . . . [and] Price report . . . the balance of factors in favour of prosecution would certainly have been weaker, but I share the judge's view that the advice and decision would probably have been the same. More importantly, I take the view that on the evidence as a whole . . . there were reasonable grounds for bringing the prosecution.*

Simple, Speedy, Summary Justice programme

The notion of Simple, Speedy, Summary Justice (SSSJ) (2006) is aimed at making the CJS, and in particular the courts, more responsive to the concerns raised by local communities. It includes measures to change the way that courts handle cases, as well as a range of sanctions that include immediate penalties, community punishments and prison.

- *Simple*: cases that are best dealt with by way of a warning, caution or other means of deterring reoffending will not enter the court process.

- *Speedy*: those cases that require the court process will be dealt with as quickly as possible.

- *Summary*: a much more proportionate approach, for example by dealing with appropriate cases the day after charge or during the same week.

The SSSJ programme includes the 'Virtual Courts' pilot scheme, launched in May 2009 (Flanagan. 2008, para. 5.45). It links police stations in central London with a local Magistrates' Court, allowing defendants to have their cases heard via a secure video link at the police station within hours of charge. Sentencing after a guilty plea can be carried out the same day, which frees up police and Magistrates' Courts' time. Other benefits of the scheme include:

- reducing the delays caused by defendants who fail to turn up to hearings;

- reducing prisoner movements, which saves on transport costs;

- reducing the risk of prisoners absconding.

The scheme was implemented after the *Review of Policing* report by Sir Ronnie Flanagan (2008), Her Majesty's Inspectorate of Constabulary/Her Majesty's Crown Prosecution Service Inspectorate's *Joint Thematic Review of the New Charging Arrangements* (HMCPSI, 2008) and the Berry (2008) interim report, *Reducing Bureaucracy in Policing*.

These all report the success of the Statutory Charging Scheme as well as suggesting improvements. Sir Ronnie suggests that the Police Service can, and should, make full use of its charging powers. He points out that this doesn't happen across all police forces because of uncertainty around existing CPS guidance. By improving the guidance and quality of police supervision, the waiting time for CPS charge decisions could be substantially reduced (paras 5.52–5.54). Flanagan also endorses the SSSJ initiative and recommends the full roll-out of the Virtual Courts scheme by 2012 (Flanagan, 2008, recommendation 22).

Berry highlights issues around 'wasted time' and bureaucracy, particularly where the police refer minor cases to the CPS for charging decisions. She suggests an extension of police charging powers to include all summary offences, regardless of plea, and possibly some further either-way offences (Berry, 2008, recommendation 6).

Finally, the *Joint Thematic Review of Charging Arrangements* highlights wasted time, duplication of effort and missed opportunities and concludes that there is still some way to go if the CJS is to take best advantage of the Statutory Charging concept (HMCPSI,

2008, para. 15.42). Like Berry, HMCPSI suggests extending police charging powers to include all summary offences, regardless of plea, to include some additional either-way offences.

C H A P T E R   S U M M A R Y

Within this chapter we have briefly examined the history, key events and milestones that have shaped and influenced the prosecution system in England and Wales.

Key legislation has been identified and explored, along with the main measures that are intended to improve the prosecution process. We have explored a variety of disposal methods that are available to the police and the CPS, as well as issues around case management and case progression. We have examined contemporary initiatives that continue to drive the government's agenda to place victims at the heart of the CJS.

Opportunities have been provided for further research and analysis of issues relating to the prosecution process. These provide stimuli, sources and evidence for completion of NOS and assignments. Further reading around this topic area will provide a clearer and more detailed understanding of the key role that the police, CPS and courts play within the prosecution process.

REFERENCES

Ashworth, A and Redmayne, M (2005) *The Criminal Process*. Oxford: Oxford University Press.

Auld, Rt Hon Lord Justice (2001) *A Review of the Criminal Courts of England and Wales*. London: The Stationery Office.

Berry, J (2008) *Reducing Bureaucracy in Policing: An Interim Report*. London: Home Office.

Crown Prosecution Service (CPS) (2002) *Annual Report 2001-2002*. Available online at www.cps.gov.uk/publications/reports/annualreport02.html#SectionTwo (accessed 11 November 2009).

Department for Constitutional Affairs (DCA) (2006) *Delivering Simple, Speedy Summary Justice*. London: The Stationery Office.

Devlin, Lord Patrick (1979) *The Judge*. Oxford: Oxford University Press.

Director of Public Prosecutions (DPP) (1986) *Code for Crown Prosecutors*. London: HMSO.

Flanagan, Sir Ronnie (2008) *The Review of Policing: Final Report*. London: Home Office.

Gibb, F (2008) Charging suspects: why it's a job for prosecutors. *The Times*, 27 November 2008, p79.

Glidewell, Sir Iain (1998) *The Review of the Crown Prosecution Service* (Cm. 3960). London: HMSO.

Godfrey, B and Lawrence, P (2005) *Crime and Justice 1750–1950*, Cullompton: Willan.

Hansard (1951) *House of Commons Debates*, Volume 483, Column 681, 29 January.

Her Majesty's Crown Prosecution Inspectorate (HMCPSI) (2002) *Thematic Review of Attrition in the Prosecution Process: The Justice Gap*. London: HMSO.

Her Majesty's Crown Prosecution Service Inspectorate (HMCPSI) (2008) *The Joint Thematic Review of the New Charging Arrangements*. London: HMSO.

Home Office (2002) *Justice for All* (Cm. 5563). London: HMSO.

McBarnett, D (1981) *Conviction*. London: Macmillan.

McConville, M and Baldwin, J (1981) *Courts, Prosecution, and Conviction*. Oxford: Oxford University Press.

Moody, S R and Tombs, J (1981) *Prosecution in the Public Interest*. New York: Columbia University Press.

Royal Commission on Criminal Procedure (RCCP) (1981) *Philips Report* (Cmnd 8092). London: HMSO.

Sanders, A (1985) Class bias in prosecutions. *Howard Journal of Criminal Justice*, 24(3): 176–99.

Zander, M (1979) The investigation of crime: a study of cases tried at the Old Bailey. *Criminal Law Review*: 203–19.

USEFUL WEBSITES

http://police.homeoffice.gov.uk/ (Home Office's Police website)

www.cjsonline.gov. uk/the_cjs/departments_of_the_cjs/ocjr (Office of Criminal Justice Reform)

www.cjsonline.gov.uk/the_cjs/whats_new/news-3512.html (Criminal Justice: Simple, Speedy, Summary Justice initiative)

www.cps.gov.uk/ (Crown Prosecution Service)

www.cps.gov.uk/publications/reports/index.html (Crown Prosecution Service business reports)

www.hmic.gov.uk (Her Majesty's Inspectorate of Constabulary)

CASES

Alford v. Chief Constable of Cambridgeshire Police [2009] All ER (D) 232

Guest v. DPP [2009] EWHC 594

R v. Director of Public Prosecutions ex p C [1994] COD 375

LEGISLATION

County and Borough Police Act 1856

Criminal Justice Act 2003

Criminal Proceedings and Investigations Act 1996

Police and Criminal Evidence Act 1984

Prosecution of Offences Act 1879

Prosecution of Offences Act 1985

5   Crime and punishment

Introduction

The courts have a responsibility to sentence people who have been found guilty of committing criminal offences, but what is appropriate and what does society expect from judges and magistrates when they consider punishment for the crime committed?

There will always be different opinions voiced as to how an offender should be dealt with by a court and both judges and magistrates have a responsibility to make decisions to meet the needs and expectations of the offender, the victim and the community. They essentially have four options when making a sentencing decision:

* custodial sentence;

* community order;

* fine;

* discharge.

Powers of judges and magistrates

Judges and magistrates have a wide discretion when it comes to sentencing but are subject to certain restrictions. A magistrate is restricted to sentencing an offender to 6 months for one offence, 12 months for consecutive offences and a fine of £5,000 (provisions yet to be implemented within the Criminal Justice Act (CJA) 2003 will increase this to 12 months for one offence and 65 weeks for consecutive offences). If it is considered that a greater sentence is appropriate, the offender must be sent to the Crown Court for sentence. Judges have no limits; however, they will be restricted to maximum sentences of imprisonment provided by statute, for example burglary 14 years; affray 3 years; theft 10 years.

Although judges and magistrates have some discretion with sentencing, they are subject to guidance that is produced by two independent bodies: the Sentencing Advisory Panel (SAP) and the Sentencing Guidelines Council (SGC). The latter was introduced following statutory intervention in 2004 (CJA 2003, s167), and the aims of both are to:

* encourage consistency in sentencing throughout the courts of England and Wales;

* support sentencers in their decision making.

(www.sentencing-guidelines.gov.uk)

Prior to 2004, the SAP advised the Court of Appeal, which had the responsibility for providing advice on sentencing. The SAP now provides advice on guidelines for particular offences, categories of offence and other sentencing issues to the SGC.

PRACTICAL TASK

Go online to: www.sentencing-guidelines.gov.uk/guidelines/council/final.html, find the guidance that relates to a breach of an anti-social behaviour order published in December 2008 and identify the seven elements of the decision-making process (see page 7).

Sentencing practice

When a judge or magistrate is determining a sentence the following will be considered:

- the offence;

- the background of the offender;

- the aim of the sentencing.

The offence

The facts of the case will be related to the judge or magistrate who will assess the seriousness of the offence committed, the culpability of the offender and the harm done. Legislation provides for a more severe sentence if the offence was racially or religiously aggravated, or if there is evidence of hostility to sexual orientation or disability.

In considering the harm done, the court will take account of issues such as the nature of injuries caused, whether the person was in a position of trust, or whether the person was a ringleader. Where a guilty plea is offered, the law allows a reduction in the sentence (see Table 5.1).

Background of the offender

Once a person has been convicted of a criminal offence, the judge or magistrate will want to know more about the offender to help them determine an appropriate sentence. If the offence is a serious one, there may be no option other than to award a custodial sentence; however, the majority of sentences awarded are non-custodial.

Previous convictions will be an important factor to consider, and whether further offences have been committed while on bail. The Probation Service is required to produce a pre-sentence report to the court or, where appropriate, the Youth Offending Team will provide a specific sentence report. The report must contain an assessment of the nature and seriousness of the offence and its impact on the victim. It may also contain information such as the offender's background, suitability for a community or rehabilitation order, how he or she responded to an order in the past, financial circumstances and medical reports.

In 2008, the Probation Service provided 216,000 pre-sentence reports, 74 per cent at Magistrates' Courts and 26 per cent at the Crown Court. The court do not always agree

Table 5.1 Reductions in sentence when a guilty plea is offered

When guilty plea offered	Reduction in sentence
First reasonable opportunity	One third
After trial date set	One quarter
After trial has commenced	One tenth

Source: SGC (2007, p6).

with the recommendations made within the pre-sentence report, but agreed with 88 per cent custodial, 71 per cent community order and 52 per cent suspended sentence recommendations (MoJ, 2009, p9).

Aim of sentencing

Legislation (Criminal Justice Act 2003, s142) provides five aims of sentencing that the court must have regard to before deciding on the sentence:

- the punishment of offenders;
- the reduction of crime (including its reduction by deterrence);
- the reform and rehabilitation of offenders;
- the protection of the public;
- the making of reparation by offenders to persons affected by their offences.

PRACTICAL TASK

Go to www.probation.homeoffice.gov.uk/files/pdf/PC33A%202005.pdf and download the document, Pre-sentence Report Guidance for Prolific & Priority Offenders. Read through the example of a pre-sentence report that you will find on page 7 and write down the aims of the sentencing in this case.

Restorative justice

In the next chapter we shall explore the concept of restorative justice and how it contributes to putting the victim at the heart of the Criminal Justice System (CJS). This approach impacts on sentencing decisions and many of the sentencing options currently available to the courts have a restorative element, such as the community order requirement of unpaid work or a reparation order.

Key legislation

There are a number of Acts of Parliament that provide judges and magistrates with the legal power to sentence people who are found guilty of a criminal offence in the courts. The range of sentencing options that are currently available is extensive and the following Acts of Parliament provide the main sentencing options:

- Crime and Disorder Act (CDA) 1998;
- Powers of Criminal Courts (Sentencing) Act (PCCSA) 2000;
- Criminal Justice Act (CJA) 2003;
- Criminal Justice and Immigration Act (CJIA) 2008.

PRACTICAL TASK

The Office of Public Sector Information (OPSI) provides details of government legislation and full details of the statutes highlighted above can be found at www.opsi. gov.uk/legislation. A 'Google' or 'Bing' search on any of the above Acts will take you directly to the relevant part of the OPSI website. You will find that the sections of the Act are set out and split into parts and chapters. Each section can be easily viewed through a hyperlink that takes you to the full wording of the section. Access and scan through each Act and make a list of the sentencing options that are available.

You may have been surprised to find that the list of options available is quite extensive and more complex than you might have expected. You will also have noted that some of the sentencing options appear to have been repeated within some of the acts, for example supervision, action plan and reparation orders. The reason for this is that Parliament continues to review legislation and amend law on a regular basis.

PRACTICAL TASK

Find the PCCSA 2000 and access the link to schedule 12, part I, 'Acts of Parliament Repealed'. Find the reference made to the CDA 1998 and you will see the sections of the Act that have been repealed by the new legislation, e.g. sections 67 to 79 of the CDA relate to supervision, action plan and reparation orders and have been replaced by sections 63 to 75 of the PCCSA. The supervision order has further been amended and the action plan order repealed in the CJIA 2008.

We will now explore some sections of the four Acts in more detail and examine some of the sentencing options available to the courts with a focus on non-custodial sentences. It is not possible within the limitations of this chapter to discuss every sentencing option and, should you wish to explore the range of other sentencing options available, further reading and research is recommended.

Crime and Disorder Act 1998

The Conservatives have forgotten the 'order' part of 'law and order'. We will tackle the unacceptable level of anti-social behaviour and crime on our streets. Our 'zero tolerance' approach will ensure that petty criminality among young offenders is seriously addressed.

(Labour Party, 1997)

After securing power in 1997, the Labour government was determined to tackle the problem of crime and in particular the causes of crime. They felt that previous governments had not effectively tackled problems of crime and particularly disorder, which was contributing to rising levels in the fear of crime, despite evidence of falling crime levels. This Act was one of Labour's first major pieces of legislation and was an attempt to tackle the problems of crime and disorder more effectively, through a multi-agency approach, and to provide new powers and procedures to deal with young offenders. (Chapter 7 will provide further detail about the impact of the Act on youth crime.)

Within this chapter, the term 'young offender' will be used when referring to a child. Unfortunately, there is no single law that defines the age of a child, but legislation will state specific age limits. In 1991, the UK adopted the United Nations Convention on the Rights of the Child definition of a child as being under the age of 18 years (OHCHR, 1990, article 1). The law also deems that a child of a certain age cannot commit a crime and currently this is under 10 for England and Wales and under 8 for Scotland.

Some of the key sections and sentencing provisions provided by the Act are:

1   anti-social behaviour order (ASBO);

8   parenting order;

11   child safety order;

65   reprimands and warnings.

Anti-social behaviour orders

An anti-social behaviour order (ASBO) can be sought from the court where a person acts in an anti-social manner that causes or is likely to cause harassment, alarm or distress to one or more persons not of the same household as himself (*sic*). It further states that the action is necessary to protect persons from anti-social behaviour in the area where the harassment, alarm and distress were caused. The Home Office provides some examples of the types of behaviour the Act is attempting to challenge – any aggressive, intimidating or destructive activity that damages or destroys another person's quality of life. It will include incidents such as noise, vandalism, graffiti, fly-tipping, disorderly or aggressive behaviour, street drinking and letting off fireworks (Home Office, 2009a).

The ASBO is not seen as a punishment for offending, but as a means of control to prevent the behaviour from continuing, and provides a civil remedy rather than a criminal one. Prior to seeking an ASBO from a court, other remedies are now available to the police, local authorities, housing associations and Youth Offending Teams to deal with offenders and, when appropriate, parents by negotiating agreements through acceptable behaviour contracts (ABCs) and parental orders. These additional powers have been provided by the Anti-social Behaviour Act (ASBA) 2003 and the Police and Justice Act (PJA) 2006.

In essence, section 1 of the CDA 1998 provides a remedy to deal with anti-social behaviour rather than directly punishing an offender and resulting in the stigma of a criminal conviction. The Home Office (2009b) states that the main aim of this type of intervention is to:

• protect victims, witnesses and the community;

• enable the offender to understand the consequences of their behaviour;

• make sure offenders change their behaviour.

When an offender refuses to comply with or breaches the conditions of an ASBO, further court action will be required to ensure compliance. Breaching an ASBO without reasonable excuse is a criminal offence and the magistrates have a range of sentencing options, including imprisonment, community order or fine.

Where a person is convicted of a criminal offence, the courts may consider that an ASBO is necessary to further control the offender's behaviour and, in these circumstances, the order is known as a criminal anti-social behaviour order (CRASBO). Examples of this would include a shoplifter being excluded from a shopping mall or a person found guilty of drunken violent behaviour being excluded from certain licensed premises.

REFLECTIVE TASK

You may be interested in finding out more about the use of an ASBO as a means of effectively tackling the problems of neighbourhood nuisance and other minor forms of behaviour that impact on the quality of life. Consider why the Labour government introduced the order and assess its effectiveness, i.e. is the order achieving its aims?

A report was produced in 2006 on behalf of the Youth Justice Board that suggested that many youths awarded an ASBO merely saw them as badges of honour (YJB, 2006). What are the implications of this?

Consider whether victims are reassured by use of the orders and is there any evidence that they are contributing to reductions in the fear of crime and disorder?

Some of these issues may provide a good basis for the development of an assignment.

Parenting orders

The CDA 1998 introduced this innovative approach in an attempt to engage parents in the rehabilitation of their children, with the aim of controlling behaviour and to prevent reoffending. Subsequent legislation has strengthened the use of this type of order by increasing its flexibility and making it more widely available, such as the PJA 2006, which now gives local authorities powers in relation to parenting contracts and orders, allowing community safety officers, registered social landlords and others to use them for anti-social behaviour.

Research has shown that inadequate supervision of children is strongly associated with offending and in one study it was shown that, where parental supervision was low or medium, 42 per cent of children had offended compared with only 20 per cent where supervision was high. Further, where parenting was deemed to be harsh or erratic, children were twice as likely to offend (DCA, 2007, p2).

A young offender (10–17yrs) can be referred to a Youth Offending Team (YOT) by the police following a final warning or conditional caution (see page 83) or by the court where the young offender is appearing at a court for the first time and is pleading guilty to a criminal offence. The aim of this type of intervention is to repair the harm caused by the offence and address the causes of the offending behaviour.

81

The YOT will need to work with the parent of any child referred to them and, in many cases, the team will work with the parent on a voluntary basis without the need for any formal contract or order. Many options are open to the team to deal with a young offender, such as ensuring attendance at school, making them attend programmes for anger management or drug or alcohol dependence, home curfews, exclusion from certain areas, and removal from disruptive influences. The parent clearly has a pivotal role to play to ensure compliance with the requirements.

Where a voluntary agreement cannot be achieved, section 25 of ASBA 2003 allows the YOT to negotiate a formal contract with the parent to comply with the requirements of the contract and for the YOT to support the parent.

When a parent refuses to cooperate, the YOT can apply to a court for a parenting order. Failure to comply with an order will result in warnings and further meetings to resolve any difficulties highlighted but, if not resolved satisfactorily, the YOT may refer the breach of the order back to the police to investigate. This may result in the parent appearing before a court for failing, without reasonable excuse, to comply with the requirements of a parenting order, which could result in a fine or non-custodial sentence such as a community order.

Child safety orders

The child safety order (CSO) is aimed at children under the age of ten who are deemed in law to be under the age of criminal responsibility. Prior to the CDA 1998, there was nothing in place to effectively deal with those under the age of criminal responsibility who could have a major impact on some communities with their unchecked anti-social behaviour.

Where a child under ten commits a criminal offence, behaves in a way that they are at risk of offending, causes or is likely to cause disruption or harassment to local residents, or contravenes a local child curfew order, the local authority may make an application to a family court for a CSO.

If the order is granted, the child will be supervised by a responsible officer, normally a member of social services or the YOT, for a period of usually three months and, in exceptional circumstances, up to one year. The order will contain a number of requirements, with the aim of subjecting the child to proper control and preventing any repeat offending. Where a child fails to comply with the order, the ultimate sanction for the courts is a care order.

REFLECTIVE TASK

This section of the CDA 1998 has attracted some criticism from academics for bringing very young children within the parameters of the CJS (Fortin, 2003, p557). Write down your thoughts about this and produce an argument agreeing or disagreeing with the criticism made.

Reprimands and warnings

Prior to the introduction of the CDA 1998, a system of police cautioning was in place for young offenders that attracted some criticism (see Audit Commission report, *Misspent Youth*, 1996). The use of repeat cautions was found to be inadequate and there was a need for more progressive and effective interventions to prevent reoffending. This was addressed by introducing a reprimand and warning scheme for a young offender (10–17 years).

A reprimand can be used when a police officer has evidence to suggest that a young offender has committed a criminal offence and is satisfied that:

- the evidence is sufficient for a realistic prospect of a conviction;
- the offender has admitted the offence;
- the offender has not been previously convicted of an offence;
- it would not be in the public interest to prosecute.

A warning is appropriate if the young offender has not been previously warned, or, where he or she has been previously warned, the offence was committed more than two years after the date of the first warning, and the offence is considered not serious enough for a charge to be brought. Where there is no previous reprimand, a warning should be given if the offence is considered to require a warning rather than a reprimand because of its seriousness.

Guidance is provided by both the Association of Chief Police Officers (ACPO) and the Crown Prosecution Service (CPS) to assist both police officers and lawyers in determining the public interest test and the type of offences suitable for a reprimand or warning.

Following a reprimand, the young offender can be referred to a YOT, which will negotiate a plan to stop the offending behaviour or to make good the harm done. This referral is voluntary, but when a young offender has been warned, the referral to the YOT is mandatory. The plan may include requirements to meet with the YOT worker, apologise to the victim personally or by letter, or undertake a community activity.

Powers of Criminal Courts (Sentencing) Act 2000

Prior to 2000, there were many different Acts of Parliament that provided sentencing options, making the law difficult and complex for practitioners within the CJS. The Law Commission, on behalf of the government, drafted the PCCSA 2000 to consolidate existing law and to include most of the sentencing options into a single Act.

Many sections of this Act have already been updated by the CJA 2003, which will be explored later in the chapter.

Some of the key sections and sentencing provisions provided by the PCCSA 2000 are:

12 absolute and conditional discharge;

73 reparation order;

100   detention and training order;

146   driving disqualification.

Absolute and conditional discharge

There are occasions when a person appears before a court for what is considered to be a minor or technical offence and punishment may be considered to be inappropriate in the circumstances, such as evading a train fare, theft of a tin of spaghetti, or a police driver colliding with a vehicle while responding to a 999 call.

The court may rule that punishment is not appropriate and has the power to discharge a person absolutely; however, they may still be liable to court costs, compensation or disqualification, and will receive a criminal record. For example, in September 2005, boxer Chris Eubanks was required to pay £450 court costs after being given an absolute discharge for taking a vehicle without consent.

The court can also award a conditional discharge, which requires a person not to commit any further offences for a maximum period of three years. If a further offence is committed within the stipulated period, the court has the power to sentence a person for the original offence as well as the further offence committed.

REFLECTIVE TASK

In August 2006, Police Constable Mark Milton appeared at Ludlow Magistrates' Court in Shropshire, and was given an absolute discharge after being convicted of dangerous driving for travelling at speeds of up to159 mph while on duty.

Find out more about this case at http://news.bbc.co.uk/1/hi/england/shropshire/ 5284962.stm and consider whether you feel that the sentence awarded was appropriate in this case. What sentencing decision would you have made and why?

Reparation orders

A reparation order can be used when a young offender has been convicted of a criminal offence and is a good example of a restorative justice approach. It allows the offender to face the consequences of his or her criminal behaviour and make good any harm done, and discourages future offending. It also considers the feelings and needs of the victim, whose consent is required before any reparation order is made.

The reparation is usually in kind rather than financial compensation. Where financial recompense is necessary, the court has other powers to award compensation to a victim. The reparation might include repair of damage caused, cleaning up litter or graffiti, or other community work. The work can be no more than 24 hours in length and will be supervised by a responsible officer.

When a reparation order is breached, the court has the power to vary or discharge the order or deal with any non-compliance with a fine or community order.

Detention and training orders

Where a young offender under 18 years has committed a more serious offence and other sentencing options are deemed not suitable, a detention and training order may be awarded by the court. It will be applicable to those who are considered to pose a high level of risk, have a significant offending history, or are persistent offenders.

For a young person under 15, the court cannot make this type of order unless it is of the opinion that the offender is a persistent offender. Similarly, the order cannot be used for a young person under 12 unless the court is of the opinion that a custodial sentence is the only means of adequately protecting the public from further offending.

A detention and training order will be for a period of between 4 and 24 months with half the sentence served in custody and the remainder served within the community and supervised by a responsible officer. Breaches of the order can be dealt with by the court and can result in a further custodial sentence or fine.

Training during the period of custody and supervision will provide activities that will focus on the education, health, behaviour and other needs of the young offender.

Driving disqualification

Traffic legislation provides the court with specific powers for the disqualification of a driver, for reasons such as driving under the influence of alcohol, dangerous driving, or the accumulation of penalty points. Courts also have the power to disqualify a person from holding or obtaining a driving licence following the commission of an offence for a period it thinks fit, for example the power may be used for a person convicted of kerb crawling.

The Crown Court has specific powers to disqualify a person from holding or obtaining a driving licence where a motor vehicle has been used in the commission of a criminal offence that attracts a jail term of at least two years' imprisonment. It also makes specific provision for any assault case, including common assault, where a vehicle has been used in the commission of the crime.

Criminal Justice Act 2003

The Labour government clearly recognised the need to reform the CJS and a number of key reports provided the stimulus for legislative change, such as:

- *Making Punishment Work* (Halliday, 2001);

- *Review of the Criminal Courts of England and Wales* (Auld, 2001);

- *Justice for All* (Home Office, 2002), which sets out the need to reform the CJS with the aim of rebalancing it in favour of victims, witnesses and the community.

PRACTICAL TASK

Go to *www.homeoffice.gov.uk/documents/halliday-report-sppu/ and access the* Making Punishment Work *report. Find recommendations 27 to 32 relating to community sentences and compare with the provisions made in the CJA 2003, for example section 177, community orders.*

Some of the key sections and sentencing provisions provided by the Act are:

22   conditional cautions;

177   community orders;

199–215 community order requirements.

Conditional cautions

A cautioning system is also in place for adult offenders, who can be given either a simple or conditional caution for certain offences. The simple caution has a non-statutory basis but must be used in accordance with guidelines issued by the Director of Public Prosecutions. The conditional caution has further been amended by section 17 of the PJA 2006. The conditional caution is similar to a warning, seeking to reform the offender and make good the harm done to the victim, and the following conditions can be attached in order to:

- facilitate the rehabilitation of an offender;

- ensure the offender makes reparation for the offence;

- punish the offender.

(PJA 2006, s17(3))

The CPS provides guidance on the use of conditional cautions and advises that the caution must be proportionate, achievable and appropriate. Conditions may include requirements such as treatment for drug or alcohol dependency, anger management and reparation to the victim (CPS, 2003).

Community order

The community order was introduced on 4 April 2005 and replaced a series of different types of community sentence provided by other Acts of Parliament. It is a single generic community order that is accompanied by a number of requirements that are attached to the order when made. Its purpose it to combine punishment with changing the offender's behaviour, making amends for the harm done, and also dealing with problems that have contributed to the commission of the crime, such as drugs or alcohol.

Where a community order is breached the court has the power to amend it, making it more onerous, and can vary or revoke the original sentence, which may mean a custodial sentence even if the original offence committed was non-custodial. The Act provides 13 requirements that can be attached to a community order:

- Activity
- Alcohol treatment
- Attendance centre
- Curfew
- Drug rehabilitation
- Electronic monitoring
- Exclusion

- Mental health treatment
- Programme
- Prohibited activity
- Residence
- Supervision
- Unpaid work

REFLECTIVE TASK

Access sections 199 to 215 of the CJA 2003 and read through the requirements provided for community orders. Write down what you consider to be the benefits of this type of approach and any problems associated with it.

Compare your answers with a report produced by the National Audit Office in January 2008 relating to the supervision of community orders by the Probation Service (the full report is available together with an executive summary at www.nao.org.uk/publications/ 0708/the_national_probation_service.aspx).

We shall explore two of the above requirements in more detail: drug rehabilitation and curfew.

Drug rehabilitation requirement

As stated previously, it was the government's intent to tackle the unacceptable levels of crime and disorder and, prior to 1998, it was commonly believed that there were clear links between drugs and crime. For example, research commissioned by the Home Office in 1998 found:

> *The research has shown that a large proportion of arrestees are involved in drug use and many of these use addictive and expensive drugs. It has shown that a number of measures of drug use and crime are strongly correlated. A substantial proportion of arrestees (approximately half) believe that their drug use and crime are related.*

> (Bennett, 1998, p47)

Drugs treatment and testing orders were introduced by the CDA 1998 and further updated within the PCCSA 2000 in an attempt to deal with the problem of drug dependency and its links to acquisitive crime (crime committed to fund a drugs habit). Where a person is convicted of an offence, the court may make a community order and attach to it a drug rehabilitation requirement (DRR), which includes both drugs testing and treatment. The Act also allows the court to attach a DRR to a person given a suspended prison sentence.

The court can only impose a DRR if it is satisfied that the offender is dependent on, or has a propensity to misuse, drugs and that the dependency or propensity may be susceptible to treatment. The treatment will be for a period of at least six months and the offender must be willing to comply with the requirement. The court may impose residential or non-residential treatment and the offender must submit to regular drugs testing. A responsible officer will be appointed to supervise the treatment and testing.

Further powers were provided to the courts with the introduction of drugs intervention orders (Drugs Act 2005, s20). The order applies to persons aged 18 and over and is aimed at persons brought before the court for anti-social behaviour connected with drugs misuse. The order can be in place for a maximum of six months only and the aim of the order will be to take measures deemed appropriate to prevent further drugs-related anti-social behaviour. If the measures adopted are later deemed to be ineffective, the court has the power to vary or discharge the order, but if an offender fails to comply with the order he or she will commit an offence that can be dealt with summarily.

REFLECTIVE TASK

Consider how effective this type of sentencing is in resolving problems of drugs misuse and reducing crime. Are government policies making a difference or is this just another soft option of dealing with offenders who some may think should be incarcerated for the crimes they have committed?

Make a list of what you consider to be the advantages and disadvantages of the approach and then visit the UK Drug Policy Commission website (www.ukdpc.org.uk), access the 'Reports' link and find the document, Reducing Drug Use, Reducing Reoffending – March 2008. What does the evidence contained in this report suggest?

Curfew requirement

A curfew order requires a person who has been convicted of a criminal offence to remain at a specified place for a period of time between two and twelve hours per day for a maximum period of six months. The court will nominate a responsible person to monitor the curfew and, in some circumstances, electronic monitoring will be used. This is where a person is tagged with an electronic device and their movements are monitored via GPS satellite.

Electronic monitoring is controversial and questions have been raised about its effectiveness. For example, on 30 September 2003, Marion Bates was shot dead in her jeweller's shop by Peter Williams, who was being electronically monitored as part of a detention and training order. It was some weeks before Williams was arrested despite being electronically tagged.

PRACTICAL TASK

> *PRACTICAL TASK*
>
> Go online to www.crimlinks.com/electronic_monitoring.htm and find out more about electronic monitoring and curfew schemes. Then consider and make a list of the advantages and disadvantages of this type of order.
>
> Further, consider the failures highlighted in the Peter Williams case as a comparison (the full report can be found at www.justice.gov.uk/inspectorates/hmi-probation/docs/peter williamsenquiry-rps.pdf).

Criminal Justice and Immigration Act 2008

Some of the key sections and sentencing provisions provided by the Act are:

22 youth rehabilitation orders;

48 youth conditional cautions.

This CJIA 2008 is a further attempt by the Labour government to introduce a series of measures to cut crime, reduce reoffending and protect the public. The Act has simplified previous legislation and provides some sentencing options, including a single rehabilitation order for young offenders with a menu of requirements that was introduced on 30 November 2009.

When sentencing a young offender under the age of 18, section 9 of the CJIA 2008 states that the court must have regard to:

- the principal aim of the youth justice system to prevent offending and reoffending;
- the welfare of the offender;
- the purposes of sentencing, which are punishment, reform and rehabilitation, protection of the public, and reparation.

Youth rehabilitation orders

These orders provide a generic community sentence for young offenders and their aim is to simplify the sentencing of young offenders and improve the flexibility of interventions with a greater choice of options for the courts.

The sentencing options that are now available are:

- Attendance centre
- Curfew
- Drug testing
- Drug treatment
- Education
- Electronic monitoring
- Exclusion
- Fostering
- Intoxicating substance treatment
- Local authority residence
- Mental health treatment
- Programme
- Prohibited activity
- Residence
- Supervision
- Unpaid work

Youth conditional cautions

The youth conditional caution can be used where the offence is deemed not suitable to be dealt with by way of reprimand or warning, or where the options available under the reprimand and warning scheme have been exhausted. Ordinarily these cases would most likely have been referred to a court and the conditional caution provides a further opportunity for a young offender to avoid the court system and to stop offending.

Failure to comply, without reasonable cause, with any of the conditions attached to a conditional caution can result in criminal proceedings for the original offence. A pilot for the scheme was commenced in June 2009 and currently only applies to 16 and 17 year olds.

Prison versus community sentence

Many people believe that putting criminals into prison is the best way of reducing crime and protecting society; however, prison populations are rising dramatically and alternative solutions have had to be found to deal more effectively with offenders. In 2007, the Crown and Magistrates' Courts handed out 1,414,700 sentences and Table 5.2 shows how the large majority of sentences were distributed.

A further 362,900 offences were not dealt with by the courts but through other means, such as cautions, penalty notices for disorder, and warnings for possession of cannabis (MoJ, 2008, p2).

Michael Howard, the ex-Conservative Home Secretary, became renowned for saying that 'Prison works'. While criminals are in prison they cannot offend and the public are protected. In contrast, the Labour government's policy since their election in 1997 has been to develop community-based sentencing policies as an alternative to prison, with the aim of reforming and rehabilitating offenders.

Despite this, prison numbers continue to rise and Table 5.3 shows how the prison population continues to grow within the UK. Table 5.4 shows how the UK compares with some other countries worldwide.

Despite the shift of policy to provide more focus on the reform and rehabilitation of offenders, in contrast to deterrence and incapacitation associated with imprisonment, the prison population continues to rise. England and Wales have one of the highest prisoner rates in Europe and the USA leads the way internationally with a staggering 760 per 100,000 of the population incarcerated in prisons.

Table 5.2 Distribution of sentences

Type of sentence	No. of sentences	Percentage
Fines	941,000	66.6
Suspended prison sentence	40,700	2.9
Community sentence	196,400	13.9
Immediate custody	95,200	6.7

Source: Ministry of Justice (2008, p4).

Table 5.3 Growth of prison populations in the UK

Prison populations	1992		1998		2004		2009 (June)	
	Number of prisoners	Number per 100,000 population	Number of prisoners	Number per 100,000 population	Number of prisoners	Number per 100,000 population	Number of prisoners	Number per 100,000 population
England & Wales	44,719	88	65,298	126	74,657	141	82,818	151
Scotland	5,357	105	6,082	120	6,885	136	8,103	156
Northern Ireland	1,811	112	1,531	91	1,295	76	1,498	84

Table 5.4 Worldwide comparisons of prison populations

June 2009	Number of prisoners	Number per 100,000 population
United States of America	2,310,984	760
Russian Federation	889,948	628
South Africa	164,755	335
Israel	22,725	325
Spain	76,174	164
Turkey	110,928	154
England & Wales	82,818	151
Holland	16,416	100
Italy	58,597	97
France	59,655	96
Germany	72,259	88
Nigeria	40,193	26

Source: King's College London (2009).

REFLECTIVE TASK

Consider why the USA and UK have higher rates of imprisonment. Make a list of all the factors that may contribute to higher prison levels and consider why, e.g. government strategy; sentencing policy; law enforcement; legal system; resource availability; and financial support.

As a theme for an assignment, you may wish to develop this further by making comparisons with a country that has a lower prison population rate and exploring the effectiveness of different criminal justice strategies.

The problem of the growing prison population was reviewed by Lord Carter of Coles in 2007 and he suggested that there were five drivers that were contributing to the prison explosion:

- changes in public attitudes and the political climate;

- changes to legislation and the sentencing framework;

- more offenders brought to justice; increased custody rates and longer sentence lengths;

- greater focus on enforcement of sentences;

- greater awareness of risk and greater political prominence of public protection.

(Carter, 2007, p5)

PRACTICAL TASK

Read through the Carter review, Securing the Future, at www.justice.gov.uk/publications/securing-the-future.htm and find the recommendations he has made to improve the balance between the supply of prison places and demand for them. What are the three key principles identified when considering measures for managing the use of custody as a sentencing option? (See page 28.)

Consider some of the ideas put forward in respect of recommendation 1. How have these been adopted in practice? What has been done already and how will legislation contribute to reducing demand for prison places? (See reference to CJIA 2008 on page 27 of the review.)

The use of community sentences is regarded by some to be a much better option than prison. The rehabilitation ideal that sentencing should aim to reform the criminal is a tenet of modern penal rationale. The conundrum for politicians is not only the duty imposed on them to promote community safety and reduce crime, but also an obligation to provide programmes and other treatment opportunities to enable offenders to stop offending (von Hirsch et al., 2009).

Reform and rehabilitation of offenders are essential to reduce crime and promote community safety, and current sentencing options are now more than ever geared towards achieving this aim, but what is the evidence to date? Government will usually claim success with their strategies; however, it is useful to explore independent research.

PRACTICAL TASK

Go to www.crimeandjustice.org.uk/opus582.html and download the document, Ten Years of Justice under Labour: An Independent Audit. *Go to page 40 and identify the problems the researchers have found with the way government measures targets. The researchers suggest that the government has not been able to effectively reduce offending. Carry out your own research using other sources and argue whether this is true or not.*

C H A P T E R   S U M M A R Y

Within this chapter we have identified the aims and purposes of sentencing within the CJS and have explored how sentencing is applied by both judges and magistrates. We have seen how sentencing decisions are informed by legislative requirements, the SGC and consideration of the offender's background.

Key legislation has been identified and explored, highlighting the wide range of sentencing options that are now available and how government continues to repeal and update legislation in an attempt to provide more effective sentencing options, with an emphasis on reform and rehabilitation of offenders, victim and community reparation, community protection, and reduction of crime.

Opportunities have been provided for further research and analysis of some key issues relating to crime and punishment that will provide stimuli, sources and evidence for completion of NOS and assignments.

FURTHER READING

There are many sources available to extend your knowledge and understanding of crime and punishment and further reading will be required to add quality and substance to a theme or debate being developed within an assignment. The following academic texts are examples of sources that could be used:

Hopkins Burke, R (2008) *Young People, Crime and Justice*. Cullompton: Willan.

Muncie, J (2009) *Youth and Crime*, 3rd edition. London: Sage, chapter 9: 'Youth justice strategies II: prevention and punishment'.

von Hirsch, A, Ashworth, A and Roberts, J (2009) *Principled Sentencing: Readings on Theory and Policy*, 3rd edition. Oxford: Hart Publishing.

REFERENCES

Audit Commission (1996) *Misspent Youth: Young People and Crime* (National Report). London: Audit Commission.

Auld, R (2001) *A Review of the Criminal Courts of England and Wales.* London: Ministry of Justice. Available online at www.criminal-courts-review.org.uk (accessed 2 June 2009).

Bennett, T (1998) *Drugs and Crime: The Results of Research on Drugs Testing and Interviewing Arrestees* (Research Study 183). London: Home Office.

Carter, Lord Patrick (2007) *Securing the Future: Proposals for the Efficient and Sustainable Use of Custody in England and Wales.* London: Ministry of Justice. Available online at www.justice.gov.uk/publications/securing-the-future.htm (accessed 15 June 2009).

Crown Prosecution Service (CPS) (2003) *Conditional Cautioning – Code of Practice and Associated Annexes – Criminal Justice Act, sections 22–27.* Available online at www.cps.gov.uk/Publications/others/conditionalcautioning04.html#types (accessed 5 June 2009).

Department of Constitutional Affairs (DCA) (2007) *Parenting Contracts and Orders Guidance.* Available online at www.homeoffice.gov.uk/documents/parenting-contracts-orders-072835.pdf?view=Binary (accessed 20 January 2010).

Fortin, J (2003) *Children's Rights and the Developing Law.* Cambridge: Cambridge University Press.

Halliday, J (2001) *Making Punishments Work: Report of a Review of the Sentencing Framework for England and Wales.* London: Home Office. Available online at www.homeoffice.gov.uk/documents/halliday-report-sppu (accessed 2 June 2009).

Home Office (2002) *Justice for All* (Cm. 5563). London: HMSO.

Home Office (2009a) *Anti-social Behaviour.* Available online at www.homeoffice.gov.uk/anti-social-behaviour (accessed 20 January 2010).

Home Office (2009b) *Tackling Anti-social Behaviour and its Causes.* Available online at www.asb.homeoffice.gov.uk (accessed 20 January 2010).

King's College London (2009) *World Prison Brief.* Available online at www.kcl.ac.uk/depsta/law/research/icps/worldbrief (accessed 15 June 2009).

Labour Party (1997) *Manifesto.* Available online at www.Labour-party.org.uk/manifestos/1997/1997-Labour-manifesto.shtml (accessed 20 May 2009).

Ministry of Justice (MoJ) (2008) *Sentencing Statistics, 2007, England and Wales.* London: Ministry of Justice. Available online at www.justice.gov.uk/publications/sentencingannual.htm (accessed 2 June 2009).

Ministry of Justice (MoJ) (2009) *Offender Management Caseload Statistics 2008.* London: Ministry of Justice. Available online at www.justice.gov.uk/publications/docs/offender-management-caseload-statistics-2008-2.pdf (accessed 27 November 2009).

Office of the High Commissioner for Human Rights (OHCHR) (1990) *Convention on the Rights of a Child: General Assembly Resolution 44/25 of 20 November 89.* Available online at www2.ohchr.org/english/law.crc.htm (accessed 19 January 2010).

Sentencing Guidelines Council (SGC) (2007) *Reduction in Sentence for a Guilty Plea: Definitive Guideline 2007*. London: Sentencing Guideline Secretariat.

von Hirsch, A, Ashworth, A and Roberts, J (2009) *Principled Sentencing: Readings on Theory and Policy*, 3rd edition. Oxford: Hart Publishing.

Youth Justice Board (YJB) (2006) Youth Offending Teams could save young people from 'badge of honour' ASBOs. *News*, 2 November. Available online at www.yjb.gov.uk/en-gb/News/ASBO researchpublished.htm (accessed 19 January 2010).

USEFUL WEBSITES

www.antisocialbehavior.org.uk (general information on anti-social behaviour)

www.cjsonline.co.uk (Criminal Justice System)

www.cps.gov.uk (Crown Prosecution Service)

www.direct.gov.uk (Directgov provides access to public services)

www.hmcourts-service.gov.uk (Her Majesty's Courts Service)

www.homeoffice.gov.uk (Home Office)

www.justice.gov.uk (Ministry of Justice)

www.opsi.gov.uk (Office of Public Sector Information)

www.probation.homeoffice.gov.uk (National Probation Service)

www.sentencing-guidelines.gov.uk (SGC and SAP sentencing guidelines)

www.yjb.gov.uk (Youth Justice Board)

LEGISLATION

Anti-social Behaviour Act 2003

Crime and Disorder Act 1998

Criminal Justice Act 2003

Criminal Justice and Immigration Act 2008

Drugs Act 2005

Police and Justice Act 2006

Powers of Criminal Courts (Sentencing) Act 2000

6 Victims and the Criminal Justice System

Introduction

Balancing the needs and interests of the victim and offender can be problematic. For example, some countries focus on offender rehabilitation and neglect the victim, who needs to be placed at the centre of the criminal justice process. This chapter will examine New Labour's pledge to put victims at the heart of the CJS in England and Wales. It will also examine the notion of restorative justice, which is aimed at providing justice for victims of crime as well as accountability for offenders.

The 'scientific study of victims' is otherwise referred to as *victimology*, with American psychiatrist Frederick Wertham pioneering early studies in the late 1940s. Before this, victims were considered as 'passive actors' in criminal events, but later studies have focused on the plight of the victim and the physical, emotional and financial harm that people suffer through illegal activities. Studies have also focused on victims' experiences with agencies in the CJS, such as the Police Service, Crown Prosecution Service and the court system itself. These studies help us to interpret victim and offender behaviour and provide useful insights in how to manage them.

Victimology also helps us to understand victims' connections to other social groups and institutions, such as the media, businesses and social movements. So-called 'radical victimology' has expanded our traditional understanding of victimhood to include real, complex, contradictory and sometimes politically inconvenient victims of crime. This arguably includes corporate and white-collar crime, people-trafficking, genocide, armed conflict, torture and terrorism. Studies of 'secondary' victimisation and the effects of crime and punishment have also drawn our attention to the families of primary victims, of prisoners and of those sentenced to capital punishment or those executed in countries that retain the death penalty.

What is now clear is that the concept of 'victimhood' has changed in the two decades since Christie's (1986) stereotypical description of a 'typical victim'. Christie suggests that the victim is weak, carries out a 'respectable project', is free of blame and is a stranger to a 'big, bad' offender. Christie also argues that 'real' victims needed to take their case to the CJS, which is problematic given that the majority of crime probably goes unreported and that most victims never come into contact with the CJS. (We shall return to this later in the chapter.) It can be argued, therefore, that current victim policy focuses on what is actually a disproportionate group of mainly vulnerable witnesses, rather than victims per se! It is also recognised that the victim is a key player in the criminal justice process, without whose cooperation in reporting crime, providing evidence and acting as a witness in court even more crime would go unreported and unpunished.

Victim models

Hans von Hentig (1948) went on to construct a category or 'typology' of victims, which includes the notions of 'proneness' and 'culpability'. He argued that some people are vulnerable and therefore more prone to becoming a victim, or are perhaps blameworthy and therefore 'culpable'. It can be the victim's actual status, their physical appearance or their behaviour that makes them prone or blameworthy, for example the elderly, women, children and the mentally ill, or those who openly display signs of wealth:

> *In a sense the victim shapes and moulds the criminal . . . [and] it would not be correct nor complete to speak of a carnivorous animal, its habits and characteristics, without looking at the prey on which it lives. In a certain sense the animals which devour and those that are devoured complement one another.*

(von Hentig, 1948, p27)

Building on this, Wolfgang (1958) conducted a major study of 'victim-precipitated' homicides in Philadelphia between 1948 and 1952. Similar to victim culpability and proneness, precipitation considers the extent to which a person can encourage or even contribute to becoming a victim by their own actions and behaviour, for example by failing to lock a house, car door or window, or by leaving valuables on show.

REFLECTIVE TASK

Consider the following in terms of 'victim precipitation' and initiate a discussion between family or work colleagues.

> *A woman freely consents to intercourse, engages in heavy petting but resists the man at the last moment. The man ignores this resistance and has sex with the woman against her will. She becomes frightened and stops resisting.*

Do you consider that, by heavy petting, the woman has largely contributed to the outcomes and precipitated her own victimisation?

(You may wish to refer to sections 1(1) and 1(2) of the Sexual Offences Act 2003, which refer to rape, consent and reasonable belief. Section 74 further defines consent.)

The emergence of victim movements and protecting victims' rights

It has been argued that the role of the CJS is to determine the guilt of someone suspected of an offence, and for victims to give evidence as witnesses in trials against the accused. The term 're-victimisation' has been associated with the marginalisation of some rape victims, who described being treated as pieces of evidence, like a fingerprint or photograph, and not as feeling, thinking human beings. Indeed, the modern victims' movement began with the opening of American Rape Crisis Centres by feminist groups in the early 1970s.

Other factors appear to have raised the profile of the victim, victimisation issues and the victims' movement, which rose to prominence in the late 1960s and 1970s. These include the move towards a centre-right in British and North American politics, along with a tough, penal approach to law. This was linked to a rise in the crime rate and incarceration as a preferred way of dealing with offenders. Around the same time there appears to have been an increasing recognition of vulnerable groups, particularly women who were suffering domestic abuse and children who were subject to abuse. This gave rise to the emergence of 'rights-based' victims' movements and, in 1972, volunteers founded the first three victim assistance programmes in the USA:

- Aid for Victims of Crime – Missouri;

- Women against Rape – San Francisco;

- The Rape Crisis Centre – Washington, DC.

Here in the UK, the interests of victims were championed by penal reformers such as Margaret Fry, who campaigned for better services for both suspects and victims. The media have also assisted by highlighting the plight of victims or particular categories of victim.

Victim organisations in the UK

Victim organisations include the National Society for the Prevention of Cruelty to Children (NSPCC) and ChildLine, which merged with the NSPCC in 2006. The first refuge for battered women was established in 1972 and the Women's Aid Federation, founded in 1974, is responsible for coordinating local and regional services. Rape Crisis Centres were first opened in London and Birmingham in the 1970s to offer emotional support and legal and medical advice to women who had been sexually assaulted or raped. Contributions by specialist, victim-help organisations include the Zito Trust, which campaigns for victims of mentally disordered offenders, while Support After Murder and Manslaughter (SAMM) works with Victim Support and the Office of Criminal Justice Reform to provide support to bereaved families and friends as a result of murder or manslaughter. (The Office of Criminal Justice Reform is a cross-departmental organisation that reports to the Ministry of Justice, the Home Office and the Attorney General's Office. It provides local Criminal Justice Boards (CJBs) with the overall framework and guidance to facilitate reform at a local level.) SAMM has been influential in shaping government policy, with pilot projects set up following consultation on victims' advocates for homicide survivors. Justice for Victims also campaigns on behalf of the families of murder victims.

Victim Support originated in Bristol in the early 1970s and its rapid expansion resulted in the launch of a national association in 1979. It works largely with the Police Service in providing emotional and practical support and information to victims and witnesses of crime. During the 1980s, the focus moved away from supporting victims of burglary, robbery and theft to supporting victims of racial harassment and sexual and violent crime, and the families of murder victims. It maintains a relatively low-key political profile, but lobbying contributed to the introduction of the Domestic Violence, Crime and Victims Act 2004, which gives statutory protection to victims' interests.

Although, generally speaking, the victims' movement has been careful to avoid political involvement in penal policy, certain victims' organisations have been vocal in demanding greater severity in sentencing. Examples include 'Megan's Law' in the USA and the campaign for 'Sarah's Law' in Great Britain, which provide the public with information about known sex offenders in an effort to assist parents and potential victims in protecting themselves from dangerous offenders. Here, victims' groups have argued for more extensive controls and additional punitive measures, which is something we will return to later under 'service' and 'procedural' rights.

REFLECTIVE TASK

The victims' rights movement has become increasingly influential in setting criminal justice policy. Form an informal discussion group with your colleagues and consider the following.

A report by the Justice Committee (JUSTICE, 1998) is concerned that domestic abuse victims are being burdened with prosecution decisions. Asking victims whether they would support a prosecution implies that the state is unwilling to fulfil its duty to police and prosecute such crimes!

To what extent do you think victims' rights movements should have influence over the implementation and adjudication of law and policy making?

Criminal justice theory

There is a general assumption that the criminal process should be invoked when it appears that a crime has been committed and there is a reasonable prospect of convicting the offender. Paradoxically, there is an assumption that there needs to be oversight and control over law-enforcement activities, and that the rights and privacy of the individual should not be invaded at will; and that the alleged offender is not merely an object within a process but an independent entity (in the CJS) with legal rights. Herbert Packer (1968), who was a professor of law at Stanford University, develops these assumptions further by suggesting that criminal justice is the balancing of two competing value systems, or models: those of 'crime control' and 'due process'. These are abstract models that identify characteristics of the CJS, but nowhere does he argue that either represents one ideal to the exclusion of the other. Rather, these models exist to help us identify where the balance of the CJS lies as well as the relative weighting of both models.

Crime control

The primary objective of the crime control model is the prevention or reduction of crime. Emphasis is placed on the criminal investigation and the interrogation of suspects, but little emphasis is placed on suspects' rights. While accepting that mistakes sometimes occur, some collateral damage is acceptable in the bigger task of controlling crime. Indeed, the model values and prioritises the conviction of the guilty, even at the risk of convicting innocents and infringing the liberties of suspects.

Due process

Due process argues for safeguards against the coercive and arbitrary use of state powers. The model emphasises the importance of equality and fairness, the presumption of innocence and adherence to the legal rules that govern state powers, and the admissibility of evidence. This can be seen in pre-hearing and courtroom procedures, for example by allowing the accused every opportunity to discredit the police and to clear their name. Packer likened the due process model to an obstacle course.

> With each of its successive stages designed to present formidable impediments to carrying the accused any further along in the process . . . It resembles a factory that has to devote a substantial part of its input to quality control.
>
> (Packer, 1968, p163)

The values of due process appear to be contrary to the utilitarian view that it is acceptable to inflict suffering or retributive justice on an individual provided that this confers benefits to the remainder of the population. Conventionally, we might assume that, if a person commits a serious wrong against another, the resulting injustice needs to be corrected. We might also assume that, to do this, the offender must undergo some form of pain or suffering in proportion to the seriousness of the offence. This is discussed by Johnstone and Van Ness (2007), who suggest that some form of pain and suffering is necessary if equilibrium is to be restored and justice seen to prevail. While in some circumstances punishment might be appropriate, due process argues for the primacy of the individual's interests, even if this means limiting state power and reducing its effectiveness to control crime.

REFLECTIVE TASK

Alex and Billie are brothers aged 15 and 16 respectively. Their parents are separated. Their father has parental responsibility and is a habitual criminal, unemployed and in receipt of benefit payments. They live on a tough, inner-city estate and Billie was excluded from school at the age of 14. Both he and Alex have convictions for possession of cannabis, burglary, taking vehicles without consent and domestic assaults.

In groups, discuss how the crime control and due process models should be applied in this case. Can these models work together effectively?

Restorative justice

A simple concept!

Restorative justice is arguably the most common approach to criminal justice throughout history. It can be seen, for example, in Roman and Sharia law, but it is debatable whether these precedents make it compatible with the principles and 'rule of law' that emerged during the eighteenth-century European Enlightenment.

Marshall (1996) suggests that restorative justice is the coming together of stakeholders to resolve the aftermath of offending, as well as its future implications. This clearly recognises that crime is much more than an offence against the state. It includes the offender, the victim and their families and supporters, as well as members of their respective communities. It recognises the need for participation, communication and negotiated agreements for restorative outcomes or resolutions and repairing the harm caused by the crime to those directly and indirectly affected by the demonstration of some shame. In practice this includes apologies, compensation or direct reparation to the victim for the harm done and indirect reparation to the wider community. Stakeholders' participation is central to the values of restorative justice and various models have been produced to illustrate how direct stakeholders are involved in the process. Johnstone and Van Ness (2007) describe four typical core elements of restorative justice.

The encounter

This involves a meeting or series of meetings, usually face to face between the parties, where each explains his or her behaviour. It concludes with an achievable agreement.

Reparation and restorative justice

Here, the offender makes amends or 'repairs' the harm caused. Reparation should reflect the seriousness of the offence and the harm caused, and is first made to the direct victim. But this ultimately depends on the ability of the offender to make reparation in a timely and feasible way. While some form of material reparation would normally follow mediation, some victims are satisfied instead with an apology and explanation, and perhaps agreement for the offender to carry out some kind of community service or programme that addresses the cause of the behaviour.

Some supporters of reparation argue that simply inflicting pain upon offenders is neither necessary nor sufficient to repair any harm done and it seems that, while this might provide a short-term resolution, it often fails to deliver an enduring experience of justice. This is based on a number of ideas and, in particular, one that argues that, in cases dealt with by conventional criminal justice means, victims lose their sense of personal power. They are neglected and are expected to play a passive role while 'professionals' make key decisions. To repair the harm done, victims need some control or involvement in the resolution of their own cases. They also need to be able to express their feelings about what happened to them and for others to understand this.

Reintegration

This is the re-entry of each party into community life and involves the creation of relationships characterised by mutual respect and shared values that lead to an understanding of intolerance of deviancy.

Participation

This refers to the opportunity for full and direct involvement of the stakeholders in the encounter, reparation and reintegration.

Victim–offender mediation

An intermediary communicates with the opposite parties, acting as a conduit to find solutions to their problems, but hasn't the authority to make a decision or force a settlement. In most instances this involves separate negotiations between the parties. English schemes have tended to rely upon this indirect approach with the first systematic use of mediation being introduced by the Exeter Youth Support Team in 1979 to supplement the formal police caution where this was considered too limited a response. The Forum for Initiatives in Reparation and Mediation (FIRM) was subsequently established in 1984 to act as an umbrella organisation. Later renamed Mediation UK, it includes Victim Support on the management committee.

A late 1980s' evaluation of victim and offender mediation schemes in the UK by Marshall (1991) indicates that the majority of victims offered the chance of meeting with their offender thought that this was a positive thing and those given the opportunity believed the experience to be worthwhile. Other more recent studies confirm high levels of victim satisfaction with mediation, particularly with direct victim–offender meetings. As a result of mediation victims felt less angry and fearful, felt personally vindicated and experienced a degree of emotional healing (Umbreit et al., 1997). Despite these promising findings, other research has been critical of the way that the needs of victims are often subordinate to the aims of diverting the offender from custody or mitigating their subsequent court sentence (Davis et al., 1988). So while some programmes are intended to divert offenders away from the courts, and reduce costs and delays, their use without similar attention to victims' needs and future prevention can also lead to the accusation that they don't take crime seriously.

PRACTICAL TASK

Visit the website http://police.homeoffice.gov.uk/operational-policing/crime-disorder/ index.html/, which refers to fixed penalty notices for disorder. Access the link to 'Penalty Notices'.

Follow the links to the document, Penalty Notices for Disorder: Police Operational Guidance. You can either download the PDF file or access it via http://police.home office.gov.uk/publications/operational-policing/penalty-notices-guidance/index.html.

Look at the aims and purposes of the fixed penalty scheme for upper-tier offences only. Make notes of key information and then consider the following four questions.

- *Who do you consider are the victims in these upper-tier offences?*

- *How does issuing a fixed penalty notice deliver swift and effective justice for them?*

- *When issuing a fixed penalty ticket, what are the drawbacks for the victim?*

- *What, if any, tensions exist between fixed penalty notice policy and policing in practice?*

Crime statistics and victims' rights

Until a quarter of a century ago, debates about crime rates usually focused on the annual police records published by the Home Office. The British Crime Survey now provides an additional set of statistics based on interviews with samples of the population. Since 2001, the annual volume on crime in England and Wales includes data from both sources, but before an event can be recorded as a crime it must first become known to the police and then be recorded by them. This can be problematic, particularly when a victim is reluctant to report or answer questions about their experiences. For example, they might live with the offender or be too embarrassed to discuss the circumstances of the offence. The victim's intellect might also cloud their judgement and their ability to make rational and informed decisions. Think of this as a 'cost/benefit' assessment. It might be that the offence is thought too trivial and/or involves no loss and, therefore, there is little point in reporting because the police either cannot or will not do anything about it. There can also be inconvenience in reporting.

In some cases, the victim may be unaware of the crime, for example children may be aware of their suffering but unaware that it amounts to a criminal act. Similarly, adult victims of fraud and theft may be unaware of the deception or believe that they have actually lost the property involved. Many crimes do not have clear individual victims; drug taking and those relating to prostitution and gambling are known as 'consensual' offences, where the victim is seen as a willing participant.

Lastly, the victim might be the general public. Examples include tax evasion, smuggling and insider-trading, motoring and public-order offences. But victims who do not report crimes to the police may nevertheless be taking action themselves, which includes seeking compensation or restitution from insurance companies and state-based schemes.

The National Crime Recording System

The National Crime Recording System was introduced in April 2002 to make crime recording more victim-orientated and to standardise national recording practices. This was based on a previous assumption that some reported incidents weren't being recorded because the police doubted that an offence had been committed. Despite these policy changes, Burrows et al. (2000) suggest that police officers are continuing to exercise discretion about whether and how to record reported crimes. The result is that some are being recorded differently from the initial report or not being recorded at all.

Growing awareness of the limitations and biases of police recorded crime statistics has resulted in the development of a variety of alternative measures since the 1960s. Like the British Crime Survey, victim surveys measure crime trends over time and establish useful insights into police reporting and recording procedures, as well as police statistics themselves. The benefits of victimisation surveys are that they aren't reliant on what comes to the attention of the police and they enable questions to be asked about the nature and impact of crime.

Refer to the National Crime Recording Standard: General Principles. *They can be found at www.countingrules.homeoffice.gov.uk/files/pdf/countrecstan03.pdf.*

- *Consider how and why the* General Principles *might lead to inconsistencies in the recording of crime complaints.*

- *As a patrol officer, consider the steps that you should take to ensure the accurate recording of a crime complaint.*

Read the extract below from The Daily Telegraph *and, as a group, decide whether:*

- *it's ethical to screen out some categories of crime;*

- *what impact might screening out certain crime(s) have on the alleged victims.*

> *Police who refuse to visit every victim of crime have been accused of 'arrogance' by one of the country's most senior officers. Bernard Hogan-Howe . . . said it was intolerable if officers did not appear to care or listen to what victims needed. In a public attack on the tactic of 'screening out' certain crimes, the chief constable said that . . . instead of selecting which offences were worthy of attendance . . . every victim should be offered a visit, no matter how minor the crime. Police chiefs have defended the system of screening calls as a way to target resources towards the most serious and solvable crimes. Mr Hogan-Howe dismissed concerns that, without screening, police would be swamped by demands on their time.*
>
> *(Whitehead, 2009)*

Placing victims at the heart of the criminal justice process

The criminal justice process has been referred to as an adversarial contest played out by actors on opposite sides, in which victims have traditionally been excluded, for example by poor or delayed information or by the unexplained decisions of the Crown Prosecution Service (CPS) when discounting cases. This can undermine victims' willingness to cooperate or lead them to withdraw from the criminal justice process. Thus, a central theme of current government policy is its pledge to rebalance justice in favour of victims and to promote victim justice.

'Tough on crime, tough on the causes of crime'

In 1997, when elected to power, the Labour Party's soundbite on criminal justice was 'tough on crime, tough on the causes of crime'. This was aimed at controlling the rising crime figures in the 1990s and the growing 'justice gap' – the difference between the number of crimes committed and the number of successful prosecutions. This has resulted in a wealth of policy and legislation changes, but what does putting victims at the heart of the CJS actually mean in practice? To the extent that it is possible to refer to victims' rights, this can be categorised under the headings 'service rights' and 'procedural rights'. Service rights include respectful and sympathetic support, information and court facilities, but exclude direct participation. Conversely, 'procedural' rights allow victims to influence sentencing such that their preferences are sought and applied by the CJS. Consultative participation is where victims' preferences are taken into account when making decisions. Information provision involves victims providing information required by the criminal justice process.

Service rights

The Home Office has made progressive attempts to improve the way in which victims are kept informed by police and prosecutors. Two Victims' Charters (Home Office, 1990, 1996) established service standards to ensure that victims received better information about case progress, that their views were obtained and considered, and that they received appropriate service facilities and assistance in court. These have since been replaced by a Victims' Code of Practice under the provisions of the Domestic Violence, Crime and Victims Act 2004. The code was introduced in 2006 and applies to the Police Service in England and Wales, the British Transport Police, the Ministry of Defence Police, the CPS and Her Majesty's Courts Service. It sets out minimum standards of service that victims and witnesses can expect. For example, most victims have the right to information about decisions relating to bail and remand decisions. The white paper, *Justice for All* (Home Office, 2002) sets out the government's long-term strategy to modernise the CJS, with proposals that include a new Independent Commissioner for Victims and Witnesses. The actual role of the Commissioner is to promote the interests of victims and witnesses, and take steps to encourage good practice in their treatment.

Victims' Advisory Panel
The national Victims' Advisory Panel, which was placed on a statutory footing by the Domestic Violence, Crime and Victims Act 2004, is chaired by the Minister of State with responsibility for victims' issues. The panel aims to bring together officials, representatives of victims' organisations and lay members who have been victims of crime to discuss the impact of crime and to consider formal recommendations for change.

In 2003, the government published a national strategy to deliver improved services for victims of crime and witnesses who are called to give evidence in court. Entitled *A New Deal for Victims and Witnesses* (Home Office, 2003), the report draws together previous strands of government policy – the proposal for an independent commissioner and a Victims' Code of Practice, compensation, support for vulnerable and intimidated witnesses, funding for the witness service and the introduction of Victim Personal Statements.

The Witness Service
Operated by Victim Support, the Witness Service provides advice, information and support to assist in preparing victims and witnesses for their court experience. Typically, this includes the provision of separate waiting areas and pre-trial visits to court. Whether the service is able to remove the ordeal of cross-examination and explain court decisions is a more problematic consideration. But, in an effort to address victims' anxieties, a number

of witness care units have been introduced across England and Wales. These units bring the police and CPS together to improve information flow and to provide additional reassurance. Witness Care Officers act as a single point of contact. Other procedural changes include, in the case of children, judges and barristers removing robes and wigs, the provision of screens, live video links and pre-recorded videotaped interviews.

Special measures for dealing with vulnerable and intimidated witnesses

Special measures were introduced as a result of a number of recommendations in the government paper, *Speaking up for Justice: Victims in Criminal Justice* (Home Office, 1998). Part II of the Youth Justice and Criminal Evidence Act 1999 now provides for screening in court, giving evidence by a live video link, the examination of witnesses through an intermediary, and the admissibility of video-recorded evidence-in-chief and cross-examination. It also restricts the cross-examination of rape complainants about their sexual history. The Criminal Justice Act 2003 allows any witness to give evidence via a live video link. Although these various measures appear to have improved the experiences of some victims, they do not appear to have improved the conviction rate for rape victims, which have declined over the past few decades (Home Office, 2009).

Procedural rights

Unlike service rights, procedural rights convey victims' views into public decision making. But this isn't without some controversy and many countries with adversarial criminal justice systems have opposed procedural reform, arguing that it undermines legal tradition and the defendants' due process rights; that it unrealistically raises victims' expectations; that it places unacceptable pressures on the court in high-profile cases; that it results in sentencing disparity and causes delays, longer trials and additional expense for the CJS. While there has been an expansion of some victims' rights – consulting about caution and charge decisions, plea negotiations, sentencing, parole and prison release – research by Erez and Rogers (1999) suggests that procedural rights have failed to transform court practices in ways that were first envisaged by both supporters and critics.

Victim impact statements

One way of affording procedural rights is through the victim impact statement (VIS). Developed in the USA, the VIS allows victims to bring details of personal injury and loss to the attention of judges, juries and prosecutors. It also reminds them that, behind the state, lies a victim with an interest in judicial outcomes. Impact statements were adopted in Britain in 2001 as 'victim personal statements' (VPS), although in England and Wales victims' comments on sentencing are excluded. Studies suggest that, while criminal justice professionals have generally welcomed the VPS, they are divided as to whether the statements should influence sentencing decisions, not least because the information provided is rarely unexpected and sometimes irrelevant, exaggerated or uncorroborated. Research by Sanders et al. (2001) appears to show that the VPS has little effect on sentencing, but it is unclear whether this is because of resistance by criminal justice professionals or because the statements are 'misconceived in principle and unsatisfactory in practice'. From 2005, the Victim's Code of Practice no longer requires the police to solicit a VPS, except in cases of murder and manslaughter.

Access Westlaw or Lexis Library online and find the cases below. Familiarise yourself with the judgments of Lord Justice Potter and Mr Justice Garland (R v. Perks) and Mr Justice Crane (R v. Griffith) and reflect on the issues raised in both cases.

- *Do you agree with their findings?*

- *How might these cases influence your working practices?*

R v. Perks [2000] All ER (D) 763

In allowing an appeal against a sentence for robbery, the Court of Appeal issued guidelines on the use of victim statements. In this case, the complainant's statement was treated with caution and a statement made by the complainant's husband was disregarded.

R v. Griffith [2006] All ER (D) 26 (Dec)

The Queen's Bench Division considered issues around mitigation and the VPS. While the court considered moving statements from the mother and father of a murder victim, it concluded that their views should not influence the tariff for cases of this type.

Criminal justice inspectorates – a thematic review

In November 2007, the Home Secretary, the Secretary of State for Justice and the Attorney General published a *National Community Safety Plan* (Home Office, 2008), part of which focuses on improving the experiences of victims and witnesses. In May 2009, the three criminal justice inspectorates – HM Crown Prosecution Service Inspectorate, HM Inspectorate of Constabulary and HM Inspectorate of Court Administration – reported jointly in a thematic review of the experiences of a number of victims and witnesses as their cases progressed through the CJS. The inspection found that the level of service and support provided to victims and witnesses was generally good and that Witness Care Units had contributed to this improvement. The review concluded that, while a great deal had been achieved overall, there was still scope for improvement, particularly in the area of 'special measures' and the VPS.

Special measures
The review found that special measures for vulnerable and intimidated victims and witnesses were sometimes overlooked, and that some officers had insufficient knowledge or understanding of the legislative provisions. This is problematic if special measures are offered but it then transpires that a victim or witness is ineligible to receive them. Conversely, it can lead to those who are eligible either not receiving them or the need being identified late in the process, which creates uncertainty for victims and witnesses.

Victim personal statements

There was considerable variation in the knowledge and understanding of front-line police officers, with the result that some victims were denied the opportunity of making a VPS when it was appropriate to do so. The absence of a VPS was sometimes overlooked by prosecution lawyers or Witness Care Officers and the type of information recorded in statements by police officers varied markedly. It was also noted that the needs of victims and witnesses weren't always being fully assessed and recorded by front-line police officers. Despite this, inspectors found that the police were keen to provide a good service to victims and witnesses, and took pride in what they did. While the lack of a fully joined-up approach frequently made their tasks more difficult, the report concludes that staff had worked hard to overcome these difficulties.

CHAPTER SUMMARY

Within this chapter you have been provided with a brief history of victimology as it relates to the harm that people suffer through illegal activities. You have considered the supporting role of the victims' movement and its influence in policy making and critical debate. The notions of 'due process' and 'crime control' have also been examined, along with the emergence of restorative justice as a way of providing 'procedural rights' and 'service rights' to victims. Finally, you have been given an insight into some of the problems and inconsistencies in police crime reporting and recording procedures. The government pledge to put victims at the heart of the CJS has also been examined through various papers and policies. Opportunities have been provided for further research and analysis that will provide evidence for completion of Qualification and Credit units.

REFERENCES

Burrows, J, Tarling, R, Mackie, A, Leis, R and Taylor, G (2000) *Review of Police Forces: Crime Recording Practices*. London: Home Office.

Christie, N (1986) The ideal victim, in Fattah, E (ed.) *From Crime Policy to Victim Policy*. Basingstoke: Macmillan, pp17–30.

Davis, G, Boucherat, J and Watson, D (1988) Can reparation be made to work in the service of diversion? The subordination of a good idea. *Howard Journal of Criminal Justice*, 27(2): 127–34.

Erez, E and Rogers, L (1999) Victim impact statements and sentencing outcomes and pressures. *British Journal of Criminology*, 39(2): 216–35.

Home Office (1990) *Victims' Charter: A Statement of the Rights of Victims*. London: HMSO.

Home Office (1996) *Victims' Charter: Standards of Service for Victims of Crime*. London: HMSO.

Home Office (1998) *Speaking Up for Justice: Victims in Criminal Justice*. London: HMSO.

Home Office (2002) *Justice for All* (Cm. 5563). London: HMSO.

Home Office (2003) *A New Deal for Victims and Witnesses: A National Strategy to Deliver Improved Services*. London: HMSO.

Home Office (2008) *National Community Safety Plan for 2008–11: Working Together to Cut Crime and Deliver Justice.* London: Home Office.

Home Office (2009) *Crime in England and Wales: Findings from the British Crime Survey and Police Recorded Crime.* London: Home Office.

Johnstone, G and Van Ness, D W (2007) *Handbook of Restorative Justice.* Cullompton: Willan.

JUSTICE (1998) *Victims in Criminal Justice: Report of the Justice Committee on the Role of Victims in Criminal Justice.* London: JUSTICE.

Marshall, T (1991) Victim–offender mediation. *Home Office Research Bulletin,* 30: 9–15.

Marshall, T (1996) The evolution of restorative justice in Britain. *European Journal on Criminal Policy and Research,* 4(4): 21–43.

Packer, H (1968) *The Limits of the Criminal Sanction.* Stanford: Stanford University Press.

Sanders, A, Hoyle, C, Moran, R and Cape, E (2001) Victim impact statements: don't work, can't work. *Criminal Law Review,* June: 447–58.

Umbreit, M, Coates, R and Roberts, A (1997) Cross-national impact of restorative justice through mediation and dialogue. *ICCA Journal on Community Corrections,* 8(2): 46-50.

von Hentig, H (1948) *The Criminal and his Victim.* New Haven, CT: Yale University Press. (See also Jacoby, J (ed.) *Classics of Criminology.* Long Grove, IL: Waveland Press, chapter 5.)

Whitehead, T (2009) Arrogant police must visit every crime victim. *The Daily Telegraph,* 2 September, p1b.

Wolfgang, M E (1958) *Patterns in Criminal Homicide.* Philadelphia, PA: University of Pennsylvania Press.

USEFUL WEBSITES

http://cjsonline.gov.uk (Criminal Justice System)

http://restorativejustice.org.uk (Restorative Justice Consortium)

www.homeoffice.gov.uk (Home Office website, which lists publications, news and links on the CJS)

www.victimsupport.org.uk (Victim Support)

CASES

R v. Griffith [2006] All ER (D) 26 (Dec)

R v. Perks [2000] All ER (D) 763

LEGISLATION

Criminal Justice Act 2003

Domestic Violence, Crime and Victims Act 2004

Sexual Offences Act 2003

Youth Justice and Criminal Evidence Act 1999

7 Youth justice

Introduction

[This] marks the last stage in that slow and tedious journey . . . before it was generally realized that it was not by throwing children and young persons automatically and indiscriminately into gaol, that the grave problem of juvenile delinquency was going to be solved.

(Ruggles-Brise, 1921, p101)

The above quotation by the then Chairman of the Prison Commission, reflecting on some of the provisions contained in the Children's Act 1908, summarises the key issue relating to youth justice.

This chapter provides a brief historical perspective on youth justice in order to contextualise the current situation. The primary focus is then on the changes to the youth justice system since the early 1990s, in particular following the election of the Labour government in 1997, together with some of the subsequent provisions contained in the Crime and Disorder Act 1998.

We are only concerned here with children as alleged or perceived offenders within the Criminal Justice System (CJS), not children as victims of crime.

Historical perspectives

Until the nineteenth century, children and young people were treated exactly the same as adults in respect of the CJS and the age of criminal responsibility was set at seven years. The full range of sentencing was available to the courts, including capital punishment and transportation, often leading to extreme sentences for minor offences – on one given day in 1814, five children were hanged for petty theft (Hopkins Burke, 2008, p47).

Criminal justice in England and Wales at this stage was just emerging from the era of the 'Bloody Code'. (The Enlightenment period, which prompted criminological writers such as Beccaria and Bentham (see Chapter 9, page 148), had not fully taken effect.) Children were dealt with on a par with adult offenders, under a harsh, punitive criminal justice regime, based almost entirely on retribution.

REFLECTIVE TASK

The 'Bloody Code' was a major feature of criminal justice in the seventeenth and eighteenth centuries. A lot has been written about it, from varying perspectives. Access the text about the Code at http://forums.canadiancontent.net/history/47165-bloody-code.html and read it through. Find out why the 'Bloody Code' existed and consider which social class it was targeting and for what purpose, e.g. protection of interests.

Nineteenth-century developments

Innovations in respect of the socialisation of children were sequential throughout the nineteenth century. The embryonic changes were not solely connected with the CJS; the century witnessed reforms in a number of key areas that affected children. Employment, education and welfare provision all featured and culminated in a shift in ideology from the punitive (punishment) model, often referred to as the crime control model, to the welfare model; or certainly a mixture of the two.

Organisations with a special interest in reforming the plight of children in society emerged during the early nineteenth century. These nineteenth-century developments pre-date any statutory welfare aid, such as was implemented after the Second World War in the potentially instant availability of state welfare aid based on the notion of 'cradle to the grave' provision, as perceived in the Beveridge Report (1942), which laid the foundations for the contemporary welfare state.

Welfare availability was charity based; for example, the National Society for the Prevention of Cruelty to Children (NSPCC) was formed in Liverpool in the mid-1880s at a meeting of the RSPCA. Interestingly, it was, and is to this day, a charity. Perhaps the charitable status of the NSPCC is a surprise to some, given the high-profile and pivotal role it has undertaken over the years in respect of the neglect of children in the late nineteenth century initially, and more recently in respect of physical and sexual abuse. Another well-known charity, the Children's Society, linked to the Church of England and formed in 1881, was initially concerned with the plight of children in respect of poverty, particularly on the streets of London. Its welfare role has expanded somewhat since those times.

Certain key events in the nineteenth century are worthy of further comment and analysis.

The early shift to the welfare approach

In 1817, the issue of a 'one size fits all' CJS was commented upon by the Society for the Improvement of Prison Discipline and the Reformation of Juvenile Offenders, who were eager to avoid the spread of unwelcome morals from adult to young offenders (Hopkins Burke, 2008, p48). Later, in 1823, separate prison ships (known as hulks) were introduced and, in 1838, the first penal institution purely for juveniles was opened at Parkhurst.

Clearly, societal consciences were being pricked and concerns were growing and, in 1840, a select committee of the House of Lords took the issue on board for investigation, leading to the eventual passing of the Youth Offenders Act 1854. This required the Home Office to certify specific and recognised establishments and these became known as 'certified reformatories' and 'certified industrial schools' (Hopkins Burke, 2008, p48).

These measures reflected the shift from a completely punitive approach in respect of young offenders towards more welfare-based attitudes, a sea change that began in the early part of the century, but gained ground in the latter part, bolstered in particular by the inauguration of charitable organisations, with overriding and stated welfare objectives.

In 1850, there were some 2,000 young people in reformatories, but by 1870 this had expanded to 7,000. Furthermore, although the industrial schools were envisaged as remaining part of the educational system, by the 1860s they were also administered by the Home Office, like reformatories (Crawford and Newburn, 2003, p6).

However, perceptions of deviant youth began to manifest themselves in the mid-nineteenth-century period, with references to youth subcultures such as the 'scuttlers' and 'peaky blinders' (Maguire et al., 2007, p576).

This was reinforced by the groundbreaking work of the social reformer Henry Mayhew and the notion of the 'dangerous classes' (a term used to associate the threat to social order and the emerging middle classes). This was a feature of the developing capitalist system and was also linked to emerging industrialisation, particularly in the urban areas of Britain. Mayhew covered considerable ground in his publications, but chapters devoted to the rookery of St Giles (a destitute area of London), the activities of so-called 'costermongers' and the street children of London provide an excellent and first-hand insight into what was clearly becoming a major issue (Mayhew, 1851/61, in Fitzgerald et al., 1981).

Go online to www.victorianlondon.org/publications/mayhew1-1.htm and read Mayhew's account of 'costermongers'. Not all of this is devoted to young people, but the account provides a flavour of inner-city life during this influential and arguably colourful period. Consider how Mayhew deals with the labelling of young people and the threat to social order, particularly in the sections entitled 'Of the uneducated state of the costermongers' and 'Habits and amusements of costermongers'.

Think about modern-day youth subculture. Write down a list of identifiable groups among young people, e.g. skateboarders. Consider whether these groups pose a threat to society, particularly the middle and upper classes, and argue whether they pose a threat to social order or not.

Twentieth-century developments

During the 1890s, the then Home Secretary, Herbert Asquith, instigated two investigative committees, the 'Gladstone' and the 'Lushington', charged with examining various aspects of the CJS. The Gladstone Report recommended the notion of treatment in prisons, especially with young offenders. The Lushington Report recommended alternatives to punishment, including education, as one of the responses to offending by young people. By the end of the nineteenth century, juvenile courts had been established in many towns (Crawford and Newburn, 2003, p6). Following the election of a Liberal government in 1906, juvenile courts were given a statutory footing in 1908.

Juvenile courts provided a venue to separate a youth court from an adult court. Consider the implications of this and write down what you consider to be the advantages and disadvantages of separating the two courts.

The newly established courts were given powers to act in both punitive and welfare mode, separate from adult courts. As the minister overseeing the legislation said at the time, 'Courts should be the agencies for the rescue as well as the punishment of juveniles' (Hopkins Burke, 2008, p51).

However, it should be noted that the juvenile courts remained firmly within the remit of the criminal law. The inception of the courts introduced the notion of the 'juvenile delinquent' – previously known as the 'young offender', the same term used today within the CJS.

However, perhaps the term 'delinquent' was an all-encompassing description that embraced all notions of apparent misbehaviour and activities that were frowned upon by the so-called 'respectable' classes, not merely crime in itself. It is a pattern that we will see repeated almost 100 years later.

At the turn of the century, young people in the industrial areas in particular were enjoying more leisure time and the association between 'youth' and 'crime' was being made. At the same time, words such as 'delinquency' and 'hooliganism' began to be used (Hopkins Burke, 2008, p51).

The dual-track approach to youth crime was witnessed in 1907/08 by the passing of legislation that heralded in community supervision by probation officers as an alternative to imprisonment.

In 1908, imprisonment for children under the age of 14 was no longer allowed. However, this ruling was followed by the introduction of specific detention facilities for young people aged 16–21 (Crawford and Newburn, 2003, p7). The first establishment was opened in Borstal, Kent (Hopkins Burke, 2008, p52) and today similar facilities are named after this. 'Borstal' was synonymous with young people and offending throughout the twentieth century, and, following a period of detention at a Borstal, most young offenders were labelled as 'juvenile delinquents'. However, there was a certain latent element of rehabilitation within their programmes. Trainees (a term for the juvenile inmates) were confined for between one and three years within a regime founded on strict discipline, hard work and drill (Muncie, 2009, p331).

Critics pointed to the inordinately long periods of detention, for example three years for offences that normally attracted a sentence of six months. Yet the first ever survey of reoffending rates from Borstals showed what in the contemporary period appear to be unattainably low rates of reoffending – between 27 and 35 per cent (Muncie, 2009, p331). These relatively low rates of reconviction remained at around 30 per cent until the Criminal Justice Act 1961 reduced the age for Borstal training to 15 and at the same time integrated Borstals into the wider prison system. The ethos of training was lost as the system lurched towards a more punitive regime and, in turn, the reconviction rate soared to 70 per cent (Muncie, 2009, p332).

In 1982, Borstals were renamed 'youth custody centres' and six years later were incorporated into the wider remit of 'young offender institutions' (YOIs). However, there is a dominant view that they now merely represent adult prisons in a young offenders' context (Muncie, 2009, p332).

The overriding principle of 'welfare' was apparent during the period between the two world wars, as emphasised by the Children and Young Persons Act (CYPA) 1933, which contained many provisions and promoted the existence of a separate juvenile justice system, founded on an ideology of welfare. The notion of 'treatment' within the juvenile system grew about this time (Crawford and Newburn, 2003, p7).

The Criminal Justice Act 1948 abolished the barbaric practice of corporal punishment in respect of young people, but introduced the 'detention centre', initially as an experiment, although it actually lasted some 40 years. These facilities allowed the courts to sentence offenders aged 14–21 to short periods of detention at an institution that was deliberately punitive. There is a view that asserts that the introduction of the detention centre was a trade-off in lieu of the abolition of corporal punishment (Muncie, 2009, p335).

Two subsequent statutes, the CYPA 1963 and CYPA 1969, cemented the idea that youth offending needed to be both understood and dealt with, within an overriding principle of welfare (Kirton, 2005, p387). The statutes raised the age of criminal responsibility to ten (1963) and the 1969 legislation directed that children under the age of 14 should be dealt with via care and protection rather than via the criminal route (Hopkins Burke, 2008, p60).

Doli incapax

Attaining the age of 14 years was symbolic in criminal justice procedure for two reasons, one of them a key legal requirement. In the case of a young person under the age of 14, the prosecution needed to prove that, while accepting that the defendant was over the age of criminal responsibility, that is, over ten years of age, the defendant actually knew that he or she was doing wrong. This is known as the principle of *doli incapax*, which was an ancient presumption, meaning 'incapable of evil' (Kirton, 2005, p390).

In practice, this was achieved by a police interviewer establishing that the defendant knew that what they had been arrested for/suspected of was a criminal offence. If the defendant elected to remain silent or the acknowledgement of wrongdoing had not been obtained by other means, such as a written statement, the task to establish knowledge of wrongdoing fell to the prosecutor in any subsequent criminal trial. Obviously, this was an additional protection for the young person and is known as a 'due process' measure (that is, working within the rule of law and ensuring the rights of an offender).

Charging of young offenders

To be charged with a criminal offence under the age of 14, consent was required from a senior police officer, normally at least of the rank of Inspector. The authorising Inspector, in turn, needed to justify in writing the reasons for charging the young person. Once charged, the young person then entered the criminal justice process, that is, the court system. In practice, most senior officers when approached with a view to immediate charging, as opposed to another course of action outlined below, would acquiesce with the recommendation for prosecution. Prosecution should only have been considered as a last resort and the context of the prosecution must be remembered because the spirit of the statute (CYPA 1969) has been described as:

> An attempt to decriminalise the juvenile court and the most welfare-oriented legislation ever enacted with regard to the treatment of juvenile offenders in England and Wales.
> (Goldson, 2009, p19)

Also at that time, within the Police Service the position of Juvenile Liaison Officer (JLO) existed and cases awaiting decisions as to *disposal* – that is, whether to charge or not – would be routed via the JLO, rather than a sudden decision being made while the young person was still in custody. This was known at the time as 'discharge for consultation' (DFC). The JLO would then look into the family/school background of the young person, which was very much within the spirit of the CYPA 1969, and link in with other agencies, such as educational welfare.

At the conclusion of the process, the JLO would make recommendations as to charge or caution, which again senior officers normally concurred with. A young offender stood more chance of receiving a caution than an immediate prosecution if he or she had been subject to a DFC, which, in practice, was normally applied to the less serious offences.

It must be said that the procedure of immediate charging was often used as a means of usurping any background investigations by the JLO, whose function received little sympathy from most operational police officers, who had had the experience of dealing with the victims and the general aftermath of the offence. However, such emotions were generally not in accordance with the best interests of the young person and the law recognised this. This illustrates the different approaches to youth justice, including both the punitive versus welfare approaches that have already been referred to.

Youth subcultures

We can identify a number of landmark events involving youth and crime that have gone a considerable way to reinforcing the perception that the link between youths and issues such as hooliganism exists. Within this section we will identify a number of key groups that influenced both public and state reactions to youth justice: Teddy boys, mods and rockers, and skinheads.

Teddy boys

The first post-war group was the 'Teddy boys', so called because of their Edwardian dress of long jackets with velvet collars, drainpipe trousers and suede shoes and their greased combed-back hairstyle with the quiff at the front and the infamous 'DA' at the rear (Maguire et al., 2007, p578). Perhaps, when viewed in a contemporary light, this may appear comical, but there was an aspect to the activities of this group that was far from amusing.

We can associate outbreaks of violence around this time with the use of and prevalence of weapons, which resulted in the government passing the Prevention of Crime Act 1953. This statute designated items such as flick knives and knuckledusters as offensive weapons and, as a consequence, banned possession, sale and importation of them.

REFLECTIVE TASK

Go online to www.rockabilly.nl/general/teddyboys.htm and find out about the type of music/lifestyle that the Teddy boys were involved with. Consider why the government felt the need to enact the Prevention of Crime Act 1953 and write down any reasons that may have led to this from the information contained within the text, e.g. the use of certain types of weapon – see, particularly, the section, 'Coshes, chains and razors'.

Mods and rockers

The 'mods', who were clearly identifiable by their sharp suits, parkas (waterproof coats) and Vespa motor scooters, were often pitched against a group called the 'rockers'. Drawn from a similar social background to the mods, the rockers were unfashionable, unglamorous and identified with leather jackets, motorbikes and an often violent machismo (Maguire et al., 2007, p578). Both of these groups were predominately drawn from a white, working-class background.

The groups came to the attention of the public during the spring of 1964, with a series of clashes over bank holiday weekends at Clacton and Margate (Muncie and McLaughlin, 2001, p51), promoting what is known as a 'moral panic' among the public.

Skinheads

The 'skinheads', easily identified by their closely cropped hair in an era in which long hair on young males was the vogue, also wore clearly identifiable clothing, braces and the infamous Doc Marten boots. They were involved with violence at football matches and attacks on both ethnic minorities and gays. It is as a result of the skinheads era that the phrase 'Paki-bashing' became familiar in British society. There was clearly a racial element to this subculture as, later in the 1970s, the British political movement the 'National Front' attracted a keen following of members dressed in skinhead garb. They rejected all notions of the values associated with 'hippies' that had developed during the 1960s and made no secret of their social background, that is, unskilled working class (Maguire et al., 2007, p578).

The above is an opportunity to familiarise yourself with three groups of young people that emerged in post-war Britain. Violence was associated with these groups, but we would be deluding ourselves and doing them a massive disservice if we were left with the impression that their sole objective was the proliferation of violence. That is not the case, but the perception was cemented in the mindset of the public that groups of young people such as those mentioned above were responsible for crime and disorder.

The first British Crime Survey (BCS) in 1982 identified the problem of the 'fear of crime' and its links to youth subcultures.

PRACTICAL TASK

Go online to: http://www.aber.ac.uk/media/Students/hrb9701.html and read through the text provided about the concept of 'moral panic' and then identify a recent youth subculture that has caused a moral panic, e.g. the hooded youth. When you have identified a group, make a list of the factors that contribute to moral panics within society.

Fear of crime

The year 1982 was a watershed for issues surrounding youth justice.

First, there was the publication of a piece of academic work by James Wilson and George Kelling in 1982 entitled 'Broken windows', which has been seen as groundbreaking work in respect of community safety. We will look at this in more detail in Chapter 8; however, suffice it to say that this laid the foundation for dealing with low-level disorder, or what has subsequently become known as 'anti-social behaviour'.

Second, the results of the first UK British Crime Survey were made known and it contained some interesting returns. For the first time ever, the issue of the 'fear of crime' was measured. The fear of crime became an almost tangible issue within the sphere of policing and criminal justice in the years that followed.

Subsequent academic work identified that certain environmental factors, such as incivilities, loud parties and street-corner rowdyism (Muncie and McLaughlin, 2001, p59) added to anxieties around the fear of crime. All of these activities could be associated with young people and contributed to strengthening the links between young people and crime.

PRACTICAL TASK

Go online to www.homeoffice.gov.uk/rds/bcs1.html and, under 'Key publications', access the document entitled British Crime Survey – Measuring Crime for 25 Years. *Having located the document, turn to page 26, 'Emerging issues in the 1990s: anti-social behaviour' and identify what factors most cause people to fear anti-social behaviour.*

Influence of Conservative government, 1979

This period is contradictory to say the least; in 1979, there was a Conservative government (the Tories) led by Margaret Thatcher, elected with law and order policy at its core. For example, the Tories implemented in full and within days of taking office a substantial pay rise for the Police Service that the previous Labour government had wanted to award in phases. Such was their commitment to the law and order agenda and their assertion that the Police Service, underpaid and understaffed for too long, was pivotal in that aspiration.

In respect of youth crime, the then Home Secretary, William Whitelaw, announced that regimes at detention centres would be designed to provide a 'short, sharp shock' (Kirton, 2005, p388). Overtly at least, the Tories appeared as if they would be as tough on crime as they were being with the UK economy, and in Margaret Thatcher's ruthless pursuit of anti-inflationary policies and the associated, but considerable, cost in terms of unemployment.

As the Tories' term of office continued, the rate of cautioning for youth offenders grew steadily; for example, 36 per cent of males and 60 per cent of females in 1984 increased to 59 per cent and 80 per cent respectively in 1994 (Kirton, 2005, p388).

One piece of legislation, the Criminal Justice Act 1991, dictated that custody was only to be used as a last resort and promoted community sentences as a 'tough alternative' (Kirton, 2005, p388). There was also recognition that, by this period, *managerialism* (applying business processes to public services) had arrived within the CJS and the costs incurred in sending young people to periods of custody were inherently high.

As a consequence, custody became the last resort and the procedure of multi-cautioning became normal practice. This is where police continually caution young offenders for individual criminal offences, before finally placing them before a court.

A series of incidents occurred throughout the country, involving young people, where it appeared that the offenders were 'cocking a snook' at the criminal law and any associated sanctions. This came to the attention of the public, who expressed outrage and perceived that offenders were getting away with crime time and time again. Clearly, it was time for change and it was one incident that arguably had the greatest influence on the future of youth justice.

CASE STUDY

The murder of James Bulger

In 1993, James Bulger, who was two years of age, was with his mother Denise in the New Strand shopping centre, Bootle, Merseyside, when he was abducted by two young boys. CCTV coverage showed James being led away by the two boys and provided the police with early investigation leads. His mutilated body was found two days later on a disused railway line in the Walton area of Liverpool, ironically close to a police station.

He had been brutally murdered. Two boys aged ten, Jon Venables and Robert Thompson, were arrested shortly afterwards and subsequently convicted of James's murder at Preston Crown Court in the November of that year.

In an era when instant communication and news had recently arrived and was global in coverage, the shock of what had happened resonated around the world with utter and total condemnation and complete disbelief that a child aged ten could be capable of such an act.

Consequently, the case had profound implications for future youth justice policy and critics of the system pointed to the shortcomings of the system. Youth justice was in crisis and it was clear that profound changes were imminent.

In the September of 1993, Michael Howard, the then Conservative Home Secretary, announced a 27-point plan for criminal justice at the Conservative Party conference. It was in this speech that he coined the now famous phrase, 'Prison works'. Criminal justice policy was moving sharply towards a more punitive model and young offenders were included.

For example, more restrictive bail conditions were made available to police/courts, the practice of multi-cautioning was discouraged and the longer custodial sentences were extended to young offenders. Secure training centres for offenders aged between 12 and 14 were opened and brought about a 40 per cent rise in custody for young offenders in the years 1992 to 1997 (Kirton, 2005, p390). Almost as a means of highlighting the punitive element in these changes, custodial regimes were modelled on US-style 'boot camps'. Remember, this was the government that had introduced the 'short, sharp shock' sentence in taking up office in 1979.

REFLECTIVE TASK

Go to:

http://news.bbc.co.uk/onthisday/hi/dates/stories/february/14/newsid_2541000/2541171.stm

http://news.bbc.co.uk/1/hi/uk/991562.stm

Read through the news accounts of the Jamie Bulger murder and subsequent investigation. Consider the implications for government at this time, together with public expectations and concerns. Write down any thoughts that you may have about the need for change within the youth justice system following the murder.

Audit Commission

We have already identified issues such as the fear of crime and the factors that contribute to it; the ever increasing concern regarding youth being out of control; the media coverage; and the ramifications of the James Bulger case, which all added to heightening concerns over youth crime.

The government responded, via Michael Howard's reforms, after Prime Minister John Major had set the tone to 'condemn a little more and understand a little less' (Kirton, 2005, p389). Arguably, the final strand manifested itself in 1996 with the Audit Commission report, *Misspent Youth*, which concerned youth justice in England and Wales (Muncie, 2009, p299).

The report concentrated on the ineffectiveness of the youth courts, in respect of the lengthy period of time in particular – an average of four months for a prosecution process, and even then only half of the defendants were actually convicted. The main thrust of the report was to recommend that resources should be moved from punitive to preventive measures. The report also argued that there was a lack of direction at national level and local authorities tended to act in the mode of an emergency service rather than a preventive one. Interestingly, it recommended the diversion of a fifth of young offenders from the courts altogether, citing a scheme in Northampton as being particularly successful. It also commented that efforts to prevent offending and 'anti-social behaviour' should be coordinated by a multi-agency approach targeting deprived areas with high crime rates (Muncie, 2009, p299).

Disorder and its contribution to the fear of crime were being attributed to youth but, in respect of many minor disorder offences, for example youths causing a nuisance in the street, there was very little the police could do, apart from possibly reporting youngsters for breaching local by-laws. This was recognised by both the police and the youths themselves as a toothless tiger and action was hardly ever taken; if it was, it was completely ineffective as a deterrent and this seems to have been acknowledged by the report and the incoming Labour government. Also, the seeds had been sown in respect of disorder by the publication of 'Broken windows' (Wilson and Kelling, 1982). This raised questions that had not been previously considered, or had certainly been overlooked, in respect of activities associated with anti-social behaviour and, accordingly, it justifies its almost iconic status in contemporary policing ideology.

The references in the report to the multi-agency approach to tackling crime and disorder should not have come as a surprise, given that much of the rhetoric emanating from government at this time was to move in this direction, as we will see in the next chapter.

New beginnings

In 1997, the incoming Labour government was elected with a pledge to be 'Tough on crime and tough on the causes of crime' and, as a soundbite at least, it stuck.

As a consequence it introduced its criminal justice flagship, the Crime and Disorder Act (CDA) 1998. Some of the changes made by this legislation in respect of youth justice were referred to in Chapter 5, and we will now focus on the main thrust and provisions of the Act in respect of young offenders. These included:

- abolition of doli incapax;
- standardisation of warning procedures;
- anti-social behaviour orders;
- curfews;
- parental responsibility;
- formulating a national Youth Justice Board (YJB);
- Youth Offending Teams (YOTs) to be established locally.

(Kirton, 2005, p390)

A typical YOT will consist of the following members:

- police officers;
- social services;
- education welfare officers;
- probation officers;
- housing officers;
- victim workers;
- drug treatment order workers;

- substance misuse workers;

- child abuse medical health workers;

- reparation officers;

- court assessment team;

- administration support staff.

Doli incapax

The revocation of doli incapax is a crime-control measure implemented as a direct result of the Bulger case. Hence, the 'due process' protection has been removed (see page 116).

Youth Justice Board

The inauguration of the national YJB and the establishment on a local level of YOTs is a direct response to the recommendations made in the Audit Commission report (1996). The report referred to the then role of local authorities and their reactive approach to youth justice. The CDA 1998 directed that annual youth justice plans be formulated and implemented in order that the authorities' effectiveness could be measured, and local authorities in England and Wales had a statutory duty 'to prevent offending by young people' (Muncie, 2009, p300).

Youth Offending Teams

Prior to the CDA 1998, youth justice was managed through local authority Youth *Justice* Teams and the move to Youth *Offending* Teams reflects a more punitive-led approach. The multi-agency composition reflects a shift to problem solving, rather than merely using the CJS as the sole means of social control. There is now some means of central direction via the YJB that was lacking previously (Muncie, 2009, p300).

The issue regarding warning procedures requires some further clarification. Prior to the CDA 1998, multi-cautioning had been a common practice, tempered somewhat by the aftermath of the Bulger case; nevertheless, practice was varied. Consequently, the Act directed that the first offence, which must be readily admitted to the police, should be dealt with via a reprimand. This is delivered and administered by a senior police officer, normally an Inspector. Any subsequent offence, which again must be admitted, must be dealt with by final warning, subject to seriousness. However, this is not automatic and is only administered by the YOT, if considered by them to be appropriate in the circumstances. Any further transgressions must go straight to court. Where a young person has been arrested, but denies the offence, the police, provided they have sufficient evidence, must charge and the court will decide on guilt or not. The police and the YOT do not decide on guilt or innocence; that is a function only for the courts.

Return to welfare?

Following the violent and tragic death of eight-year-old Victoria Climbié in London in 2000, the government ordered an inquiry into the events surrounding the case, which was chaired by Lord Laming. The subsequent report was far-reaching and contained some 108 recommendations.

As a result, the government produced a green paper entitled *Every Child Matters* (DfES, 2003), which formed the basis for the Children Act 2004. A primary theme highlighted within the paper was a move towards a more joined-up approach to providing welfare services for children. This has led to the establishment by local authorities of 'Children's Trusts', through which, it is hoped, integrated services for children will provide a safer, more comprehensive model, avoiding previous shortcomings that have led to tragedies such as that involving Victoria Climbié. At the time of writing, it is clear that there still remains much work to do, and Lord Laming has had to further review child protection services in England (Laming, 2009) and has made additional recommendations. This is in response to the inquiry into child protection following the tragedy of 'Baby Peter', which involved the same local authority as that of Victoria Climbié.

At first glance it appears that *Every Child Matters* has signalled a return to the welfare approach for youth justice and there has been a partial shift in responsibilities at government departmental level.

However, a companion document to *Every Child Matters*, entitled *Youth Justice: The Next Steps*, did not enthusiastically embrace the welfare approach and used phrases such as 'preventing offending' (Muncie, 2009, p302) and did not recommend that youth justice should be incorporated with mainstream children's services. We must also remember that these measures were implemented by a government that was elected on a slogan of being 'Tough on crime and tough on the causes of crime'. Youth offenders are still perceived to be offenders first and children with welfare needs second (Muncie, 2009, p303).

Effective – or new wine in old bottles?

There has been considerable change in the approach to youth offending since 1998. The Audit Commission looked at the changes implemented in its report, *Youth Justice 2004*, and reached the following mixed conclusions:

- improvements in the time between arrest and court appearance;

- applauded the emphasis on achieving the statutory aim of prevention;

- noted that minor offences clogged the system;

- too many offenders being sent for custodial sentences;

- intensive community sentences being under-resourced.

(Muncie, 2009, p300)

PRACTICAL TASK

For the final task in this chapter go to *www.crimeandjustice.org.uk/youthjusticeaudit structure.html* and access the independent report entitled Ten Years of Labour's Youth Justice Reforms: An Independent Audit, *published in 2008.*

Access the link 'View press release' and identify the key findings from the report. Note the differences between these findings and those listed above and determine why this could be.

CHAPTER SUMMARY

The chapter will end where it started, at the introduction stage, where the quotation refers to a 'slow and tedious' journey. Written in 1908, it could well have been written over 100 years later and still carry the same validity as the intervening sections of this chapter have hopefully shown. How things will progress in the future remains uncertain, but society seems to have agreed on one point over the last 100 years: dealing with young offenders requires a different approach from dealing with adult offenders; whether that approach is right will be subject to further argument, as the past 100 years have shown. Previous form is often a good indicator of future performance.

In the chapter various tasks have been set for you and, if you have undertaken them diligently, they will have provided you with some key information in the development of youth justice.

Other debates are starting to emerge and are suggesting a move away from the traditional models of 'punitive versus welfare', to 'inclusion', 'reconciliation' or 'problem-solving' (Muncie, 2009, p303) – the latter of which seems to be more congruent with other contemporary developments in policing.

We wait with interest.

REFERENCES

Audit Commission (1996) *Misspent Youth: Young People and Crime* (National Report). London: Audit Commission.

Audit Commission (2004) *Youth Justice 2004*. London: Audit Commission.

Beveridge, Sir William (1942) *Social Insurance and Allied Services* (Cmd 6404). London: HMSO.

Crawford, A and Newburn, T (2003) *Youth Offending and Restorative Justice*. Cullompton: Willan.

Department for Education and Skills (DfES) (2003) *Every Child Matters* (Cm. 5860). London: HMSO.

Fitzgerald, M, McLennan, G and Pawson, J (1981) *Crime and Society: Readings in History and Theory*. London: Routledge.

Goldson, B (2009) What 'justice' for children in conflict with the law? Some reflections and thoughts. *Criminal Justice Matters*, 76(1): 19–21.

Hopkins Burke, R (2008) *Young People, Crime and Justice*. Cullompton: Willan.

Kirton, D (2005) Young people and crime, in Hale, C, Hayward, K, Wahidi, A and Wincup, E (eds) *Criminology*. Oxford: Oxford University Press.

Laming, Lord William (2009) *The Protection of Children in England: A Progress Report*. London: The Stationery Office.

Maguire, M, Morgan, R and Reiner, R (2007) *Oxford Handbook of Criminology*, 4th edition. Oxford: Oxford University Press.

Muncie, J (2009) *Youth Crime*, 3rd edition. London: Sage.

Muncie, J and McLaughlin, E (2001) *The Problem of Crime.* London: Sage.

Ruggles-Brise, Sir Evelyn (1921) *The English Prison System.* London: Macmillan.

Wilson, J Q and Kelling, G L (1982) Broken windows. *The Atlantic Monthly*, March.

USEFUL WEBSITES

http://forums.canadiancontent.net/history/47165-bloody-code.html (information on the Bloody Code)

http://news.bbc.co.uk (search for articles on the murder of James Bulger)

www.aber.ac.uk/media/Students/hrb9701.html (Hayley Burns's essay about 'moral panics')

www.audit-commission.gov.uk (Audit Commission)

www.childrenssociety.org.uk (The Children's Society)

www.history.ac.uk/ihr/Focus/welfare/articles/bradleyk.html (Kate Bradley's essay on juvenile delinquency c.1900–50)

www.homeoffice.gov.uk/rds/bcs1.html (British Crime Survey)

www.nspcc.org.uk (National Society for the Prevention of Cruelty to Children)

www.rockabilly.nl/general/teddyboys.htm (article about 'Teddy boys')

www.umich.edu/~ece/student_projects/bonifield/pardons.html (more information on the Bloody Code)

www.urbandictionary.com/define.php?term=skin+head (article about 'skinheads')

www.victorianlondon.org/publications/mayhew1-1.htm (Mayhew's essay on costermongers)

LEGISLATION

Children Act 2004

Children and Young Persons Act 1933

Children and Young Persons Act 1969

Children's Act 1908

Crime and Disorder Act 1998

Criminal Justice Act 1948

Criminal Justice Act 1961

Criminal Justice Act 1991

Prevention of Crime Act 1953

Youth Offenders Act 1854

8 Multi-agency approach

CHAPTER OBJECTIVES

By the end of this chapter you should be able to:

- understand the development of multi-agency working;
- appreciate the reasons for the emergence of multi-agency partnership working;
- identify some of the key events that contributed towards partnership working;
- explain the role of the Crime and Disorder Reduction Partnership (CDRP);
- identify key functions of the CDRP.

LINKS TO STANDARDS

This chapter provides opportunities for links with the following Skills for Justice, National Occupational Standards (NOS) for Policing and Law Enforcement 2008.

IA2	Communicate effectively with members of communities.
IB11	Contribute to resolving community issues.
IB12	Design out crime.
IB4	Determine the concerns and priorities of communities in relation to safety, social inclusion and the prevention and reduction of crime and anti-social behaviour.

Introduction

This chapter will focus mainly on the requirements placed upon the police in respect of the provisions contained in the Crime and Disorder Act (CDA) 1998. This has brought about some major changes, not only in the approach to crime itself, but also in placing the multi-agency approach or partnership working on a statutory footing.

This is also an interesting cultural shift for the Police Service, in that it has historically strived to remain as neutral as possible and not show any leanings that could be perceived to be favouring one individual or organisation over the next, especially in operational matters that could impinge on the Criminal Justice System (CJS). The CDA 1998 has radically altered that stance and, in fact, police would be open to criticism if they approached problems without first considering a partnership approach and consulting with the public.

It has taken some considerable time and some major events to arrive at this state of affairs and this chapter will discuss some of the main landmarks along that road and consider the contemporary situation.

Historical perspectives

On occasions, the Police Service has worked together with other organisations, for example during the war years with the Security Service (MI5) and, more recently, during the 'troubles' in Northern Ireland. In the wake of the terrorist attacks in New York ('9/11' – 11 September 2001) and in London (7 July 2005), this arrangement is now much more formal. The Joint Terrorism Analysis Centre (JTAC), based at MI5 headquarters, contains personnel from 16 government agencies and departments, including police officers (Hayman, 2009, p38).

In respect of planning for major events such as floods, storm damage, air disasters and terrorist attacks, emergency plans are drawn up by police in conjunction with local authorities and other emergency services. This is both established good practice and routine procedure, and a new legislative framework has recently been developed with the introduction of the Civil Contingencies Act 2004.

Perhaps the area of police work that is most commonly linked to working with other agencies is in the field of child protection. This has received considerable media coverage since it was introduced into this country in 1973, following the inquiry into the tragic death of Maria Colwell. As we have identified in the previous chapter, the child-protection system is being refined, in the wake of further tragic cases, such as those concerning Victoria Climbié and 'Baby Peter'. Police have a core role to play, alongside medical and social work professionals.

Since 1 April 2006, each area has had, by law, to establish a multi-agency Local Safe-guarding Children Board.

Scarman Report

Leading up to the weekend of 10 April 1981, the police at Brixton, London, were becoming increasingly concerned with an upturn in reported street crime, including thefts from motor vehicles. An operational decision was taken to deploy more plain-clothes officers with a view to deterring/detecting offences. This operation came to be known as 'Operation Swamp' and the Brixton police did literally flood the area with officers. Unfortunately, the backdrop to this had been set in 1978 when the government had ordered the Royal Commission into Criminal Procedure (RCCP), to enquire into issues relating to the CJS. A major consideration was the enforcement of the so-called 'sus laws', which related to police stop and search tactics.

During the course of the operation, police made some 950 'stops' and over half the people stopped were black. This resulted in 118 arrests, but only one of these was for robbery and only another 21 for crime-related matters (Newburn, 2003, p88). Tension soon grew between the police and the local community, and the area around Railton Road became known colloquially as the 'Front line'. Eventually, tensions spilled over and three days of large-scale disorder commenced, which saw buildings burnt out and destroyed, widespread looting, and police attacked by bricks, bottles and petrol bombs. On the Saturday, in particular, a large number of police officers, and some members of the public, were injured and police vehicles were damaged, many being burnt out.

The intensity of the rioting shocked the whole country and the then Home Secretary, William Whitelaw, after touring the area in the aftermath of the riot, ordered an inquiry, chaired by Lord Scarman. Further disturbances took place across Britain that summer. Following major disturbances at Toxteth in inner-city Liverpool in July, where one person died, CS gas was used for the first time on the British mainland and a police station was attacked by a mob, the remit of the Scarman Inquiry was extended to consider the Toxteth disturbances. One fact was clear to all observers even before Scarman reported: the concept of 'policing by consent' had completely broken down.

Brixton and Toxteth shared several common features: they were both areas with significant ethnic minorities, mainly Afro-Caribbean; unemployment was extremely high, especially among the youth; and both were acknowledged as deprived inner-city areas with acute social problems.

PRACTICAL TASK

Go online to http://news.bbc.co.uk/1/hi/programmes/bbc_parliament/3631579.stm, read the section subtitled 'What did the report say?' and answer the following questions.

- *What did Lord Scarman say about relations between the police and the local community?*

- *What recommendations did he make in relation to police and local community relations?*

Following the publication of the Scarman Report, some of the recommendations were placed on a statutory footing by inclusion in the Police and Criminal Evidence Act (PACE) 1984, which resulted from the 1981 report of the RCCP. This included regular consultative meetings between the police and the local communities, known as 'community forums', and the introduction of a monitoring system whereby arrested persons were visited in the police station.

Independent persons known as 'lay visitors' were appointed by Police Authorities to undertake unannounced visits to police custody suites to interview persons in custody about their treatment. These still play a part in everyday police life and are now known as 'custody visitors'.

Post-Scarman, the expression 'community policing' began to be heard and, given the emphasis on 'community' in the report, some Chief Constables took up the initiative. In the case of Toxteth, the Merseyside Police formed its own 'Toxteth Section' of hand-picked officers who had the task of both policing the area and attempting to repair the shattered community relations and rebuild the concept of 'policing by consent'. Officers not belonging to the Toxteth Section were not allowed into 'the triangle', as the area was known, without the express permission of the duty Inspector. Other agencies were also involved and consulted in relation to the policing problems of the area and, although it was nothing like the formalised arrangements that exist nowadays, it was an early attempt at a multi-agency approach to policing (McLaughlin, 2007, p66).

Home Office Circular 8/84

Perhaps the next significant event was the publication by the Home Office of Circular 8/84, which urged a multi-agency approach to crime prevention (McLaughlin and Muncie, 2001, p305). It laid the foundations for future major change. However, at the time there was an official acceptance that police could not tackle crime as a single agency and, in an attempt to control crime, as opposed to trying to deal with its aftermath, crime prevention (now referred to as reduction) emerged as a prominent issue.

This was directly linked to two factors: the impact of the first British Crime Survey in 1982, which indicated that the level of actual crime was about four times the figures recorded by police, and the establishment of the Home Office Crime Prevention Unit in 1983 (McLaughlin and Muncie, 2001, p304). This was prompted by the growing influence of the 'Right Realism' school of thought in relation to criminological theory, which we will look at in more detail in the next chapter.

In the first instance following Circular 8/84, the Police Service tried to establish 'crime prevention panels' that involved other agencies and businesses. It was an early attempt to harness the community into crime reduction and was administered by the local crime prevention officer. In the early days, they appeared unsure as what their role actually was, given that, until that point, any role of this sort was a matter only for the police; however, some of the more proactive panels produced ideas such as biro pens with crime-prevention advice written on the stem, as a means of raising awareness generally.

Another means that was introduced, and one that is more familiar, was via the intro-duction of 'Home Watch' or 'Neighbourhood Watch' in some areas. Many of these schemes exist today, but were started in the early 1980s (the first scheme was in Mollington, Cheshire in 1982), and involve several properties in a residential street or small area. The idea is that each homeowner looks out for the others and any suspicious activity is reported to the scheme co-ordinator, who reports it to the police. The police, in turn, alert the co-ordinator of the scheme to any relevant intelligence that they may have, regarding possible threats to the security of their properties. Home Watch certainly had some success, if only to make people feel safer, and the principle has been extended to other areas of everyday life, such as 'Pub Watch' and even 'Church Watch' – schemes that are probably hybrid versions of 'Home Watch' and the crime prevention panel.

Safer Cities Programme

In 1988, the Home Office initiated the 'Five Towns Project' as a working example of the 1984 circular. The initial towns selected were Bolton, North Tyneside, Croydon, Swansea and Wellingborough and the project ran for 18 months, although some of the crime-prevention measures that were implemented ran for longer than this (McLaughlin and Muncie, 2001, p305). Following the apparent success of Five Towns, in 1988, the government announced the 'Safer Cities Programme', which initially involved 16 cities. This, like the earlier project, was overseen by the Home Office and eventually introduced titles such as 'Safer Salford' to participating cities, clearly showing the way to what we now see on a daily basis. The underpinning principle of this is the prevention of crime. An organisation called 'Crime Concern' was established, whose function was to promulgate good practice within crime prevention (McLaughlin and Muncie, 2001, p306).

Morgan Report 1991

Despite the above developments, the government was not happy with the slow take-up of crime-prevention partnerships and Circular 8/84 generally and, as a result, the 'Standing Committee on Crime Prevention' (Rogers and Blakemore, 2009, p30) established an inquiry under James Morgan, which reported in 1991 and is known as the Morgan Report. The report contained some 19 recommendations, three of which are outlined below.

- Introduction of a statutory responsibility on local authorities (with the police) for the 'stimulation of community safety and crime prevention programmes, and for progressing at a local level a multi-agency approach to community safety'.

- Establishment of a local authority co-coordinator with administrative support.

- More specific attention at a local level to involving businesses as partners 'instead of regarding them solely as a possible source of funds'.

(Rogers and Blakemore, 2009, p30)

PRACTICAL TASK

Go online to www.crimereduction.homeoffice.gov.uk/toolkits/p010301.htm and read through the article entitled 'Multi-agency approach: background'. Answer the following questions.

- *What did the Morgan Report say regarding crime reduction for major agencies?*

- *What does it say about the 'holistic' approach to crime reduction?*

Somewhat surprisingly, given the background context of the Morgan Report, the recommendations were not taken up by the then Conservative government (Gilling, 2007, p2). Two reasons may account for this: first, at the time of Morgan, the Royal Commission into Criminal Justice (RCCJ), which had begun taking evidence in 1990, was yet to report; and, second, the government in 1993 announced via the Home Secretary at the

Conservative Party conference that 'prison works' – heralding in a new era in penology, where imprisonment was to become a major plank in crime control.

'Broken windows'

The previous chapter mentioned the influence of 'Broken windows' on matters such as anti-social behaviour (ASB) and it is now appropriate to look at this in more detail. The 'Broken windows' article was published in the 1982 *Atlantic Monthly* journal and it has been described as 'arguably the most influential article published in contemporary police studies' (McLaughlin, 2007, p73). When the article is considered carefully and reflected upon, it is clear that there are direct links with what we now call 'neighbourhood policing'. Other factors have played a part, but the impact of 'Broken windows' should not be underestimated.

The theory behind the article is simple: if a building is left unrepaired when one window is broken, others follow, often in rapid sequence. The culmination is that the surrounding area is affected and becomes derelict and lawless, where no one, including the police, appears to care. The fear of crime is raised and, as a result, the law-abiding public abandons the area. Low-level criminality, including disorder, goes unchecked, which in turn leads to more serious crime, and the area gains a reputation as a lawless place where anything goes, as the police and the law-abiding community have effectively moved out.

The 'Broken windows' theory has also influenced policing styles, despite arguments to the contrary, and has been credited with reductions in crime and disorder. The most famous of these has been in New York City during the 1990s, when police implemented a mode of policing that has become known as 'zero tolerance'. The Chief of the New York Police Department (NYPD) at this time was William (Bill) J. Bratton. Prior to his appointment, he was Chief of the New York Transit Police, where George Kelling, one of the authors of 'Broken windows' was the academic adviser to the Transit Authority and was instrumental in the appointment (Bratton, 1998, p140).

Bratton as Transit Chief faced three major policing problems: fare evasion, disorder and crime (Bratton, 1998, pp143–4). Many of the New York public refused to use the subway, especially after dark, and the Authority was losing revenue. This is where the theory of 'Broken windows' was first applied in policing:

> We began to apply this concept to crime in the subways. Fare evasion was the biggest broken window in the transit system. We were going to fix that window and see to it that it didn't get broken again.

(Bratton, 1998, p152)

The principle of 'zero-tolerance policing' has not been applied in the UK, mainly as it is very resource intensive in respect of police officers: first, to provide a visible presence on the street in order to provide reassurance for the public and, second, to detect and deal with the most minor of offences, particularly ASB, that the zero-tolerance approach targets.

A version of it has been applied in specific areas such as town centres, for short periods of time, for example operations against street drinking and minor disorder on Friday and Saturday evenings. An example of it in a UK context was during the 'Street Crime Initiative' in 2001/02 when, in London, half of the capital's traffic officers were redeployed to divisions with a high recorded robbery rate (Stevens, 2005, p254) and city centre 'vagrants' were proactively targeted.

The most famous UK example comes from Cleveland Constabulary in the late 1990 period under the leadership of Superintendent Ray Mallon (now Mayor of Middlesborough). It is claimed that, within three months of the strategy having been implemented, a 22 per cent reduction in ASB, burglary in a dwelling and other quality-of-life offences had resulted (Rogers, 2006, p156). The policy was controversial and not without criticism and was reviewed when Superintendent Mallon moved on; however, it certainly brought these issues to the attention of the public at large.

REFLECTIVE TASK

Go online to www.theatlantic.com/doc/198203/broken-windows#, access the article 'Broken windows' and read through the first three pages. Reflect on what is being said and answer the following questions.

- *What do Wilson and Kelling say about the breakdown of community controls and why this happens?*

- *What will happen if the panhandler (beggar) remains 'unchecked' and who might be encouraged by this?*

- *What is the core role of police in maintaining order and what are they unable to do?*

- *What do you consider to be the core role of the police in the area where you live?*

- *How do your responses compare with those of the authors, Wilson and Kelling?*

Problem-oriented policing

The idea of 'problem-oriented policing' stems from research in America by Herman Goldstein, adviser to the Chicago Police Department, and emerged towards the end of the 1970s. It is often closely associated with community policing, because of its community focus.

Since the introduction of the motor vehicle and personal radio into policing, a 'fire-brigade' approach to calls for service has become ingrained. Officers on mobile patrol were told via the radio operator where to go, when and why, in order to perform their role. As we have just seen, the 'Broken windows' theory refers to this mode of policing. Visits were made to incidents, often minor, that repeated themselves, for example ASB (youths playing football), and very little, if anything, was done to address the problem. Officers saw their role as enforcement and would look only to their powers of arrest, rather than considering issues in the wider context. This had several disadvantages in that police managers had little or no control over the calls process and it was a continuous waste of resources for police to be making numerous visits to the most minor of incidents. They mattered to the members of the public who made the calls in the first place, as they affected their quality of life. As this response function required so many officers in order to meet the demand, other pressing problems that required some priority and substantial periods of evidence gathering, for example drug dealing, could not be properly addressed.

Goldstein went some way to addressing these issues, with his approach to problem-oriented policing (POP). Basically, a 'problem' is considered to be something that promotes substantial community concerns and police are encouraged to consider problems in 'clusters' as opposed to single incidents. POP dictates that police research into the underlying problems that affect the safety of the community they serve (Ratcliffe, 2008, p71). By doing so, it is hoped that solutions can be found to perennial problems that blight communities and are a constant draw on police resources. Importantly, the solution to many of these problems often lies *outside* the CJS or, in other words, cannot be properly addressed merely by enforcement, such as making arrests or issuing fixed penalty notices or reporting offenders for summons.

POP is used on a day-to-day basis as an approach to problem solving mainly by 'Neighbourhood' or 'Local Policing Teams'. Since 2001, there has been an ongoing police reform agenda that requires the Police Service to adopt this method of policing to resolve community problems. The system is closely aligned to community policing, which is defined as policing *with* and *for* the community, rather than policing *of* the community (Newburn, 2003, p315). As the solutions often lie outside the CJS, it is more successful in a multi-agency approach to problems.

There are 'tools' available to assist with this problem-solving approach. Two of the most common are the 'SARA' and 'PAT' models that are outlined below. The idea of the SARA/PAT models is to break crime and disorder problems down into manageable and solvable scenarios.

SARA model

- Scanning
- Analysis
- Response
- Assess

Remember, the overriding principle is to solve problems by using these tools. In order to do that the full facts of the situation must be fully known and understood, prior to any proposed solutions being put in place. So below is an example of how a SARA may look, after a referral of ASB to the police – in this case, youths playing football in the street.

- **S** Calls to the police, complaints to the councillor, letters in local papers.
- **A** Consider *all* the information available, before deciding actually what the complaint is about.
- **R** Put action plan in place with partners; provide 'all-weather' five-a-side pitch with floodlighting.
- **A** Revisit in three months and evaluate effectiveness of action plan.

The above is just an example and very few problems are resolved as simply as that.

PAT: the problem analysis triangle

PAT (Figure 8.1) is derived from routine activity theory by Marcus Felson that emerged initially in the late 1980s. It argues that, for a crime to occur, three elements must be present:

- a victim;

- a suitable location or venue;

- a motivated offender.

Take away any one of these components and the problem no longer exists. PAT is more commonly used in cases of 'situational' problems, which we will look at in the next section.

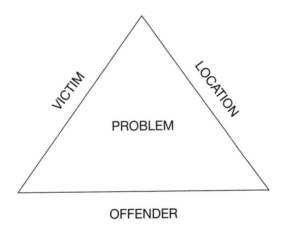

PROCTOR

There is also another tool available called PROCTOR.

- **PRO**blem

- **C**ause

- **T**actic or Treatment

- **O**utput and **R**esult.

The SARA model is currently preferred by the Police Service, but PROCTOR is listed here for comparison and is an alternative methodology to consider.

REFLECTIVE TASK

Go online to www.chiltern.gov.uk/neighbourhood/site/scripts/documents_info.php? documentID=348&pageNumber=2 and read through the case study using SARA and PAT.

Reflect on the circumstances outlined in the first paragraph, which involves a case of ASB, and consider how the SARA model has been used to break the problem down and offer a solution to the problem.

- *Now, from your own knowledge, list the agencies/local authority departments that could be involved in the proposed solution.*

- *If it were left to the police alone to address this recurring problem, what resources might they need to successfully resolve it? (Consider 'Broken windows'.)*

Situational crime prevention

The concept of 'situational crime prevention' is linked to the Right Realism school of criminological thought that emerged in the 1980s and directly to rational choice theory, of which Ronald Clarke of the Home Office Crime Prevention Unit was one of the main proponents. The underpinning principle of situational crime prevention is very simple.

Criminals make a rational decision to commit crime (which we will look at in more depth in Chapter 9) and, for that to happen, similarly to routine activity theory (see 'PAT' above), all necessary elements, such as opportunity, motivation, etc., need to be in place.

It is possible to control the behaviour of people, as a study of suicide rates in Birmingham in 1972 illustrated (McLaughlin et al., 2003, p361). The poisonous content of gas, which was used in domestic cooking and heating, had been removed and the research examined an eight-year period between 1962 and 1970 and found a dramatic decrease in the rate of suicide. It was no longer possible to turn on the gas taps and inhale poisonous fumes.

Perhaps a more appropriate example comes from West Germany and relates to motor vehicles. In 1963, steering column locks were made compulsory on all vehicles irrespective of age; this is accredited with a 60 per cent decrease in incidents of the unauthorised taking of motor vehicles (McLaughlin et al., 2003, p363).

What situational crime prevention seeks to do, as the above examples illustrate, is to prevent the *opportunity* for crime. The motivation of people who intend to commit crime, or are successful in doing so, is not the concern; it is preventing them from doing it in the first place that is the only consideration.

Situational crime prevention has led to developments that are now very familiar, such as CCTV in town centres and the erection of secure metal gates at the rear of terraced properties, known as 'alley-gating'.

Crime and Disorder Reduction Partnerships

The introduction of Crime and Disorder Reduction Partnerships (CDRPs), known as Community Safety Partnerships (CSPs) in Wales, is a result of the CDA 1998, which was passed by New Labour following their 1997 election victory. The CDRP is largely based on the Morgan Report (1991), which the Conservative government chose not to implement. Not all of the Morgan recommendations are implemented and there are 376 CDRPs across England and Wales, which broadly reflect local authority boundaries.

The word 'reduction' is in the title and has replaced the word 'prevention'. The change is made as 'reduction' is seen as a more interventionist proactive role for the here and now, whereas 'prevention' is much more future-orientated (McLaughlin and Muncie, 2001, p308). The inclusion of the word 'disorder' reflects the growing influence by this stage of the 'Broken windows' theory.

The shift to partnerships is not merely a British phenomenon, as there is partnership working in one form or another across both Europe and North America (Rogers, 2006, p27). This development has also been endorsed by the United Nations Congress on the Prevention of Crime and the Treatment of Offenders and dates as far back as 1990 (Rogers, 2006, p27).

The CDA 1998 created two 'responsible authorities' in respect of the CDRP – the police and the local authority. In practice, this was the local police commander and the local authority chief executive, although subsequently the Primary Care Trust has been added. It was also becoming clear to the Police Service, prior to the CDA, that statutory partnership working was on the horizon; hence, several forces altered their divisional boundaries to mirror those of the local authorities, in order to facilitate partnership approaches to crime and disorder. Most, if not all, have followed suit.

The central feature of the CDRP is that it is *local* in both structure and vision. This reflects the central tenor of the 'Broken windows' philosophy as the full title of the article suggests: 'Broken windows – police and *neighbourhood* safety'.

Initially, the Act placed a responsibility upon the police/local authority, in partnership with other agencies, to produce a 'strategy for the reduction of crime and disorder in the area' (Newburn, 2007, p570). In order to do this, CDRPs were expected to complete an audit of crime (survey) of their communities every three years.

Remember, the underpinning motivation for this from Home Office Circular 8/84 onwards has been crime prevention, or reduction as it is now called. The CDRP exists to *reduce* crime and disorder, not to *investigate* and *prosecute* via the CJS. That is a role for the police and the Crown Prosecution Service. The CDRP does not replace that function but seeks to augment it.

The Chair of a CDRP is usually the local divisional police commander and members of CDRPs include the following:

- Police Service;

- Crown Prosecution Service (CPS);

- local authorities;

- Probation Service;

- voluntary sector;

- Youth Offending Team (YOT);

- drugs intervention teams;

- Fire Service;

- Health Service;

- Victim Support;

- registered social landlords (RSLs) (housing associations);

- parish councils.

The following examples highlight in practice their multi-agency approach to reducing crime and disorder.

- The most obvious evidence of a CDRP in operation is the existence of the CCTV systems, normally operated by local authority employees. Some cameras are equipped with a loudspeaker that allows the CCTV operators to communicate directly to people within close proximity to the camera and which is normally used to issue verbal warnings regarding any witnessed ASB.

- Physical intervention measures include alley-gating, by restricting access to private dwellings and reducing the opportunity for crime, especially burglary. This feature has now been copied by numerous private developers, who erect several properties in a small estate or close that allows only one entry and exit, and is now known as a 'gated community' – the overriding principle is crime reduction, not merely enhanced privacy.

- In respect of ASB, the provision of youth shelters is a direct attempt to reduce disorder, by diverting young people away from activities that could impinge on the quality of life of the local population.

The above illustrate how a Neighbourhood or Local Policing Team adopting a POP approach would seek to solve problems by working alongside their local communities and other CDRP partners, such as local authority housing, education and leisure services, and registered social landlords (RSLs). This approach to policing is totally different from that in the era that witnessed the Brixton and Toxteth riots and underlines the principles of policing *for* and *with* the community, as opposed to the policing *of* the community.

All forces have been required to move towards neighbourhood policing. The role of response officers, those who deal with 24/7 calls for service, is to *support* neighbourhood policing and allow their colleagues to work alongside the community and with other CDRP partners in a problem-solving approach. In some forces, student officers commence their operational phase by being posted to a Neighbourhood Policing Team. This is designed to develop their problem-solving and partnership working as early as possible.

Bill Bratton has commented on this and describes the journey in policing from what was purely an enforcement role to a more community role as a change from the 3Rs:

1. Rapid Response

2. Random Patrol

3. Reactive Investigation

to a more community-focused approach to policing – the 3Ps:

1. Partnership

2. Problem-Solving

3. Prevention.

He expanded further:

> Remember in the 1970s and 1980s police said: 'If you give us additional personnel, equipment and resources we'll take care of your problems and control crime.' This didn't happen because there was no partnership with the community, other institutions of government and the criminal justice system; police can have a significant impact on crime and disorder. This is the basic premise behind community policing and, when properly applied, it is tougher on crime than anything else we've ever tried. New York City's experience is proof positive of this.
>
> (Newburn, 2005, pp472–4)

PACT meetings

Police and the CDRP are required to consult with their public. One of the methods that has been steadily gaining ground over the last few years is the PACT meeting. The acronym can mean either 'Police and Communities Together' as in some force areas such as Lancashire, or 'Partners and Communities Together' as in West Mercia. The principle is the same. The original idea started in Chicago in 1993, when the police department implemented its Chicago Alternative Policing Strategies (CAPS) programme. One of the successes was the 'beat meeting' held in various locations around a neighbourhood (Newburn, 2005, p434). This has now been adopted in the UK and concentrates on small geographical areas, such as a local authority ward. Meetings are normally convened by a neighbourhhood officer, assisted by community support officers and representatives of other partners such as the local authority. Minutes are kept and the top three problems from the area as identified by the public are formally adopted for action by the partners and progress is reported on, either via a designated website or at a future PACT meeting.

Go to www.ourbobby.com and follow these links:

- Neath Port Talbot;

- Pontardawe Area;

- Cadoxton;

- PACT Meetings.

Answer the following questions.

- According to the website, what is discussed at a PACT meeting?

- What are PACT priorities?

- According to the website, who actually solves the problems?

Prolific and priority offenders

A key function of the CDRP is to manage prolific and priority offenders (PPOs), who are known active offenders who commit most of the recorded crime. Many of them are youth offenders.

Go online to www.crimereduction.homeoffice.gov.uk/activecommunities/activecommunities 088.pdf and go to page 11 of the National Community Safety Plan 2008–11. Read through the case study regarding a PPO and answer the following questions.

- How has a CDRP framework facilitated this outcome?

- How does it comply with the culture of reducing crime and disorder?

- In relation to the police only, how does it adhere to the principles of problem-oriented policing (POP)?

Write down your answers and reread the relevant sections of the chapter and see if you are correct.

Following the introduction of the CDRP in 1998, which heralded a fresh approach to tackling issues of crime and disorder, and complete new agendas and responsibilities for most agencies involved, it would be unrealistic to imagine that changes of this magnitude would be problem-free.

In 2004, a review of the CDRP was implemented and reported on in 2006 (Rogers and Blakemore, 2009, p36) and recommended phased changes, which include the following.

- Removal of the need to audit every three years.

- Local three-year community safety plans will be refreshed every year.

- Plans will be integrated with other local strategies and plans using Local Area Agreements.

- Power to share information will be become a duty for the three statutory agencies, police, local authority, health service, including probation.

- National standards will be introduced.

- Scrutiny committees within local authorities will have responsibility for oversight of the work of the CDRP.

(Rogers and Blakemore, 2009, p36)

Part of the review focused on the role of RSLs and encouragement aimed at them to work closer within the CDRP.

To conclude this section, the following case study refers to a policy of an RSL inspected by the Audit Commission and highlighted as good practice. It highlights many of the RSL functions and, when considered, increases understanding of the quest to integrate RSLs within, and to strengthen further, the CDRP framework.

CASE STUDY

The South Liverpool Housing (SLH) Group Housing Association is an RSL. The following is taken from the Association's website and is presented here as a case study. RSLs have powers to apply for anti-social behaviour orders (ASBOs).

SLH has organised a range of diversionary measures aimed specifically at young people, including funding for Positive Activities for Young People (PAYP) in the South Liverpool Area, the Youth Squad, and development of a Citizenship programme in local secondary schools to raise awareness of ASB.

SLH have a comprehensive and well-designed Neighbour Nuisance and Harassment case management file which is used effectively to record incidents of ASB.

Tenants involved in the prosecution of ASB cases are offered an extensive package of support. SLH has a victim support package which includes extra security, 24 hours a day support scheme and a witness support forum held every six weeks. This scheme was shortlisted for a UK Housing Award for Excellence in Delivering Safer Neighbourhoods. SLH provides practical support, such as informing the person's employer that they are assisting in a court case and paying compensation for their absence. This is designed to encourage those experiencing ASB to give evidence against offenders, increase conviction rates and improve the quality of life for people living in the area.

141

SLH gives appropriate support to offenders of ASB including the identification of support need and, generally, a punitive approach is only adopted after the exhaustion of other possibilities.

(SLH Group, 2007)

REFLECTIVE TASK

Consider and debate the strengths and weaknesses of the South Liverpool Housing initiative to tackle ASB. What are the implications of this type of approach for other agencies, residents and perpetrators, and does it offer a viable long-term solution to this type of problem?

Multi-Agency Public Protection Arrangements

Multi-Agency Public Protection Arrangements (MAPPA) are now structured and formalised and relate to the management of potentially dangerous offenders (PDOs), who are violent and sexual offenders within the community. The overriding principle is to manage the *risk* that a PDO may pose to the public. The context to the contemporary MAPPA illustrates the important role that they now perform.

In 1997, the government passed legislation that introduced the Sex Offenders Register; the principle behind the register was that the whereabouts of *convicted* sex offenders were known to the police. A major driving influence for the register at the time was the Police Superintendents' Association, which lobbied strongly for the register, and also the increased concern regarding the management of PDOs following release from prison.

Megan's Law

The so-called Megan's Law was passed in New Jersey, USA, after seven-year-old Megan Kanka was raped and murdered in 1994 by Jesse Timmendequas, who had two previous convictions for sex attacks. The furore around the incident focused on the issue that local parents had never been warned that Timmendequas had moved into their area. Following the murder of Megan, the State of New Jersey passed legislation that allowed details of convicted sex offenders to be available publicly, and this became federal law in 1996 and available to all states. What occurred in the USA did not go unnoticed in the UK.

PRACTICAL TASK

Go online to *www.meganslaw.ca.gov/*, which provides access to the Attorney General's Office for the State of California, and answer the following questions.

- In paragraph two on the website, how many persons are required to register in California as sex offenders?

- How many home addresses of registered offenders are available via the website to the public?

- In paragraph three, after signing the disclaimer, what are you able to search?

Sarah Payne

Sarah Payne was abducted and murdered by convicted offender Roy Whiting in July 2000. Whiting had already served a four-year sentence for abducting a child and, following the discovery of Sarah's body some two weeks later, he was arrested and eventually convicted. Comparisons were quickly made with the New Jersey case and sections of the media were quick to point out that no such law existed in the UK and labelled any potential legislation as 'Sarah's Law'.

Shortly after the discovery of the body, the *News of the World* published names and addresses of convicted sex offenders throughout the country and this led directly to outbreaks of public disorder on the Paulsgrove housing estate in Portsmouth, where one of the named people resided. A group known as RAP (Residents Against Paedophiles) was formed and the disturbances, which involved several hundred people on that estate and the neighbouring Wymmering estate, led to over 50 arrests (Hill, 2001). Properties and cars were attacked and burnt out, and it took several days for Hampshire Police to fully restore order.

The Paulsgrove disturbances act as an example of what can occur when information of the most sensitive nature concerning members of the community is released to the public at large, and the vigilante action of RAP sealed the fate on any impending legislation that may have been comparable to Megan's Law.

Local arrangements between police, probation and other agencies throughout the country had emerged during the 1990 period in response to the greater public concern. In 2000, the government passed the Criminal Justice and Courts Services Act, which placed MAPPA on a statutory footing to manage risks posed by sexual and violent offenders (Ireland et al., 2009, p266). In 2003, legislation was passed that increased the restrictive orders available and added prisons as a 'responsible authority' alongside police and probation agencies. These three agencies now form the core of a MAPPA panel that operates on three levels of risk management (Ireland et al., 2009, p266).

Go online to www.probation.homeoffice.gov.uk/output/Page434.asp and answer the following questions.

- *How many levels of management are there?*
- *What are the categories of offenders that are managed?*
- *How does this differ from the Californian site in the last task?*
- *Having read this section and the information contained in the two sites, list your reasons as to why that might be the case.*

Bichard Inquiry

Although the Bichard Inquiry did not relate directly to MAPPA, the circumstances of it do relate directly to the management of a PDO in the wake of the murders of Jessica Chapman and Holly Wells by Ian Huntley in Soham, Cambridgeshire, in August 2002.

Following the conviction of Huntley, it was reported that he had been subject to eight separate sexual allegations between 1995 and 1999 within the Humberside area, where he then resided (Rogers, 2006, p47). None of these allegations resulted in convictions at court, but the police were made aware of them. When Huntley applied for employment as a caretaker at Soham Village College, a routine vetting process was put in place and Cambridgeshire Police requested information from their colleagues in Humberside. The fact that Huntley had come to the attention of Humberside Police, but was never convicted, was not passed on. This is the area focused on by Sir Michael Bichard, who led the Inquiry.

When the report was published in 2004, it contained 31 recommendations. As a result, an online facility called VISOR (Violent and Sexual Offenders Register) was made available to all police forces from 2005 (Rogers, 2006, p48) and will be a key tool not only for the Police Service to share intelligence and exchange information, but also for MAPPA.

National Offender Management Service

The establishment of the National Offender Management Service (NOMS) is a merger of the management of the Prison and Probation Services. The idea developed from a report by Patrick Carter, published in 2003, in which he recommended a single management structure and 'end to end offender management' (Newburn, 2007, p678). The actual service is being developed via ten Regional Offender Managers (ROMs) and the management of the newly amalgamated service commenced in June 2005.

CHAPTER SUMMARY

The Police Service has travelled a long way since the time of the Brixton riots in 1981. At that time, the service largely worked as a single entity and even employed its own solicitors as a prosecuting service (the Crown Prosecution Service did not come into existence until five years later). At that time, the Police Service saw its position as remaining isolated from other agencies, given its enforcement function. The Scarman Report (1981) was the first to move the Police Service closer to the community, and this trend continued and culminated with the CDA 1998. Police now take the lead in many multi-agency forums around the country and this has led to the development of new skills for police managers and practitioners alike. It has also enhanced the ethos of 'policing by consent' and overall public accountability; and by consulting with the public, there has been an improvement to policing services in the communities they serve.

REFERENCES

Bichard, Sir Michael (2004) *The Bichard Inquiry Report* (HC 653). London: The Stationery Office.

Bratton, W J (1998) *Turnaround.* New York: Random House.

Gilling, D (2007) *Crime Reduction and Community Safety: Labour and the Politics of Local Crime Control.* Cullompton: Willan.

Hayman, A (2009) *The Terrorist Hunters.* London: Bantam Press.

Hill, D (2001) After the purge. *The Guardian*, 6 February.

Ireland, J, Ireland, C and Birch, P (eds) (2009) *Violent and Sexual Offenders.* Cullompton: Willan.

McLaughlin, E (2007) *The New Policing.* London: Sage.

McLaughlin, E and Muncie, J (2001) *Controlling Crime.* London: Sage.

McLaughlin, E, Muncie, J and Hughes, G (eds) (2003) *Criminological Perspectives: Essential Readings.* London: Sage.

Morgan, J (1991) *Safer Communities: The Local Delivery of Crime Prevention Through the Partnership Approach.* London: Home Office.

Newburn, T (2003) *Handbook of Policing.* Cullompton: Willan.

Newburn, T (2005) *Policing: Key Readings.* Cullompton: Willan.

Newburn, T (2007) *Criminology.* Cullompton: Willan.

Ratcliffe, J (2008) *Intelligence-led Policing.* Cullompton: Willan.

Rogers, C (2006) *Crime Reduction Partnerships.* Oxford: Oxford University Press.

Rogers, C and Blakemore, B (eds) (2009) *Problem Oriented Partnerships: A Reader.* Cullompton: Willan.

Scarman, Lord Leslie (1981) *Scarman Report: The Brixton Disorders.* London: HMSO.

South Liverpool Housing (SLH) Group (2007) *Anti-social Behaviour.* Available online at www.audit-commission.gov.uk/housing/goodpractice/Tenancyandestatemanagement/Pages/asbsouthliverpool.aspx (accessed 20 January 2010).

Stevens, J (2005) *Not For the Faint Hearted.* London: Weidenfeld & Nicolson.

USEFUL WEBSITES

www.audit-commission.gov.uk (Audit Commission)

www.crimereduction.homeoffice.gov.uk (Home Office's Crime Reduction site)

www.homeoffice.gov.uk (Home Office)

www.probation.homeoffice.gov.uk (National Probation Service)

LEGISLATION

Civil Contingencies Act 2004

Crime and Disorder Act 1998

Criminal Justice and Court Services Act 2000

Police and Criminal Evidence Act 1984

9 Criminological perspectives

Introduction

The study of reasons why people commit crime has fascinated societies for centuries. Contributions have been made by jurists, or people who study the impact of law in society, the medical profession, journalists and sociologists. All have added considerably to a discipline that is still developing and one that is more popular, or more intriguing, than ever. The number of criminology-related courses on offer in higher education and the number of applicants they attract is testimony to that assertion. Very few, if any, other disciplines promote such debate among groups of people as do ideas of or reasons why people commit crime. We all may have our own thoughts and what this chapter will seek to do is to provide an insight into the main theories of criminality, which will allow for reflective, informed consideration and future debate. There is no one-size-fits-all theory; if it existed, the remedies to it would have been addressed in one form or another well before now.

The word 'criminology' is first attributed to the French anthropologist Paul Topinard in 1879 and sought to explain criminology as the 'science of understanding the criminal' (Muncie et al., 2010, p13). This was during a period when medical science was challenging existing theories of crime. Before we can look at that in any detail, we need to start with a theory that is as influential today as the day it was written: the theory of Classicism.

Bloody Code – recap

To appreciate fully the impact of Classicism we need to recall what we looked at in Chapter 7 and the references to the 'Bloody Code'. Over 200 offences at the time of its existence carried the death penalty, from the most minor to the most serious. Penalties were disproportionate to the offence, were far too draconian and most were aimed at punishing the body by inflicting pain, or worse. Sentencing was uncertain, however, and often dependent on mercy pleas to the judiciary. As a result, minor offences were dealt with far too harshly and more serious ones merely admonished.

The Criminal Justice System (CJS) was inconsistent, inhumane and iniquitous.

Classicism

It was from this backdrop that a philosopher called Cesare Beccaria, a founder of the Italian school of criminology, published his essay *On Crimes and Punishments* (1764), within a Europe that by now had entered the Enlightenment period (Taylor et al., 1973, p1). Beccaria's theory of Classicism can be summarised as follows.

- All men are equal before the law.
- People make a choice when they commit crime.
- It is freely chosen.
- It is a rational decision.
- It is taken having considered the inevitable punishment in relation to detection.

Beccaria also referred to the issue of punishment and this can be summarised as follows.

- It should be prompt.
- It should be proportionate to the harm to society.
- It should act as a deterrent.

The ideas of Beccaria were in accordance with the philosophy of another writer in England at that period, Jeremy Bentham, who later played a major part in the design of the modern prison. Bentham wrote about the principle of *Utilitarianism* or, as it is often described, 'the greatest happiness of the greatest number'.

The aim of criminal law should be to deter crime, thereby protecting the community, not merely to punish offenders. The law existed for the well-being of all of society, not just the middle and upper classes, who benefited most from the 'Bloody Code'.

Classicism looks forward and seeks to act as a deterrent. It is not eye-for-an-eye and tooth-for-a-tooth, which is *retribution* (punishment) only and backward looking. The central thrust of this theory is *deterrence* and, unlike the 'Bloody Code', it is aimed at the *mind* not the *body*. By fully understanding what a 'sure and certain' punishment would be, a decision is made in the mind of an individual who may be considering committing a crime – a harm against society. A fully informed and conscious decision is taken in the mind of an offender *before* an offence is committed.

This principle or ethic, which is the central core of Classicism, is known as *mens rea* or the 'guilty intent' within criminal law and is the foundation of the CJS today. Without it, a defendant cannot be convicted. Often, in practical terms, it can be described as the *motive*, derived from the *motivation* of the offender.

In practice, the prosecution in a criminal trial must prove three points:

- an offence occurred;

- the offender committed the act;

- the offender intended to do it.

This, together with proportionate sentencing, is Beccaria's lasting legacy to the CJS. Police officers, when gathering evidence against alleged offenders, encounter this principle on a daily basis.

Positivism

As with any theory within criminology, there is an inevitable challenge and, in the case of Classicism, this came initially from within the medical profession, based on research of the natural sciences and the study of social behaviour (McLaughlin and Muncie, 2006, p302). The theories that come under the banner of Positivism are called that because the key elements within them are tangible and can be identified – hence positive. There are three branches to the Positivist school, as shown in Figure 9.1.

The first two theories of the Positivist school are known as the *individual theories*, as they relate to individual people and specific features within them. This is the area where medical science has been focused and where it offered the first challenge to Classicism. This came via another Italian, Army doctor Cesare Lombroso, and his *biological* theory,

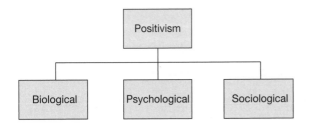

Figure 9.1
Branches of the
Positivist school

published in 1876 as *L'Uomo delinquente* ('The criminal man') (Hale et al., 2005, p65). Lombroso was the founding father of the Positivist theories and part of the Italian school of criminology, who were pioneers of the discipline. Similar to other theories in criminology, there is overlap between the individual theories of *biological* and *psychological positivism* and that will be noticeable here.

Biological positivism

Lombroso conducted studies among serving army personnel and Italian prisoners. He concluded that criminals bore specific physical features, such as enormous jaws, high cheek bones, large ears and head shapes that differed from those typical for the race. People falling into this category were often labelled by him as being 'atavistic' – throwbacks to a primitive age, a term first suggested by Darwin in 1881 (Taylor et al., 1973, p41). Lombroso also carried out studies among prostitutes and concluded that female criminals bore physical features similar to those of males. He continued to research and publish, developing his theory as he did so and, given its significance, other researchers published their work regarding biological features.

What Lombroso did in respect of criminology and criminal justice was to offer an explanation for crime that directly challenged the notion of free will contained in Classicism. For Lombroso and other Positivists, the issue is that criminal behaviour in people possessing these positive features is *determined*; in other words, it is inevitable that criminal behaviour will occur. The remedy, therefore, is not punishment but treatment, in this case medical.

Looking back to the work of Lombroso, at first glance a natural reaction may be one of scepticism, but he laid the foundations for far-reaching research, albeit some of it grossly misplaced. His work led to the development of the eugenics movement, particularly in the USA, where laws were passed restricting immigration from certain parts of the world. Some states passed laws allowing psychosurgery, including the frontal lobotomy – practices that continued into the 1970s. The most distasteful eugenics ever practised were those of Nazi Germany during the Second World War (Lilly et al., 1989, pp43–4).

Biological positivism also had benign influences on the criminal law in England and Wales, by mitigating the impact of Classicism and recognising the determinism within an individual, as the following illustrates.

REFLECTIVE TASK

Go to the following website, which lists the provisions of the Infanticide Act 1938: www.opsi.gov.uk/RevisedStatutes/Acts/ukpga/1938/cukpga_19380036_en_1.

Access paragraph 2 and answer the following questions.

- *What verdict may be reached in place of murder?*
- *What have the jury to be satisfied of before deciding the above?*
- *How old does the child have to be?*

REFLECTIVE TASK *continued*

Linked to the above, there has been recent debate regarding this law. Go to www. independent.co.uk/news/uk/crime/scrap-outdated-infanticide-law-say-judges-495016.html and, having read the article, answer the following questions.

- *What do the judges feel about this law?*

- *What is of 'particular concern'?*

Having read part of the Act and what the senior judges have said recently, list any reasons that you feel may directly affect a mother after the birth of a child.

Psychological positivism

The issue of psychology plays a major and ever increasing role in numerous aspects of crime and criminal justice. The current techniques connected to police investigative interviewing were written by psychologists and this discipline is being proactively pursued further by several academic research centres. Television programmes such as *Cracker* have projected the role of the 'offender profiler' into the public domain and several universities offer courses on this subject. Research is taking place in many areas linked to psychology, but the search for the 'criminal mind' is ongoing.

Mental disorder is often temporary, but under English and Welsh law mental disorder is not a defence to crime, only mitigation. There are exceptions that apply in circumstances that are encountered on occasions within the CJS.

One theory that is recognised as having considerable credibility is the work of Hans Eysenck, initially published in the 1960s. He looked at three areas of the personality:

- extraversion;

- neuroticism;

- psychoticism.

Criminals scored highly on all three counts (Newburn, 2007, p162).

REFLECTIVE TASK

Consider the issues Eysenck raised as to causes of crime and complete your own list. Try to keep it to psychological or mental disorder issues, e.g. withdrawn personality, anxious disposition.

Having completed the list, go to www.docstoc.com/docs/2216719/Eysenck%EF%BF%BDs-Theory-of-Personality—Crime (it may take time to download – please be patient).

Having accessed the site, go to Slide 10 and see if your list tallies with that of Eysenck.

REFLECTIVE TASK *continued*

Now answer the following based on the slide presentation.

- *6 – What did he argue against?*
- *6 – How does criminal behaviour occur?*
- *14 – Who are most likely to be criminals?*
- *14 – What personality traits will they display?*
- *36 – In relation to psychology, what does it say about the work of Eysenck?*

Sociological positivism

One of the earliest sociologists to write about crime was Emile Durkheim. His 1897 work paved the way for the American 'Chicago School' of criminology to flourish and heralded a major new beginning in criminology. Durkheim wrote that crime was an inevitable part of society and will never be eradicated. It serves a purpose by laying down and reinforcing the moral boundaries within society, which is a sign of a healthy one.

PRACTICAL TASK

Go to http://news.bbc.co.uk/1/hi/uk_politics/1627061.stm and read the article that refers to a case where a British couple arranged to adopt twin girls from the USA. The arrangement was a private one and made via the internet. While there is sympathy and understanding for childless couples such as the one featured here, the affair triggered off a public reaction.

Having read the article, answer the following questions.

- *What did Dr Fox say about the reaction of the House?*
- *What did Mr Milburn say about the purpose of adoption?*
- *What profit motive did he condemn?*
- *What should not be the main interest?*

The above is a good example of what Durkheim means by the moral boundaries of society; although it was perfectly legal at the time, it has since become an offence for the reasons outlined in the article.

Anomie
Durkheim also wrote about the changes in society, from what he called the mechanical to the organic, and their effect on individuals. What he was concerned about was social

integration and solidarity, and where human ambition fits into that equation. For Durkheim, solidarity was brought about by two forces:

- *integration* – cohesion brought about by common beliefs;
- *regulation* – the restrictions on behaviour and ambitions.

During a study into suicide rates across Europe, where to attempt suicide was a criminal offence in most countries at the time, Durkheim identified that rates rose during periods of social change, due to insufficient regulation. This situation he called *anomie* or 'normlessness'. This assertion is perceived as a critique of modern industrialisation and the changes in the economic structure, with specific references to the personal ambition that may be inspired (Newburn, 2007, p173). This particular point is the one that was later developed by Robert Merton in his *Strain Theory*. Although Durkheim makes reference to the economy, he is not writing from a Marxist perspective on crime, where theory is dictated totally by economic issues.

Chicago School

So far we have looked at crime being a rational act performed by a free-thinking individual who has exercised choice in doing so, and crime being an unavoidable occurrence due to either a biological or psychological feature or features within the individual. The latter theories were very much set in a medical model. Criminology had developed from philosophers writing about law to medical researchers publishing the results of their research – whatever the theory, there is an inevitable challenge. We have looked at the contribution of Durkheim to the debates, but the arrival of the social theories of crime was heralded by the research of the University of Chicago from the 1920s onwards. The first, conducted in 1925 by Robert Park and Ernest Burgess, focused on the ecology of the ever developing industrialised city and, as regards crime, one area in particular that signalled that crime was not something to do with an individual's genetic make-up, but arose from the social environment or society itself. In keeping with other Positivist theories, sociological positivism sees the improvement in the environment, such as improved employment opportunities, good schools, and stable backgrounds and communities, as the way to address crime, not punishment as per Classical theories.

Zones in transition

Park and Burgess studied the city of Chicago and concluded that the city developed in zones, called 'concentric zones' (Jewkes and Letherby, 2002, p23) or circular rings, from the centre outwards. This depiction of the city with the concentric rings has become known as the 'Burgess model' (Figure 9.2) and is widely used in subjects such as urban geography.

The city centre contained the high street shopping and businesses, and the areas further towards the city suburbs and the outer zones became more affluent and were subject to less crime. But the zone in between these was run down and contained the cheapest housing, dilapidated buildings and acute social problems, such as unemployment, poor

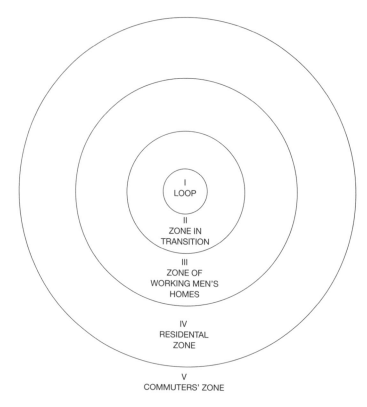

Figure 9.2 Burgess model of a city, depicting the zone in transition

health and education, and the highest crime rates. It seemed to be an area that people aspired to get away from as quickly as possible, and one where people seemed unwilling to put down social roots and hence community ties. They labelled this area as the *zone in transition*. They named it thus as this was exactly what it was – an area to which immigrants came and where they found low-rent accommodation and jobs, but when their economic circumstances improved, they immediately moved to the outer suburbs. Industrialisation was creating communities that were transitory, and as a result traditional norms and values had broken down (Jewkes and Letherby, 2002, p23).

It is important to stress that this research and the applied criminology does not seek to *blame* any immigrant group or racial or ethnic minority regarding the zone in transition; it is merely highlighting the social pressures and chaotic lifestyle encountered by many people living there.

In the last few years, many inner cities in the UK have benefited from substantial inward investment, much of it from private sources, such as property developers. That is easily recognised from the numbers of builders' skips that have been seen outside Victorian buildings in inner cities; clearly, major refurbishments have been made. However, negative images of the inner city still abound and, in relation to perceptions concerning the fear of crime, the inner city is still a place in the eyes of some that is not safe.

REFLECTIVE TASK

In the previous chapter we mentioned problems associated with two of Britain's inner-city areas, Brixton and Toxteth. In keeping with that theme, go to http://news.bbc.co.uk/1/hi/uk_politics/965111.stm and answer the following questions.

- *In order to receive the money, what do councils have to do?*

- *What did the Deputy Prime Minister say that the money would do?*

- *What did the Conservative Party spokesman say he would do?*

Write down the social factors that are frequently associated with the inner city and consider how many of them, in your opinion, are causes of crime.

Social disorganisation

Work published in 1942 by Chicago School theorists Clifford Shaw and Henry McKay, who looked at juvenile offending rates, confirmed much of the findings by Park and Burgess; as such, the zone in transition concept became influential in criminology and the idea of social or environmental factors being causes of crime a powerful one. Despite critiques, it remains so to this day, as we can see from the BBC news article in the last task.

Shaw and McKay took things a stage further. They concluded that children living in such an area are often subject to contradictory standards and behaviour as opposed to a stable, consistent and conventional pattern (Newburn, 2007, p192). They pointed out that children in the wealthier suburbs had traditional and recognised organisations and groups, such as churches, schools and a more structured family background. Due to the nature of the zone in transition, families were under greater strain and offending was a product of *social disorganisation.* Children mixed with children from similar backgrounds and became involved in delinquency via a *cultural transmission* of values passed from generation to generation (Newburn, 2007, p193).

Differential association

Edwin Sutherland, another member of the Chicago School, developed his theory of *differential association* in 1947. It clearly builds on the social disorganisation of Shaw and McKay, but, unlike disorganisation, which implies a hit-and-miss approach and something of a lottery, Sutherland sees differential association as being much more structured and linked to community groups and values, but, as for Shaw and McKay, more likely in areas where crime rates were higher. People, he believed, learned criminality by being exposed to criminal values and learned the techniques of doing so in exactly the same way as other skills are acquired, via communication and interaction with others. Sutherland argued that persons may come into contact with 'definitions favourable to violation of law' or 'definitions unfavourable to violation of law' (Lilly et al., 1989, p56). This theory is more than just 'who you mix with' – although that is an element, it is more associated with criminal families and careers.

It perhaps goes some way to explaining why we see a proliferation of criminal gangs associated with specific geographical areas.

Strain Theory

Although written by another American academic at a similar time as the Chicago School, Robert Merton, who published his work on *Strain Theory* in 1938, was not a member of it. He did draw upon the work of Durkheim and his anomie thesis but, while social change and lack of regulation were the causes for Durkheim, Merton saw cultural goals as the cause of anomie.

For Merton, the overriding cultural goal in American society is material success and this is measured by material possessions and wealth. American society prides itself on an ethic of opportunity for all and, as a consequence, any member of American society, via hard work, can achieve the American dream. Anybody can go from 'the Little House on the Prairie to the White House'. In reality, that is all it is – a dream. There can only be one Donald Trump in New York City.

In a capitalist society, there will inevitably be winners and losers, irrespective of the success or otherwise of the economy. Capitalism creates inequality; you take your social class from your economic position within it. As a consequence, if you are unemployed or employed in a low-wage menial job, you will be at the bottom of the economic pile and your chances of making it to the White House are extremely slim at best. At the time that Merton published this work, racism was endemic in American society; it was 30 years before Dr Martin Luther King, the great civil rights leader, made his famous 'Promised land' speech.

Strain Theory was aimed at the lower working classes and those ethnic minorities who were discriminated against on the grounds of race, as the structure of society limits the opportunities for some groups more than others. The majority will still conform and lead law-abiding lives (Newburn, 2007, p176). These issues, economic deprivation and race, are examples of the *strains* in American society and, in that context, offenders could be perceived to be victims of the system. Merton is quoted as saying, 'A cardinal American virtue, ambition, promotes a cardinal American vice, deviant behaviour' (Newburn, 2007, p175). Of course, the theory can be applied to any capitalist society, such as the UK.

The non-conformers or victims of the anomie can utilise four *deviant adaptations* (Newburn, 2007, p176):

- innovation;
- ritualism;
- retreatism;
- rebellion.

They are shown in Table 9.1; the final adaption (conformity) signifies acceptance, or in this case adherence to social norms and the criminal law.

Table 9.1 Merton's typology of individual adaptations to environmental pressures

Type of adaptation	Cultural goal	Institutionalised means
I. Conformity	+	+
II. Innovation	+	−
III. Ritualism	−	+
IV. Retreatism	−	−
V. Rebellion	±	±

Note: + signifies acceptance, − signifies rejection, and ± signifies rejection of prevailing goal or means *and* substitution of new goal or means.

Source: Adapted from Merton (1957, p150).

Innovation is worthy of further comment. The *cultural goal* is accepted by innovative individuals, but they may not have the legal means to achieve it because of the structure in society. To do so, they may resort to criminality.

PRACTICAL TASK

In relation to Merton's 'innovation', what offences/offenders readily spring to mind; and what offences do not readily spring to mind? List your reasons for both answers.

Go to www.rart.gov.uk and follow the links to:

- *North West RART;*

- *News: 2009;*

- *Sep 2009: Smuggling couple go to prison.*

Read the content of the report and answer the following questions.

- *Why was the couple sent to prison?*

- *What offences were involved in total?*

- *What did the spokesperson from the SOCU say about the legislation?*

Merton's 'innovation' could easily be applied to serious and organised crime. Drug trafficking for large profits perhaps comes to mind first and it was those activities that the government had in mind when the Proceeds of Crime legislation was passed. Something that does not feature as prominently is what we call 'white-collar crime', also known as 'crime of the suites', as much takes place hidden from public view. If your answers contained that aspect, that would be a legitimate critique of Merton, given that the theory is clearly aimed at lower working-class deviancy.

157

Labelling Theory

Labelling Theory falls under the heading of 'interaction theories' and offers a challenge to the main theories that we have looked at so far: Classicism, Positivism and Strain Theory. It actually started being formulated in the 1930s, but it was the 1960s before it finally arrived. It is based on how certain acts within society are perceived and how particular individuals behave, hence the interaction element. There are two main components to the theory.

1. The manner of how a particular behaviour is labelled as deviant.

2. The effect of that labelling on an individual.

(Jewkes and Letherby, 2002, p27)

In respect of the first element, what the researchers looked at was *why* a specific act was labelled as criminal, not who did it or why. It is often written within criminology that crime is a 'social construct' – that means simply that crime is what society deems it to be. There is no fixed or immovable definition of what crime is. Take homicide – is it *always* treated as a crime, that is, murder?

REFLECTIVE TASK

Write down as many forms of homicide as you can think of, e.g. deaths resulting from an escape of chemicals from a factory.

- *How many are classed as murder and are triable via the CJS?*

'Social rules are the creation of specific social groups' (McLaughlin et al., 2003, p246). This means that certain groups in society have power over others and the power to decide the issue over social construction, that is, what is crime? The groups we are talking about here are the middle and upper classes having power over the lower classes, where the focus of the criminal law has traditionally been focused. For example, definitions of crime alter from place to place and over time; remember that, when we looked at Durkheim earlier in the chapter, to attempt suicide at the time of Durkheim's work was a crime. That changed with the Suicide Act 1961 and to attempt suicide was no longer considered a crime in England and Wales. Currently there is an ongoing debate regarding assisted suicide, which remains a criminal offence in England and Wales, but not so in Switzerland, and there are signs that the situation may alter shortly in this country. So to apply Labelling Theory to that situation, does it mean that a person assisting with the suicide of a chronically sick person in England and Wales is a criminal per se and, therefore, the act is wrong and punishable by society, or a saint acting in the interests of the person suffering and, therefore, the act is an act of mercy?

REFLECTIVE TASK

Consider the above paragraph and write down your thoughts and answers in relation to the question posed in the last sentence.

The second element to Labelling Theory relates to the reaction of others to people who have been labelled and how that label affects them.

Once labelled, people tend to behave in a manner that fits the label. For example, those at school who have special educational needs are routed that way within the education system and, once thus labelled, are socialised that way and *behave* accordingly. The interaction with others will be on the basis of the individual having special needs, thus being labelled first and foremost, and considered a person and individual second. The same applies to people who have been dealt with via the CJS; they are considered 'different' from the rest of society. Also, as others become aware of the label, they *expect* them to behave in a way that fits the label; in other words, they are victims of stereotyping. In the case of a convicted shoplifter, if that person is seen in a shop, people will *expect* him or her to be there for the purposes of theft and for no other reason.

REFLECTIVE TASK

Cast your mind back to school and the pupils who consistently breached school/class discipline and answer the following.

- *Were the offending pupils different each time or were they the same on most occasions?*

- *When a new staff member arrived to teach the class, who did they first look to when an incident occurred in class?*

- *When a punishment was consistently applied to a pupil, what effect did it have on that individual?*

Marxist Theory

Karl Marx wrote very little about crime per se; however, his work has been interpreted and applied to crime and criminal justice by others. Having just discussed Labelling Theory and the power of social groups over others, it is natural to turn to Marx. Everything for Marx emanates from the 'means of production' or, to put it another way, the economy. As we mentioned in the section on Strain Theory, capitalism creates inequalities in terms of social class, and increases the power of certain groups over others.

Capitalism relies on mass consumption and maintaining society's insatiable wants. To do that, it is crucial that there are workers who are both consumers and producers. It is in the interests of the ruling classes that the wages paid to workers are as low as possible, in order to maximise profits. This will no doubt lead to conflict; however, in order to mitigate the conflict it is important to create a reserve army of workers, the unemployed for example, who are ready to take the jobs of the errant workers. Also, in respect of the criminal law, laws are passed that criminalise the actions of the proletariat, or the working class, and protect the interests of the bourgeois or ruling class, in order to maintain the means of production and their class interests (McLaughlin et al., 2003, p250).

Crime also acts in the following ways in society.

- [It] reduces surplus labour by creating employment within the criminal justice system; (consider the number of private companies that are delivering services within the criminal justice system).

- [It] creates a situation where the exploited proletariat focus their attention on their own class, who have been deemed criminal, rather than concentrate on their own exploitation by the bourgeoisie.

(McLaughlin et al., 2003, p250)

The next task will focus on the miners' strike in 1984–85 and the part that the Police Service played in it. Most police officers who served in that long industrial dispute will privately admit that it was not the finest hour for the Police Service. Forces from all around the country were drafted into the main coalfields and pit villages, and some of the tactics implemented were controversial, for example manning roadblocks on motorways to prevent pickets from attending at nearby pits where miners were still working. For this, police used the common law provisions of preventing a breach of the peace. After the collapse of the court trials following the major pit disturbances, the government passed the Public Order Act 1986.

PRACTICAL TASK

Go to http://news.bbc.co.uk/1/hi/uk/3494024.stm and, having read the report and the above paragraph, answer the following questions.

- *What was Margaret Thatcher not going to let happen?*

- *Who had she appointed and why?*

- *What were despatched around coalfields and which area was a specific target?*

- *What happened at Orgreave and what did the police do to combat it?*

- *What did the pickets fail to do?*

Realist criminology

Right Realism

This theory within criminology first emerged in the mid-1970s, but it was at the end of that decade that its influence began to be felt in terms of policy. An expression that has become familiar within criminology nowadays is 'What works?'. This means that any practical measures that can be implemented that reduce crime and disorder should be seen as successful and considered good practice. This emanates from *Right Realism.*

Right Realism challenged the apparent failure of the rehabilitation policies, largely based on sociological positivism, that were implemented after the Second World War. It pointed to the ever rising recorded crime rates, especially since the 1950s. This, to the main advocates of Right Realism – James Q Wilson in particular, who was co-author of 'Broken windows' – was sufficient evidence of failure. Also, the issue of the *fear of crime*, particularly street crime, had come to the fore, mainly through crime surveys (1974 in the USA and 1982 in Britain) and, as we saw with 'Broken windows' in Chapter 8, the focus is primarily concerned with street-crime offences and their prevention.

The ideas of the Right Realists are closely aligned to those of the American political right wing and, following the election of Republican President Ronald Reagan in 1981, the influence of these ideas was enhanced by the appointment of James Q Wilson as the crime adviser to the President. In terms of the UK, politically there was a 'meeting of minds' across the Atlantic between Ronald Reagan and Conservative Prime Minister Margaret Thatcher, elected in 1979. This formed the alliance of the 'New Right' and saw Right Realist policies influencing British institutions, for example in the establishment of the Home Office Crime Prevention Unit in 1983, as mentioned in the previous chapter.

Wilson also advocated the return of *deterrence* in sentencing (McLaughlin et al., 2003, p335) – clearly influenced by Classicism. For Wilson, the overreliance on rehabilitation practised since the end of the war had not worked and had certainly had not reduced crime in any way. In fact, we had witnessed great rises. While Wilson does not go into detail about the causes of crime, he does reject any notions of sociological positivism. He urges government to find measures that bring about 'desirable changes in the level of criminal victimisation' (Newburn, 2007, p274). In practical terms, this explains the rise of *situational crime prevention*, as mentioned in Chapter 8.

This is linked to the thoughts of another proponent of Right Realism, Charles Murray, who is famous for a number of controversial publications, one of them being *Does Prison Work?*. Up until the 1990s we had seen the prison population at around 45,000 in the UK, but by 2009 it had risen to around 85,000. Murray was targeting the so-called 'soft sentencing' of community-based sentences and pointing to their failure. These thoughts certainly did not fall on deaf ears within the New Right, and American prisons saw major increases in their populations. His ideas were formally adopted by the then Conservative government by the public announcement at their annual conference in 1993 of 'Prison works' – this was in the wake of the James Bulger case (see Chapter 7).

Murray introduced the concept of the 'underclass'. For Murray, people coming into this category are not just poor but are identifiably so by their behaviour. This can be evidenced by unkempt homes, drunken behaviour and the inability to retain employment for more than weeks at a time. Their children follow a similar pattern of poor schooling and behaviour, and feature highly among local juvenile offenders (Newburn, 2007, p273). On this tack he referred to the decline in marriage and hence the stable background for children as a breeding ground eventually for crime. This is linked to an overreliance on state benefits. In particular, he refers to single parents as being incapable of providing a suitable and stable background for children (Newburn, 2007, p273).

This undoubtedly led the then Prime Minister Margaret Thatcher to set up the somewhat ill-fated Child Support Agency and certainly led her successor, John Major, to target apparent abuses of the state welfare system by single parents.

Left Realism

The development of *Left Realism* was a break away from the mould of twentieth-century American-led theories, as this was a British initiative, mainly the work of criminologist Jock Young.

One of the key features of Left Realism in respect of the causes of crime is that it introduces the issue of *relative deprivation* – the level of deprivation in relation to other social groups. There are similarities here with Strain Theory and perhaps recognition that social welfare policies since the Second World War have brought about improved living standards and have largely banished absolute deprivation, or poverty per se. However, the issue of deprivation remains a contributory factor in the causes of crime.

Young introduced what he called the 'square of crime', detailed in Figure 9.3.

Both realist theories, in contrast to other criminological theories, involve the *victim* and a key component of Left Realism focuses in that area, as can be seen on the figure. Right

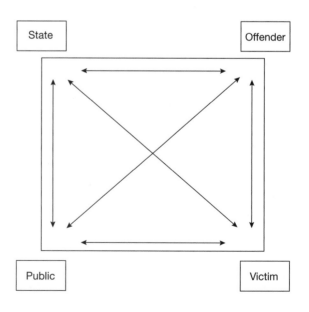

Figure 9.3 The square of crime

Realism includes the victim by highlighting the fear in relation to street crime and argues for control mechanisms, such as a return to deterrence via sentencing, high-visibility policing and situational crime prevention measures, such as CCTV.

Left Realism is far more holistic in approach, which is where the square of crime plays its part. Crime rates are caused by the social relationships of the four points in the square and any explanation that omits one or more is inadequate (Newburn, 2007, p267).

For Young, this presents itself as follows:

> *To control crime from a realist perspective involves intervention at each part of the square of crime: at the level of the factors which give rise to the putative offender (such as structural unemployment), the informal system (such as lack of public mobilisation), the victim (such as inadequate target hardening) and the formal system such as ineffective policing.*
>
> (cited in Newburn, 2007, p267)

Left Realism takes issues in relation to the victim seriously; it refers to matters such as domestic violence and advocates the use of victim surveys, in order to gauge the level of victimisation in that regard. While some theories give the impression that criminality is played out as a working-class offender preying on a materially comfortable middle-class victim, Left Realism rejects that view. It points out that most crime is in fact *intra-class*, that is, working class on working class, and victims are likely to be from that social group.

Left Realism provided the intellectual framework for some governmental policy implementations, particularly in relation to the measures under the Crime and Disorder Act (CDA) 1998, as we discussed in the previous chapter. For example, local crime surveys or the audit of crime have clear links, but other government policy issues such as 'New Deal', aimed at the unemployed, would be in this category. The improved availability of nursery places for young mothers of preschool children is aimed at allowing parents the opportunity to access further training or employment. This would alleviate their reliance on state benefits, as depicted by Right Realists such as Charles Murray, and also reduce the potential for relative deprivation and causes of crime, as per Left Realism.

These are often called *social crime prevention* policies and at first sight do not directly relate to potential causes of crime. However, in respect of Left Realism, the concept of relative deprivation as a cause of crime should not be underestimated.

C H A P T E R   S U M M A R Y

The theories that we have looked at in this chapter have at some stage been the basis for government policy and this is how research informs practice.

As we have seen, some of the theories overlap or draw on each other in some way; all have added greatly to the discipline or science of criminology, from Classicism to the Chicago School. The initial Positivist research was based in the medical field and it is this legacy that causes some commentators to refer to criminology as a science. As we look at human beings and search for the reasons why they do, or do not, commit crime, it seems a fair description.

Often, the theories influence policy but we are not aware of them. For example, one of the most quoted soundbites of the late twentieth century in the UK became famous via Labour Prime Minister Tony Blair. He first quoted it while in Opposition and prior to his first election as Prime Minister in 1997. If we look closely at it, we can see the criminology at work:

> *Tough on crime and tough on the causes of crime.*

Being 'tough on crime' – Right Realism; being 'tough on the causes of crime' – Left Realism.

The 'catch-all' theory has yet to be researched and written. Whether you are a Marxist or a Right Realist, you will agree at least on one point: criminology remains an intriguing and ever developing discipline.

Hale, C, Hayward, K, Wahidin, A and Wincup, E (2005) *Criminology.* Oxford: Oxford University Press.

Jewkes, Y and Letherby, G (eds) (2002) *Criminology: A Reader.* London: Sage.

Lilly, J, Cullen, F and Ball, R (1989) *Criminological Theory: Context and Consequences.* London: Sage.

McLaughlin, E and Muncie, J (2006) *The Sage Dictionary of Criminology*, 2nd edition: London: Sage.

McLaughlin, E, Muncie, J and Hughes, G (eds) (2003) *Criminological Perspectives: Essential Readings.* London: Sage.

Merton, R K (1957) *Social Theory and Social Structure*, revised edition. New York: Free Press.

Muncie, J, Talbot, D and Walters, R (2010) *Crime: Local and Global.* Cullompton: Willan.

Murray, C, with Davies, M, Rutherford, A and Young, J (2000) *Does Prison Work?* London: Civitas/Sunday Times.

Newburn, T (2007) *Criminology.* Cullompton: Willan.

Taylor, I, Walton, P and Young, J (1973) *The New Criminology.* London: Routledge.

www.anzsoc.org (Australia/New Zealand Society of Criminology)

www.asc41.com (American Society of Criminology)

www.britsoccrim.org (British Society of Criminology)

www.crimlinks.com (the CrimLinks site is maintained by Teesside University)

www.manhattan-institute.org (Manhattan Institute for Policy Research, but contains good links to criminology)

Crime and Disorder Act 1998

Infanticide Act 1938

Public Order Act 1986

Suicide Act 1961

10 Future directions

Introduction

Within this chapter we shall revisit and summarise some of the information provided in previous chapters, and consider the future direction of the CJS. We do not have a crystal ball to map out the direction and future of criminal justice accurately, but we can consider what factors may shape future state responses to criminal justice.

Recent history provides a number of examples of events that have had a significant impact on criminal justice policy and direction, such as the Brixton riots, miscarriages of justice, the Stephen Lawrence Inquiry and the murder of James Bulger. More recent events, such as the terrorist atrocities in New York, Madrid and London, the growth of technology and the worldwide credit crunch, provide new challenges for effective criminal justice responses.

We have already seen evidence of how the Labour government has approached criminal justice since 1997. No area of the CJS has been left untouched and wholesale reform has taken place. Whether these interventions have been effective or not is still open to debate, but one thing that is certain is that government will continue to be challenged to find effective solutions for the problems of crime and disorder, and to deal effectively with offenders, victims and witnesses.

In Chapter 1 we considered various models of criminal justice, highlighting the welfare and justice models, and the crime control and due process models, and considered punitive/ retributivist regimes, contrasting them with those adopting a rehabilitative/treatment approach. Examples have been provided of the different approaches adopted and, as the nature of politics changes and certain events dictate, these approaches will continue to be modified.

Change of government

The year 2010 will see another general election and the likelihood of a different party in government. If the Labour Party is able to retain power, its current criminal justice strategy will continue (see page 5). But what are the implications should another political party, such as the Conservatives or Liberal Democrats, be voted into power? Further change will be inevitable and it is likely, once again, that significant change and reform will take place within the CJS. David Cameron, in his keynote address to delegates at the Conservative Party conference in Manchester (8 October 2009) made it quite clear that the Conservative Party would reform the police, the courts and the prisons.

REFLECTIVE TASK

Consider the implications of a change of government and how this would manifest itself within the management and delivery of criminal justice. Write down the advantages and disadvantages of change and, in particular, consider the impact on offenders, victims and witnesses.

Let us consider some of the changes that the two main opposition parties to the Labour government are considering, starting with the Conservative Party:

> *Britain's prison system is not working. Half of all crime is committed by previous offenders, and 65 per cent of prisoners re-offend within two years of release.*
> *Our measures will restore confidence in the criminal justice system, re-design prisons for the 21st century, and launch a sentencing and rehabilitation revolution.*
>
> (Conservative Party, 2009a, p7)

Plans for change include increasing the capacity of prisons, making community sentences tougher and more effective, including withdrawing benefit from those who do not attend, enforcing drug rehabilitation requirements, introducing a scheme for offenders to compensate victims, and accelerating the deportation of foreign prisoners.

Planned changes for the Police Service include the removal of bureaucracy, such as stop and search account forms, and certain surveillance authorities (permissions), tougher action on knife crime, and empowering local communities to ensure that police are accountable and that they are meeting the needs of the community.

> Labour's catastrophic mismanagement of the criminal justice system has led to prisons bursting at the seams; the creation of over 3,600 new criminal offences since 1997; and an unprecedented criminalisation of our children.
>
> (Liberal Democrats, 2009)

The Liberal Democratic Party, similarly to the Conservatives, provides a range of proposed changes, such as employing 10,000 more police officers, introducing community justice panels, restorative justice, and rigorous community sentences as an alternative to short-term prison sentences.

PRACTICAL TASK

Prior to the general election in 2010, each of the three main political parties (Labour, Conservatives and Liberal Democrats) will have published their respective election manifestos containing more detailed information about their proposals for criminal justice. Find the election manifesto for each party (each party has its own website), make a list of CJS changes/reforms proposed and compare the different approaches.

We shall now revisit some of the information provided in previous chapters and consider some of the issues that may contribute to reform of the CJS in the future. When considering each chapter, a task will be set that may provide you with a potential theme to develop an academic debate for an assignment.

Courts of Justice

The courts system (see Chapter 2) continues to be modified and governments aspire to introduce services that are fair, efficient and effective. Recent innovations have seen the introduction of Community Justice Courts, the increasing use of specialist courts in an attempt to deal more effectively with issues such as domestic violence, drugs or mental health, and the introduction of a UK Supreme Court.

In April 2009, the government published a green paper, *Engaging Communities in Criminal Justice*. The paper set out three proposals to improve criminal justice services by:

- strengthening the connections between the community, the prosecution, and courts services;

- ensuring justice outcomes are more responsive and visible;

- improving communication between local people and criminal justice services.

(Home Office, 2009a, p2)

Community engagement is seen by government as being the most effective means of inspiring public confidence in the CJS. It provides a vision of those agencies concerned with criminal justice working together in partnership with communities to tackle crime and disorder, deliver justice and provide quality services.

The courts in conjunction with other criminal justice agencies have an important role to play in the development of community engagement and Table 10.1 provides an overview of some of the planned innovations.

Table 10.1 Role of courts and agencies in community engagement

Community prosecutors	Will work with the community and be aware of local concerns that will be reflected in decision making. Thirty pathfinder areas to be introduced in 2009–10 and will involve the police, the courts and other partners.
Community impact statements	Allow the community to voice their concerns to criminal justice services, particularly the courts. Responses and feedback will be provided to the community of how views have been incorporated into the criminal justice process and will highlight outcomes achieved.
Problem solving	Important to help offenders deal effectively with problems that are contributing to recidivism (repeat offending). Aim is to reduce same patterns of offending and to minimise further harm. This approach has already been adopted in the 13 criminal justice areas and plans are to expand this type of approach across England and Wales by March 2012.
Continuity of judges/magistrates	Continuity recognised as being critical for judges/magistrates to build rapport with offenders, and to fully understand and keep track of the offender's personal circumstances. This is particularly useful when reviewing the progress of an offender during a community sentence (Criminal Justice Act 2003, s178).
Intensification of effort	Areas identified as having severe crime and disorder problems and social deprivation will be targeted to provide a more focused and intensive problem-solving capacity, in order to find solutions to underlying problems.
Selection and deployment	Changes in the process of recruiting judges/magistrates to better reflect diverse needs of communities. Involving the community in recruiting processes and providing community engagement and problem-solving training for new appointees.

Source: Home Office (2009a, pp3–6).

REFLECTIVE TASK

The courts have an important role to play in the continued reform of the CJS. It is evident that current government policy sees engagement with communities as the way forward, in order to deal more effectively with crime and disorder problems, and to increase the public's confidence in the CJS.

- *Consider some of the initiatives currently being adopted that involve the courts and what impact they may have on the future delivery of criminal justice.*

- *What problems are likely to occur in implementing the policy of community engagement? Make a list of potential problems and consider how such problems can be overcome.*

- *Who within the community is likely to engage with criminal justice agencies and will those who do engage be able to reflect the needs of their community?*

(Thoughts and answers provided can be compared with future government and academic papers relating to research and evaluation of the approaches adopted.)

Arrest and detention

In Chapter 3, we discussed the notion of police discretion and its influence on police arrest, report and caution or no further action decisions. This was considered in the context of the Scarman Report (1981), miscarriages of justice, and domestic legislation, policy and practice, as well as the requirements of European law and human rights. We gained some useful insights into the impact of the Police and Criminal Evidence Act (PACE) 1984 and the way that it has shaped, and indeed continues to influence, the way that the police arrest and detain suspects. The chapter also raises a number of key issues regarding interview practices and suspects' right to silence.

But planned changes by the Conservative Party will include bringing in a 'repeal bill' to scrap elements of terrorism and crime legislation that are considered contentious (Conservative Party, 2009b). This is expected to include laws on detention without charge, stop and search and, more particularly, section 44 of the Terrorism Act 2000, which some argue gives the police unfettered powers to stop and search anyone on the street. The Conservatives (2009b) point out that police officers made more than 120,000 searches in 2008 under the Terrorism Act 2000, which is a threefold increase from 2007, and yet only 1 per cent led to an arrest, let alone charges or convictions. The issue of stop and search using section 44 powers is also taken up by Lord Carlile of Berriew, QC, who describes some searches in his annual report on the operation of counterterrorism legislation as 'almost certainly' illegal:

> *I have evidence of cases where the person stopped is so obviously far from any known terrorism profile that, realistically, there is not the slightest possibility of him/her being a terrorist, and no other feature to justify the stop. In one situation the basis of the stops being carried out was numerical only, which is almost certainly unlawful and in no way an intelligent use of the procedure.*

> (Carlile, 2009, para. 140)

And so the Conservative Party has unveiled plans to abolish stop and account (when an officer requests a person in a public place to account for themselves) in its entirety as well as recommending that stop and search should be recorded by an officer radioing in search details in order to create a digitally taped or transcribed police log with no forms (Conservative Party, 2009b).

In the lay-by outside the Long Marston Airfield, venue for the Bulldog Bash, two armed officers patrol as sniffer dogs and search teams inspect the bikers they have pulled over in 'intelligence-led' operations conducted under the Terrorism Act 2000. For Slim, being stopped was insulting. The civil servant, who works for the Ministry of Defence, claimed that he had just returned home after eight months in Afghanistan, trying to prevent terrorism – 'It wasn't intelligence-led. It's because I am wearing motorcycle-club patches on my leathers.'

(Bird and Gibb, 2009)

Visit the Bulldog Bash website at www.bulldogbash.eu/ and then research the Human Rights Act 1998 and the circumstances where the police can lawfully breach article 8 of the Act. Debate and consider using anti-terrorist stop and search legislation at events such as the Bulldog Bash.

The Policing Pledge

The recent Policing Pledge seems to be a clear departure from evidence-based policy and particularly 'new public management' as a means of regulating, measuring and assessing the police through a performance framework. This is typically associated with systems, processes and risk aversion, linked to a lack of trust and confidence at all levels of government and policing. Power (1997) goes further by suggesting that new public management is nothing short of the institutionalisation of an audit culture. In marked contrast, the Policing Pledge is part of a reform agenda set out in the government's policing green paper, *From the Neighbourhood to the National* (Home Office, 2008). It provides some guiding principles about what the public can expect from the Police Service, which is now measured against one key target: to increase public confidence that the police and local councils are dealing with crime and anti-social behaviour. This is a part response to the reducing bureaucracy recommendations contained in the Flanagan Report (2008), which covers areas such as new working practices (lean principles), performance culture and risk aversion. It now appears that the Police Service is trying to find different ways of working and the Policing Pledge is intended to foster an environment that allows officers and staff to rediscover their discretion to exercise professional judgement.

The prosecution process

You will recall from reading Chapter 4 that the Crown Prosecution Service (CPS) was formed in 1986 so that prosecutions could be undertaken in the interests of fairness by someone who is legally qualified and who is not identified with the investigative process (RCCP, 1981). Since then there have been a number of reviews and fundamental changes to the powers and roles of the CPS. One significant example is the transfer of the decision on what offence an individual should be charged with from the police to the CPS in more serious cases (Auld, 2001). A recent Justice Committee review of the CPS identifies the pivotal role that the CPS has in developing a professional and robust relationship with the police and in making the police 'better'. 'The CPS, therefore, has a role to play in improving investigations, by demanding more and better evidence from the police at the charging stage' (Justice Committee, 2009, para. 27).

This responsibility isn't without its problems, however, and the position that the CPS currently occupies between the courts and the police is a difficult one, particularly in establishing a clear role and being accepted in that role by existing, older agencies. This seems to have arisen partly out of group psychology and partly from the division of responsibility with other agencies (Glidewell, 1998, para. 16).

Statutory charging

A further area in which the CPS role has changed is that of statutory charging – the decision on what offence, if any, an individual should be charged with. This was implemented as a result of the Auld Review (2001) and the subsequent enactment of the Criminal Justice Act 2003. The Statutory Charging Scheme was rolled out between 2004 and 2006 and the charge decision is now a matter for the CPS in all but minor cases. It also defines the parameters for much of what happens to an individual case in the CJS. While there seems to be broad support for the CPS in making charging decisions, some practical challenges have also been acknowledged. Stephen Wooler CB, Chief Inspector of the CPS, states:

> *Whilst the charging arrangements . . . are very sound and . . . put the decision making in the right place . . . they have, from the operational point of view, some significant disadvantages in making sure that there are quick decisions.*

(Justice Committee, 2009, para.19)

REFLECTIVE TASK

CPS decisions taken under the Charging Scheme are based on the premise that they should prevent an individual being drawn further into the CJS, and therefore succeed in reducing the likelihood that he or she will reoffend. This is in the interests of potential victims and society as a whole, as well as having a benefit to the individual.

- *Reflect on the principles of statutory charging and debate the merits, or otherwise, of the above statement.*

- *For those with experience of the police custody suite or who perhaps know a custody officer, discuss either your or their experiences of the Charging Scheme and how these met with the described principles.*

Stephen Wooler's concerns may explain why there have been proposals to move back from statutory charging. Sir Ronnie Flanagan's independent *Review of Policing* report (2008) recommended consideration of the extension of police charging powers to all cases heard at the Magistrates' Court, and to additional offences subject to trial, either at the

Magistrates' or the Crown Court. This was reiterated by Jan Berry, former Chair of the Police Federation, in her interim report (2008) on progress against the Flanagan Review. If the Conservative Party is elected in 2010, it has pledged to return charging discretion to the custody sergeant for all summary offences, citing the absence of CPS lawyers in some custody suites as part of the reason. It will also allow custody officers the power to charge some either-way offences.

Diversion from prosecution – appropriate and effective, or expedient?

The growth in the number of out-of-court disposals represents a fundamental change to our concept of a CJS. Similarly, the fact that prosecutors can now recommend that an individual be conditionally cautioned, and a prosecution suspended subject to the fulfilment of particular conditions, represents a significant change to the prosecutor's role. These out-of-court disposals have been referred to as a 'paradigm shift' in criminal justice, away from 'due process' in open court (Justice Committee, 2009, para. 59).

REFLECTIVE TASK

I think it is extremely useful to have . . . systems that allow low-level public disorder to be dealt with without prosecutions as long as it is not being used for cases which would otherwise in court be dealt with perhaps more leniently. . . . the question is [have] we drifted towards a huge increase in non-court disposals because it is cheaper [and] . . . have we adequately thought through whether it is better?

(Justice Committee, 2009, para. 49)

Consider the comments above and relate this to the issue of fixed penalty and penalty notices for disorder and minor offences where those who accept them receive the same punishment. Debate whether this is an appropriate alternative to prosecution or should a choice of sentence, where available, be a judicial one and something not available to the police?

The debate has been further ignited by proposals recently announced by the Director of Public Prosecutions (DPP) that suspects will avoid prosecution if action is considered disproportionate (Edwards and Hope, 2009). Under the new *Core Quality Standards* (CPS, 2009), lawyers will have to weigh the cost and time involved in bringing a prosecution against the seriousness of a crime and the harm it has caused. The guidance is intended to encourage 'common sense' in the justice system. For example, a householder accused of assault when arresting a burglar could have the charges withdrawn. We suspect, however, that this debate will continue to rage on!

Crime and punishment

Crime and punishment (see Chapter 5) continues to attract much debate and divide public opinion. Some members of a community would gladly see more criminals incarcerated, while others see the benefit of a more rehabilitative approach with prison seen as a last resort. The state has to find effective solutions to ensure safety within the community, provide deterrents to reduce crime and disorder, and find ways of preventing or reducing reoffending. We have already identified the problem of overcrowded prisons and questioned whether prison actually works (see page 90), and we have also recognised the importance of rehabilitative approaches to punishment. The Labour government (1997–2009) has introduced a number of key statutes that have extended the range of sentencing options, including community sentences and treatment programmes.

The recent introduction of the youth rehabilitation order has provided a generic community sentence for young offenders, has simplified sentencing, and has provided a more flexible and greater range of options for the courts. The aim of youth justice is to prevent offending and reoffending, to consider the welfare of the offender, and also to balance any punishment with the needs and expectations of the victim and community. It is too early to say whether the new legislation and innovative approach to the sentencing of young offenders will work, but there has clearly been an attempt by the government to find solutions through a range of treatment measures that have the potential to deal with some of the causes of crime.

We have already mentioned government plans to increase public confidence in the CJS, set out in their green paper, *Engaging Communities in Criminal Justice*. The paper also sets out a range of measures designed to engage communities in the sentencing process, and also provide the opportunity for the community to visibly see justice in action through a scheme called 'Community Payback'. Table 10.2 provides an overview of some of the planned innovations that directly relate to crime and punishment in England and Wales.

Table 10.2 Planned innovations for crime and punishment

Community Payback	Will target the less serious, less persistent and non-violent offenders. Is seen as a means of punishing an offender to make amends to the community. Offenders will be required to wear a uniform and more information will be provided to the public on payback projects and outcomes achieved.
Asset recovery	Part 5 of the Policing and Crime Act 2009 provides new and stronger measures for seizure of assets from those who profit from crime.
Citizen panels	Will give local people the opportunity to have a say in the type of work undertaken within the Community Payback scheme and also a say on how seized criminal assets are used. There are plans to have 60 panels in place by the end of 2009.
Restorative justice	A youth restorative disposal scheme has been piloted in seven areas during 2009 and current plans are to make restorative justice more widely available to adults in more areas in future years.
Compensation orders	There is an intention to increase efforts to improve the collection and enforcement of compensation orders.

Source: Home Office (2009a, pp6–8).

REFLECTIVE TASK

Some of the recent innovations by government, shown in Table 10.2, have resulted in much debate, with some commentators openly criticising policy and direction.

- *What do you consider to be both the strengths and weaknesses of the above plans to engage the community in Community Payback and asset recovery schemes?*

- *Will public confidence in the CJS be improved or will some of the policies create further problems?*

Human rights organisations have their own strong views – consider the following statement from Liberty:

> *However, some proposals, such as orange 'Community Payback' vests and websites that seek to name and shame, should not form part of government policy. These are cheap attention-grabbing proposals that seek to play to people's sense of revenge – they are not about ensuring justice is delivered.*
>
> *(Coles, 2009, p10)*

Consider the Human Rights Act 1998, particularly article 8 relating to the right to respect for private life, and question whether the proposals are necessary and proportionate. Also consider what sort of approach is being adopted – is it a rehabilitative or a retributive approach? A review of this policy and its implementation provides the basis for a useful academic debate and assignment topic.

Victims

One of the features of Labour's policies of criminal justice has been a marked shift towards victims' rights, which have now moved centre stage in the CJS. You will recall from reading Chapter 6 that the traditional and somewhat formal role of the victim was that of giving evidence in court as a witness, but without having much influence on the court's decision. During the 1980s, the victims' movement emerged to reverse what some have described as the 'marginalisation' of victims and the Victims' Charter now sets out the role of the victim in the CJS as well as the service that they should expect. And, of course, the Criminal Justice Act 2003 is aimed at shifting the CJS in favour of victims, witnesses and communities. Measures included in the accompanying white paper included restricting bail for defendants accused of committing offences while on bail, encouraging early guilty pleas by indicating the likely sentence for a guilty plea, and expanding the circumstances in which the defendant's previous convictions could be disclosed in court.

In October 2001, the Home Office introduced the victim personal statement (VPS) scheme in England and Wales, which was a feature of the 1996 Victims' Charter. This allows victims to submit a statement prior to trial, describing the effect that the crime has had on them. But because it is judges and magistrates who ultimately decide how an offender should be punished, the statement is of limited use in court and, indeed, you will recall that, while the court is able to take the statement into account in identifying how the offence has affected the victim, the court is unable to consider the victim's opinion when determining a sentence. In the case of *R* v. *Perks* [2000], the Court of Appeal, Criminal Division, directed that a letter from the victim's husband should be disregarded and the victim's VPS treated with an appropriate degree of caution.

The current victim-centred approach is, therefore, problematic and raises a number of issues, including what it would mean practically, legally, politically and philosophically to have a genuine victim-centred system and what such a system might look like. Most commentators agree that the current system is not victim-centred, although some argue that it is possible to convert it into one worthy of the label without fundamental reform (Hall, 2009). And, of course, there are issues based on the assumption that the victim is separate from, and distinguishable from, the offender. Thus, as in Christie's model (see page 97), the victim is blameless and relatively weak (Christie, 1986). Research, however, concludes that criminals are more frequently victimised than non-criminals and that 'victims of violent crime themselves have considerable involvements' (Fattah, 1991, p123).

It should also be remembered that there are occasions when the victim and offender are either related or are friends and, as such, they might be hesitant about the case or may suffer financially or emotionally if the offender is prosecuted. And, of course, there are the vulnerable and marginalised, such as drug addicts, beggars, street sleepers or the mentally ill, and any provisions that reduce defendants' safeguards almost always increase the danger that innocent people will be convicted, leaving offenders undetected and unpunished, an outcome that cannot be said to be in the interest of the victims of crime or the security of society as a whole.

REFLECTIVE TASK

On 26 January 2009, Sara Payne was appointed as the Victims' Champion, an 'independent public' voice for victims of, and witnesses to, crime – Sara's daughter was murdered by a paedophile in July 2000. She now liaises with victims' groups and the government's 60 neighbourhood Crime and Justice Coordinators in England and Wales. Her appointment will pave the way for the appointment of the Victims' Commissioner early in 2010.

Carry out some research on the internet to establish the role of the Victims' Champion.

- *How will the position further highlight and support the plight of victims?*

- *How does the role place the victim centre stage within the CJS?*

Make a list of the potential benefits and continue to monitor the activities of the Victims' Champion to identify the actual benefits achieved.

Youth justice

As we identified in Chapter 7, issues identified with youth crime and offending are subject to constant change. The age of criminal responsibility in England and Wales is ten; in Scotland it is eight, the lowest throughout the European Union. There does not seem any desire to alter that by raising it and dealing with incidents of youth crime in a less formal way.

There are several issues that are concerning the authorities in relation to youth justice at the moment, and these include gangs, the increase in the use of knives, and the availability of cheap alcohol, which leads to anti-social behaviour and associated health risks.

Measures have been introduced to address most if not all of the issues within the Youth Crime Action Plan, which was launched in 2008.

PRACTICAL TASK

Go online to www.homeoffice.gov.uk/documents/youth-crime-action-plan/, where you will find an updated version of the action plan, Youth Crime Action Plan – One Year On. Access the summary document and answer the following questions.

- *Page 4, paragraph 6 – What is the 'offer' to young people?*
- *Page 5 – What are the four main aims?*
- *Page 6 – What does the triple-track approach entail?*
- *Page7 – What is the purpose of the Safer Schools Partnership?*
- *Page 14 – What does it say about 'serious youth violence'?*

Multi-agency approach

It is clear that police will work in a multi-agency environment on a number of levels in the short-to-medium term (see Chapter 8). Some legal provisions have recently been made that empower the Police Service and police authorities to collaborate in respect of the provision of specific services, for example following major disasters or in major crime investigations (Policing and Crime Act 2009, ss5–13). This does not include outside agencies at this stage, but illustrates government thinking. These collaborative provisions are no surprise, given that planned mergers of police forces to form larger 'strategic forces' were strongly proposed in 2006–07 and were only overturned in the light of fierce opposition.

Crime and policing representatives

While the Policing and Crime Act 2009 was being processed through the legislature in 2008, it was proposed that direct elections to police authorities be introduced and those elected would be called 'crime and policing representatives' (CPRs). Each local authority area would elect one so, for example in the case of Merseyside, there would be five CPRs, which would reflect the five local authorities that make up the county. This was in order to enhance public accountability.

In addition to being elected to police authorities, CPRs would automatically be members of the local Crime and Disorder Reduction Partnerships (CDRPs). This was proposed country-wide, with the exception of London.

The British National Party (BNP) made a public statement that it would actively target these elections in order to secure influence over policing and, as a consequence, the provision was dropped. As a CPR and member of a police authority, the office would provide opportunities to lobby not only the most senior members of a police force, but also those of CDRPs. Although the BNP is a legally constituted political party, its ideology and policies are abhorrent to many people. While this provision was dropped by the Policing and Crime Act 2009, the commitment remains to enhance public accountability where possible and the issue of directly elected members of police authorities/CDRPs is likely to be raised again. The BNP issue will need to be addressed one way or another.

Terrorism

We are likely to see the issue regarding the prevention of terrorism being played out at grassroots level in communities, as opposed to what some members of the public think is a detached and remote function based in London. Regions around the country have formed Counter-Terrorism Units (CTUs), which combine the security services and the police. The larger police forces also nominate two police authority members for responsibility for counter-terrorism matters. They currently meet informally every three months (Hayman, 2009, p325).

In March 2008, the government launched the National Security Strategy. As well as harnessing the resources of the police and security services, it also strives to form new partnerships within communities, including the private and voluntary sectors, community and faith organisations and individuals (Hayman, 2009, p315). This is making clear inferences towards an enhanced role for the CDRP and, as this policy is refined, the role will be fully formulated.

The government's counter-terrorism strategy is called CONTEST 2 and contains four strands: Pursue, Protect, Prevent and Prepare. Multi-agency and partnership working will be a key element in the success of the strategy, for example radicalisation within communities has been identified as a problem that needs to be tackled.

> *The Prevent strategy depends upon a unique and ground-breaking range of local, national and international partners. It needs the support of communities and community organisations in this country to protect vulnerable people from radicalisation and recruitment to terrorism.*
>
> (Home Office, 2009b, p15)

REFLECTIVE TASK

The Channel Project is attempting to tackle the problem of radicalisation. Go online to www.timesonline.co.uk/tol/news/politics/article3593700.ece and read the article that explains how the project works. It is too early to make any conclusions about the effectiveness of the strategy, but consider the advantages and disadvantages of this type of approach. What impact will it have on communities and how effective do you feel this project will be in the fight against terrorism?

Criminological perspectives

Trying to predict the next criminological theory that emerges and passes the empirical test is not an easy task. Some patterns are developing and, as discussed in Chapter 9, the area of psychological studies, where research is particularly active, is more likely to witness developments. In keeping with the Positivist theories, there is considerable overlap as the following illustrates.

A study by the Sainsbury Centre for Mental Health, released in November 2009, reports that 80 per cent of crime is committed by people who experienced problems with behaviour as children and teenagers. The report noted that children with mental health issues can experience problems with education, which affect their employment chances, or lock them into low-paying jobs, teenage pregnancies and marital problems later in life (SCMH, 2009).

So far we should be able to identify the links with *psychological positivism* and *sociological positivism* as well as the issue over single parents as identified by Charles Murray (see 'Right Realism' on page 161).

The report goes on to say that the cost of crime in relation to 'conduct problems' is around £60 billion a year. These 'problems' are defined as disobedience, lying, fighting and stealing. However, it is also argued that early-intervention schemes for children identified as being at risk can pay dividends later. For example, a scheme in the USA reduced the costs of crime by $11 for every $1 invested – a considerable saving. The study claims that the most effective programmes, which include preschool-age children, can reduce offending by almost 50 per cent. The costs for the schemes are worthy of note, at about £900 per child for group-based schemes, while home-based support and therapy for the most serious cases costs about £4,000 (SCMH, 2009).

Clearly, the attraction here to any future government is the reduction of costs. We are likely to see more of these empirical studies based on criminological theories, especially in the area of psychology, given the inevitable cuts in public services.

Another area that will undoubtedly lead to further research concerns the development of *globalisation.* A definition of globalisation could be along the lines of, 'The intensification of worldwide social relations which link distant localities in such a way that local happenings are shaped by events occurring many miles away and vice versa' (Newburn, 2007, p868).

Globalisation provides opportunities for crime that were previously inaccessible and, in accordance with the definition above, policing and criminal justice have to respond accordingly. The term 'de-localisation' (Newburn, 2007, p868) is often used to describe the manner in which business, criminal or otherwise, is conducted.

The 'local' aspect is interesting given that, apart from the *individual theories* within Positivism, most of the remainder contains at least an element of local influence, for example *zones in transition* and *differential association.* Consequently, criminology has a strong 'local' core running through it. Durkheim's *anomie* may be applied to the constantly changing nature of society that globalisation brings, but given that his work was written in the late nineteenth century, before it could be credibly applied to the influences of the global world, further empirical research is warranted.

There is some evidence that members of terrorist organisations affiliated to the Global Jihad (Al-Qaeda) are motivated into doing what they are doing by *relative deprivation*, which is a key concept within *Left Realism.* Again, when this theory was formulated, the concept of globalisation was hardly on the horizon.

Therefore, further criminological theories that go some way to explain the reasons for the motivations of crime are likely to be based in a global context. They may be old theories reworked, old wine in new bottles almost, but applied to globalisation.

REFLECTIVE TASK

Go online to www.guardian.co.uk/world/2003/mar/09/terrorism and read the report from The Guardian *newspaper written by a young Algerian male who was living illegally in London. Then answer the following questions.*

- *Why do some people in the Arab world admire Osama bin Laden?*

- *What was Al-Qaeda able to provide for people?*

- *According to the author (Rachid), what is the motivation for terrorism?*

- *What are current Algerians 'bitten by'?*

- *What criminological theory do you think fits this description best of all and why?*

C H A P T E R   S U M M A R Y

This chapter has provided you with a contemporaneous overview of some of the strategies being implemented and issues being debated that will impact on the future direction of policing and the CJS. We find ourselves in an era of facing the challenge of change with the government and its agencies constantly searching for effective solutions to combating crime and disorder.

Communities demand high standards and scrutiny of criminal justice agencies is more intense now than ever before. CJS decisions, activities and performance are analysed in detail by the media and government policies are constantly being criticised despite evidence of success. Take, for example, the recent 'Baby Peter' death in Haringey, London (August 2007), which resulted in a media frenzy, and the resignation of the Haringey council leader, the council cabinet member for children and young people, and the head of children's services, who has since challenged her resignation through the courts. Prior to this event, considerable steps had been taken to provide new law, practice and procedures following lessons learnt from previous events, supported by additional resources and finance, new and more robust inspection regimes, and performance measures – not perfect by any means but a determined effort by government to make improvements. The later event, although tragic and possibly avoidable, fails to be put into perspective against the steps that had been taken to improve services for the protection of children.

Add to this offenders, being managed through the multi-agency public protection arrangements, who occasionally 'slip through the net' and commit serious crime; the courts, which are sometimes criticised for being too lenient or too harsh with sentencing; some victims who continue to feel that they are getting a raw deal from the CJS; and the police who, despite the overwhelming scope of their responsibilities and the considerable steps taken during the last decade to professionalise the service, are quickly pilloried by society when things go wrong.

We have identified that a new government will bring more changes and we hope that you agree that there are no easy answers to some of the problems faced in the struggle against crime and disorder. Government needs to engender public confidence in the CJS and criminal justice styles will continue to change to reflect political, social, economical and environmental factors. It is inevitable that the debate will continue about the balance between the rights of an offender compared to those of a victim.

Since 1997, the Labour government has made profound changes to the CJS and this chapter has provided further evidence of their commitment to continuing the development and implementation of new ideas that may provide suitable and sustainable solutions to the challenges faced. It is too early to say whether some of these initiatives will work in making inroads into reducing crime, rehabilitating offenders, appeasing communities and victims with the introduction of local measures to tackle criminal justice issues, or making communities safer. The new methods and initiatives will be evaluated in due course and, of course, when things do go wrong the media will soon let us know. Change of government during 2010 is a strong possibility and we have also identified within this chapter the potential consequences of a political change.

The practical and reflective tasks within this chapter and throughout the book should have provided you with stimuli, sources and evidence for completion of NOS and assignments. Further academic reading and research will provide you with a more detailed understanding of the CJS and will be necessary for second- and third-year HE students, who will require evidence of wider research and analysis to attain a first-class grade.

REFERENCES

Auld, R (2001) *A Review of the Criminal Courts of England and Wales*. London: Ministry of Justice. Available online at www.criminal-courts-review.org.uk (accessed 2 June 2009).

Berry, J (2008) *Reducing Bureaucracy in Policing: An Interim Report*. London: Home Office.

Bird, S and Gibb, F (2009) Police spend £1m and use terror Act to control the Bulldog Bash but the most aggressive things were pesky wasps. *The Times*, 8 August, p35.

Carlile, Lord Alex (2009) *Report on the Operation in 2008 of the Terrorism Act 2000 and of Part 1 of the Terrorism Act 2006*. London: The Stationery Office. Available online at http://security.homeoffice.gov.uk/news-publications/publication-search/general/Lord-Carlile-report-2009/ (accessed 20 January 2010).

Christie, N (1986) The ideal victim, in Fattah, E A (ed.) *From Crime Policy to Victim Policy*, New York: St Martin's Press.

Coles, A (2009) *Liberty's Response to the Green Paper: Engaging Communities in Criminal Justice*. London: Liberty.

Conservative Party (2009a) *Repair: Plan for Social Reform: Plan for Change*. London: Conservative Party.

Conservative Party (2009b) *Back on the Beat: Now for a Change*. London: Conservative Party.

Crown Prosecution Service (CPS) (2009) *Core Quality Standards*. Available online at www.cps.gov.uk/consultations/cqs_policy.pdf (accessed 30 November 2009).

Edwards, R and Hope, C (2009) New rules will let criminals off the hook. *The Daily Telegraph*, 20 October, p1.

Fattah, E A (1991) *Understanding Criminal Victimisation*. Scarborough, ONT: Prentice Hall.

Flanagan, Sir Ronnie (2008) *The Review of Policing: Final Report*. London: Home Office.

Glidewell, Sir Iain (1998) *The Review of the Crown Prosecution Service* (Cm. 3960). London: HMSO.

Hall, M (2009) *Victims of Crime: Policy and Practice in Criminal Justice*. Cullompton: Willan.

Hayman, A (2009) *The Terrorist Hunters*. London: Bantam Press.

Home Office (2008) *From the Neighbourhood to the National: Policing our Communities Together* (Cm. 7448). London: The Stationery Office.

Home Office (2009a) *Engaging Communities in Criminal Justice: Summary*. London: Office for Criminal Justice Reform. Available online at http://consultations.cjsonline.gov.uk/downloads/Engaging_Communities_in_Criminal_Justice_Summary.pdf (accessed 22 January 2010).

Home Office (2009b) *Pursue, Prevent, Protect, Prepare: The United Kingdom's Strategy for Countering International Terrorism*. London: The Stationery Office.

Justice Committee (2009) *The Crown Prosecution Service: Gatekeepers of the Criminal Justice System*. London: The Stationery Office.

Liberal Democrats (2009) *Justice and Crime*. London: Liberal Democratic Party.

Newburn, T (2007) *Criminology*. Cullompton: Willan.

Power, M (1997) *The Audit Society.* Oxford: Oxford University Press.

Royal Commission on Criminal Procedure (RCCP) (1981) *Philips Report* (Cmnd 8092). London: HMSO.

Sainsbury Centre for Mental Health (SCMH) (2009) *The Chance of a Lifetime: Preventing Early Conduct Problems and Reducing Crime.* Available online at www.scmh.org.uk/pdfs/chance_of_a_lifetime.pdf (accessed 27 November 2009).

Scarman, Sir Leslie (1981) *The Scarman Report.* London: HMSO.

USEFUL WEBSITES

www.cjsonline.co.uk (Criminal Justice System)

www.communityjustice.gov.uk (the government's Community Justice website)

www.cps.gov.uk (Crown Prosecution Service)

www.direct.gov.uk (Directgov provides access to public services)

www.hmcourts-service.gov.uk (Her Majesty's Courts Service)

www.homeoffice.gov.uk (Home Office)

www.justice.gov.uk (Ministry of Justice)

www.number10.gov.uk (official site of the Prime Minister's Office)

www.parliament.uk (Houses of Commons and Lords)

www.police.homeoffice.gov.uk (official Police website)

www.victimsupport.org.uk (Victim Support)

CASES

R v. Perks [2000] All ER (D) 763

LEGISLATION

Criminal Justice Act 2003

Human Rights Act 1998

Police and Criminal Evidence Act 1984

Policing and Crime Act 2009

Terrorism Act 2000

Index

A

adversarial approach 9–10, 59–60, 105
anomie 152–3, 156–7, 180
anti-social behaviour (ASB) 80–1, 119, 121–2,
    132–3, 138, 141–2
appeal courts 29–34
arrest and detention 44–8, 170–1
  discretion and police powers 48–55
Attorney General 14, 63
Audit Commission 121–2

B

Berry Report 50, 71
Bichard Inquiry 144
Bloody Code 112, 148, 149
Borstal 115
Bratton, Bill 132, 139
breach of the peace 4, 45
British Crime Survey 104
British National Party (BNP) 178
Brixton riots 51, 128–9
'Broken windows' 119, 122, 132–3, 137, 161
Bulger, James 10, 120
bureaucracy, reducing 50, 71, 171

C

capitalism 156, 159–60
cautioning 66, 86, 90, 120, 123, 173
charging 64–6, 71–2, 116–17, 172–3
Chicago School 152, 153–6
child protection 123–4, 128
child safety orders (CSOs) 82
children *see* young offenders
Classicism 148–9
Code for Crown Prosecutors 66–8, 69–70
community engagement 168–9, 174
Community Justice Courts/centres 35–6
community orders 86–7
community policing 129–30, 133–6, 138–9
community sentences 92–3
conditional cautions 66, 86, 90, 173
Coroner's Courts 37
Court of Appeal 31, 32–3
court procedures
  giving evidence 38–40
  witnesses 106–7, 108
  see also crime and punishment; prosecution
    process

Courts of Justice 22–4, 25, 35–8, 168–70
  appeal courts 29–34
  Crown Court 28–9, 31–2
  European Court of Human Rights 34–5
  Her Majesty's Courts Service 24–5
  Magistrates' Courts 25–7, 29–30, 64–5
  Youth Courts 27
Crime and Disorder Act (CDA) 79–83, 122,
  127–8, 163
Crime and Disorder Reduction Partnerships
  (CDRPs) 137–42, 178
crime and policing representatives (CPRs) 177–8
crime and punishment 75–6, 174–5
  prison versus community sentencing 90–3
  sentencing options 79–90
  sentencing powers/practice 76–9
  see also prosecution process; victims
crime control model 7, 100
crime prevention/reduction 130, 136, 161
  CDRPs 137–42, 178
crime statistics 104–5
Criminal Cases Review Commission (CCRC) 32–3
Criminal Injuries Compensation Authority (CICA)
  38
criminal justice 2, 3–6, 105, 166–7
  models of 7–10, 100–1
  see also Criminal Justice System (CJS)
Criminal Justice Act 85–8
Criminal Justice and Immigration Act (CJIA)
  89–90
Criminal Justice Boards (CJBs) 18
criminal justice inspectorates 108–9
Criminal Justice System (CJS)
  key agencies 14–18
  structure and management 10–14
criminology 147–8, 179–80
  Classicism 148–9
  Labelling Theory 158–9
  Marxism 159–60
  Positivism 149–56, 179–80
  Realism 130, 136, 161–3, 180
  Strain Theory 156–7
Crown Court 28–9, 31–2
Crown Prosecution Service (CPS) 63, 63–4,
  66–8, 69–70, 171–2
  Statutory Charging Scheme 64–6, 71–2,
  172–3
  Threshold and Full Code Tests 68–70

curfew requirements 88–9
custody, suspects' rights 52–5, 129

D
defence process 62
    see also prosecution process
detention and training orders 85
deterrence 149, 161
differential association 155–6
discharge, absolute/conditional 84
discretion, and police powers 48–55
doli incapax 116, 123
domestic violence courts 36
driving offences 85
drug courts 36
drug rehabilitation requirements (DRRs) 36,
    87–8
due process model 7–8, 100–1

E
either-way offences 26
electronic monitoring 88–9
European Court of Human Rights (ECHR)
    34–5
evidence 46–7, 54–5, 62
    presenting to court 38–40
evidential test, CPS 68–9

F
fear of crime 119
Flanagan Review 50, 71, 171, 172–3

G
Glidewell Report 63
government 10, 167–8, 181
    Conservative 5, 17, 119–22, 131–2, 160,
        161, 162, 170
    Labour 5–6, 17, 18, 79–80, 85–6, 90,
        105, 122–4, 168–9

H
habeas corpus 46
Her Majesty's Courts Service (HMCS)
    24–5
Home Office 11–12, 50, 130–1
House of Lords 33
Human Rights Act (HRA) 34, 46, 52
Huntley, Ian 144

I
indictable offences 26
inner cities 154–5
    Brixton/Toxteth 51, 128–9, 130
inquisitorial approach 9–10

J
judges 27, 28–9, 33–4, 35–6, 76–7
juries 29, 37
JUSTICE 8
justice, miscarriages of 32–3, 51–2, 54
justice model 7, 17
juveniles *see* young offenders

L
Labelling Theory 158–9
Laming Report 123–4
Left Realism 162–3, 180
legal advice, suspects 54
Lord Chancellor 10–11, 24

M
magistrates 26–7, 35–6, 76–7
Magistrates' Courts 25–7, 29–30, 64–5
Marxist Theory 159–60
mediation, victim–offender 103
Megan's Law 99–100, 142–3
mens rea 149
mental disorder 151, 179
miners' strike 160
Ministry of Justice (MoJ) 12–13
miscarriages of justice 32–3, 51–2, 54
mods and rockers 118
Morgan Report 131–2, 137
multi-agency approach 127–33, 177–9
    CDRPs 137–42, 178
    MAPPA 142–4
    NOMS 17–18, 144
    problem-oriented policing 133–6
multi-cautioning 120, 123

N
National Crime Recording System 104–5
National Offender Management Service
    (NOMS) 17–18, 144

O
oaths, courts 39
out-of-court disposals 173
    cautioning 66, 86, 90, 120, 123

P
PACE 45, 52, 54, 65, 129
PACT meetings 139–40
paedophiles 99–100, 142–4
parenting orders 81–2
partnerships *see* multi-agency approach
PAT (problem analysis triangle) 135
Payne, Sarah 99–100, 143–4
Police Service 15–16

Policing Pledge 50, 171
Positivism 149–56, 179–80
potentially dangerous offenders (PDOs) 142–4
poverty 49–50, 112–14, 162–3,180
Powers of Criminal Courts (Sentencing) Act (PCCSA) 83–5
prisons 17, 90–2, 113, 161
Probation Service 16–17
problem-oriented policing (POP) 133–6
PROCTOR 135
prolific and priority offenders (PPOs) 140–1
prosecution process 59–63, 173
    Simple, Speedy, Summary Justice 62, 71–2
    see also crime and punishment; Crown Prosecution Service (CPS)
public interest test, CPS 69–70

Q
QUEST initiative 50
questioning of suspects 54–5

R
race riots 44, 51, 128–9
racism 118, 156
Realist criminology 130, 136, 161–3, 180
Reducing Bureaucracy 50, 71
registered social landlords (RSLs) 141–2
rehabilitative approach 17, 36, 87–8, 89, 92–3
relative deprivation 162–3, 180
reparation 84, 102
reprimands 83, 123
restorative justice 78, 84, 101–3
Right Realism 130, 136, 161–2
rights 34–5
    suspects 46, 52–5
    victims 98–100, 104–9, 175–6
Royal Commission on Criminal Procedure (RCCP) 52, 62–3

S
Safer Cities Programme 131
SARA model 134
Sarah's Law 99–100, 143–4
Scarman Report 128–30
sentencing see crime and punishment
sex offenders 99–100, 142–4
Simple, Speedy, Summary Justice (SSSJ) 62, 71–2
situational crime prevention 136, 161
skinheads 118
SOCAP 45
social class 49–50, 113–14, 158, 159–60, 162–3
    see also criminology

square of crime 162–3
Statutory Charging Scheme 64–6, 71–2, 172–3
stop and search 44, 51, 128–9, 170
Strain Theory 156–7
suicide 153, 158
summary offences 26
Supreme Court 33–4
sus laws 51, 128–9
suspects' rights 46, 52–5
suspicion, reasonable 48

T
Teddy boys 117
terrorism 12, 128, 178–9, 180
Threshold Test, CPS 68
Toxteth riots 129, 130
treatment model 17
tribunals 37–8

U
underclass 162
unlawful arrest 46–7

V
victims 66, 97–8, 162–3
    restorative justice 78, 84, 101–3
    rights 98–100, 104–9, 175–6
Virtual Courts scheme 71

W
warnings 83, 123
welfare model 7, 115–16, 124
welfare provision 112–13, 123–4
Witness Service 106–7, 108
wrongful convictions 32–3, 51–2, 54

Y
young offenders 80–5, 141–2, 155, 162, 179
    see also youth justice
Youth Courts 27
youth justice 90, 111–16, 119, 174, 177
    charging 116–17
    government influence on 119–24
    youth subcultures 117–19
    see also young offenders
Youth Justice Board (YJB) 123
Youth Offending Teams (YOTs) 81–2, 83, 122–3, 123
youth rehabilitation orders 89

Z
zero-tolerance policing 132–3
zones in transition 153–5